34.95
1/13/09

Culture and Conflict in Child and Adolescent Mental Health

Culture and Conflict in Child and Adolescent Mental Health

M. Elena Garralda and
Jean-Philippe Raynaud

JASON ARONSON
Lanham • Boulder • New York • Toronto • Plymouth, UK

The folktale in chapter 3 originally appeared in *Enfants et sociétés d'Asie du Sud-Est* by J. Koubi and J. Massard (Paris: l'Harmattan, 1995). Copyright l'Harmattan. Reprinted with permission of the publisher.

Published in the United States of America
by Jason Aronson
An imprint of Rowman & Littlefield Publishers, Inc.

A wholly owned subsidary of
The Rowman & Littlefield Publishing Group, Inc.
4501 Forbes Boulevard, Suite 200, Lanham, Maryland 20706
www.rowmanlittlefield.com

Estover Road
Plymouth PL6 7PY
United Kingdom

Copyright © 2008 by Jason Aronson

British Library Cataloguing in Publication Information Available

Library of Congress Cataloging-in-Publication Data

Culture and conflict in child and adolescent mental health / [edited by] M. Elena
  Garralda and Jean-Philippe Raynaud.
    p. ; cm.
  Includes bibliographical references.
  ISBN-13: 978-0-7657-0592-1 (cloth : alk. paper)
  ISBN-10: 0-7657-0592-3 (cloth : alk. paper)
  ISBN-13: 978-0-7657-0593-8 (pbk. : alk. paper)
  ISBN-10: 0-7657-0593-1 (pbk. : alk. paper)
  1. Child psychiatry—Cross-cultural studies. 2. Adolescent psychiatry—
Cross-cultural studies. 3. Psychiatric emergencies—Cross-cultural studies.
4. Political violence—Psychological aspects. 5. War—Psychological aspects.
I. Garralda, M. Elena. II. Raynaud, Jean-Philippe, 1960–
[DNLM: 1. Mental Disorders—ethnology. 2. Adolescent. 3. Child. 4. Conflict
(Psychology) 5. Cross-Cultural Comparison. WS 350 C968 2008]

RJ499.C855 2008
618.92'89—dc22   2007043425

Printed in the United States of America

⊗™ The paper used in this publication meets the minimum requirements of
American National Standard for Information Sciences—Permanence of Paper
for Printed Library Materials, ANSI/NISO Z39.48-1992.

Contents

Vol.	Year	Title	Publisher	Editors
6	1982	Preventive Child Psychiatry in an Age of Transitions	Wiley	
	1985	*Prevention en psychiatrie de l'enfant dans un temps de transition*	PUF	
7	1982	Children in Turmoil: Tomorrow's Parents	Wiley	
	1985	*Enfants dans la tourmente: Parents de demain*	PUF	
8	1986	Perilous Development: Child Raising and Identity Formation Under Stress	Wiley	
	1992	*Le developpement en peril*	PUF	
9	1992	New Approaches to Infant, Child, Adolescent and Family Mental Health	Yale University Press	C. Chiland and J. G. Young
	1990	*Nouvelle approches de la sante mentale de la naissance a l'adolescence pour l'enfant et sa famille*	PUF	
10	1990	Why Children Reject School: View from Seven Countries	Yale University Press	
	1990	*Le refus de l'ecole: Un apercu transculturel*	PUF	
11	1994	Children and Violence	Jason Aroson, Inc.	
	1998	*Les enfants et la violence*	PUF	

The Leadership Series (1998–2004)

Vol.	Year	Title	Publisher	Editors
12	1998	Designing Mental Health Services and Systems for Children and Adolescents: A Shrewd Investment	Brunner/Mezel	J. G. Young and P. Ferrari
13	2002	Brain, Culture and Development	MacMillan	J. G. Young, P. Ferrari, S. Malhotra, S. Tyano, and E. Caffo

Vol.	Year	Title	Publisher	Editors
14	2002	The Infant and the Family in the 21st Century	Brunner-Routledge	J Gomes-Pedro, K. Nugent, J. G. Young, and T. B. Brazelton
15	2004	Facilitating Pathways: Care, Treatment and Prevention in Child and Adolescent Mental Health	Springer	H. Remschmidt, M. Belfer, and I. Goodyer

The Working with Children & Adolescents Series (2006–)

Vol.	Year	Title	Publisher	Editors
16	2006	Working with Children and Adolescents: An Evidenced-based Approach to Risk & Resilience	Jason Aronson	M. E. Garralda and M. Flament
17	2008	Culture and Conflict in Child and Adolescent Mental Health	Jason Aronson	M. E. Garralda and J. P. Reynaud

Preface

The world of today is complex and diverse. In some countries the population is rich and healthy, it feels free and independent and is living under democratic rules, while in other countries the population is poor and starving and living under dictatorships.

The break down of the colonial system, beginning in the 1960s, has changed the world giving us a great number of new nations and new national identities. In turn, this has led to ethnic, religious, and economical conflicts—including civil war—in many regions where the people are becoming victims of persecution.

Reflecting on the course of Western European history over the last one hundred years or so, a situation like this today will generate a great number of emigrants and refugees leaving their home countries to look for a better life elsewhere. Everyone should keep in mind the European period from 1860 to 1920, in particular, when great numbers of the populations in Europe looked for a better life in the United States. The main reasons for leaving were poverty, starvation, and political and religious persecution; in fact, one-fifth of the Swedish population immigrated to the United States.

Today, communication is developing at a speed that was unbelievable only thirty years ago. To go between continents is now a question of hours instead of days, weeks, or months. The communication of ideas and thoughts is available in seconds. Facts and fictions are continuously broadcast by television and satellites. People who suffer have many opportunities to learn about good conditions in other parts of the world, inspiring them to look for shelter, protection, and a new life in a different country. This variety is a true challenge for mental health professionals working with parents and children!

The theme of the 18th World Congress of the International Association for Child and Adolescent Psychiatry and Allied Professions—IACAPAP—is "Carrying Hope between East and West for 3 Cs: Children, Cultures, Commitments." The aim of the congress book, to be presented in Istanbul in spring 2008, is to focus interest on the effects of turmoil on children. Mental health professionals need to start planning how to meet children of immigrants and refugees and to develop the necessary services and methods to support those coming with a burden of psychiatric need.

Per-Anders Rydelius, MD, PhD
President of IACAPAP
Professor of Child and Adolescent Psychiatry at Karolinska Institutet,
Stockholm, Sweden

April 2008, Stockholm

Introduction

M. Elena Garralda and Jean-Philippe Raynaud

The International Association for Child and Adolescent Psychiatry and Allied Professions (IACAPAP) aims to disseminate emerging knowledge and good clinical practice in the area of child and adolescent mental health worldwide. It organizes international scientific as well as world regional meetings on individual topics.

It is part of IACAPAP's scientific tradition to publish a book coinciding with each world congress. A list of past volumes in the IACAPAP book series is included in this volume. This book marks the celebration of the 2008 World IACAPAP Congress in Istanbul, Turkey. It addresses the influence of culture and conflict on child and adolescent mental health.

With the increasing globalization and geographical integration of the world population—all too often in response to political conflict and war—understanding transcultural issues, but also those related to war and the effects of psychological trauma, has become central to the day-to-day activities of an ever increasing group of psychiatrists and professionals working in the field of child and adolescent mental health.

This volume aims to bring up-to-date, empirically derived knowledge on transcultural themes as they affect child and adolescent mental adjustment in order to assist those seeking to understand and ameliorate the mental health problems of children and young people.

The contributions represent expert views supported by empirical and clinical experience. They address, first, general transcultural issues of relevance for child mental health (i.e., political turmoil, the effects of stigma, anthropological considerations, international adoptions, and the adjustment of specific immigrant groups). Second, they address cultural aspects of specific child and adolescent mental health disorders (conversion disorder, depressive suicide and suicide, parental dysfunction, and posttraumatic stress disorder). Third, they cover the training of professionals in transcultural child psychiatry and setting up temporary interventions in war and conflict areas.

The developmental challenges involved in military conflict are explored by Raija-Leena Punamäki who draws on her extensive experience of researching and working with Palestinian children and young people, already the third generation engaged in an intensive political and military conflict. She explains how both Middle Eastern and Western cultures implicitly emphasize the importance of conflict and struggle for maturation; however, war violates the conditions that can make conflict into a positive influence for development. The author's account of her own research highlights how good family relations, secure attachments, and a cohesive and supportive atmosphere can protect children exposed to trauma from the development of mental health problems such as posttraumatic stress disorder (PTSD), anxiety, and aggressive behavior. She discusses not only the transgenerational transmission of trauma, characteristics of traumatic memories, the interactive influences that modulate the effects of trauma on the mental health adjustment of children, but also the possible genetic and biological mechanisms involved. Punamäki highlights the important potential healing and compensatory effects of education and academic achievement.

Stigma is never far away where mental health is concerned. Where mental and physical health problems are specially intertwined, as in countries lacking in child and adolescent mental health services provision, it is important to consider stigma in relation to both physical and mental health. Cornelius and Obeagaeli Ani address the issue from the perspective of Africa and other developing countries, where the limited medical and economic resources continue to create enormous disease burdens and where the additional social and psychological distress engendered by stigma is likely to substantially increase associated disability and hardship. They describe models of stigmatization as applicable to physical and mental health conditions affecting children and other people in Africa including HIV-AIDS, epilepsy, tuberculosis, onchocerciasis, sickle cell disease, and teenage pregnancy, in addition to mental disorders. Stigma adds to the burden by limiting access to care and psychosocial support: for disorders such as HIV and tuberculosis, this may interfere with control strategies and put whole communities at risk. The chapter discusses how stigma is also likely to worsen the already high psychosocial burden intrinsic to many childhood mental disorders for children and families. Given the serious and wide-ranging impact of stigma, the authors make a plea for clinicians and health planners to proactively incorporate antistigma strategies in their work and programs.

The anthropological perspective to help understand transcultural influences is represented by Maurice Eisenbruch's chapter. The chapter is derived from ethnographic work carried out by the author in Cambodia, a Buddhist society with a lack of trained child psychiatrists, where Buddhist monks and traditional healers minister traditional healing instead. He points out that a child and adolescent psychiatrist coming to similar resource-poor countries may play a vital role in educating others, but must be willing to increase his or her cultural competence. Among other interesting examples, the chapter outlines ways in which Cambodian society draws on religious beliefs to deal with *sKan* or potentially fatal childhood illness: problems such as convulsions for example may be regarded as an expression of the child's unbroken links with a previous life and mother, and "substitution" rituals used to sever those links and ensure the child's healthy survival into adulthood.

The phenomenon of international adoptees is one measure of the increasing contacts and interchanges between peoples on a broad worldwide scale. Frank Verhulst provides a longitudinal research perspective to the issue of mental health adjustment in these children. The studies he has led over the years show that compared to nonadopted peers reared in intact families, internationally adoptees lag behind in physical growth, attachment, and school achievement, and, to a lesser extent, in behavioral and emotional adjustment. Nevertheless, it is also clear that adoption taking place very early on—in particular before twelve months of age—offers opportunities for catch-up growth and development and generally the message is a positive one. Despite the fact that mental health problems are increased in adoptees, the majority are well adjusted psychiatrically by the time they reach adulthood, they display adequate social and educational performance and achieve an employment status comparable to those of nonadopted individuals.

Immigration across different countries has increased dramatically over the last few decades. What are the implications for child and adolescent mental health? Matthew Hodes and colleagues discuss these implications using an empirically evidence-based approach with regards to the Afro-Caribbean community in the United Kingdom. They provide a historical, anthropological, and social perspective to frame their discussion of mental health issues, including behavior in school, crime and delinquency, substance abuse, mood and eating disorders, suicide, and psychotic and developmental disorders. The picture is mixed, with indications of increased problems for this community in some areas such as psychoses, but reduced psychiatric risk in others, for example eating disorders. The authors emphasize the importance of "culturally informed" research that investigates the relevance of specific aspects of a particular culture and family as well as social organization for the shaping and onset of psychiatric disorder and of problems in social adjustment. They equally comment on the importance of investigating protective factors for specific disorders and problems as a way of understanding resilience within different communities.

The second group of chapters addresses cultural aspects of specific child psychiatric disorders, such as conversion disorder, depression and suicide, and stress disorders.

Berna Pehlivanturk and Fatih Unal describe cultural and clinical aspects of conversion disorder in Turkish children and young people. Following a historical overview, they outline the position of conversion disorder within contemporary classification systems and clinical aspects including epidemiology, neurobiological aspects of a possible somatosensory amplification tendency whereby individuals with conversion disorder may pay more attention to normal physiological sensations and the somatic components of affect, and the influence of culture. Some cultures and languages may be comparatively lacking in words to express emotions and verbal expression may be more censored in societies with more dominant traditional life styles: this could lead to an increased tendency to the expression of emotions through body language, especially in girls and women. Physical illness is generally more socially acceptable than psychiatric or emotional problems and physical symptoms allow patients to be taken seriously by their families and physicians. On the other hand, conversion can be mixed with mythical beliefs. For example, a common belief in Turkey is in the existence of "djinnies," who are potentially harmful to human beings, and patients with hysteria are handled by religious healers on the assumption that they are possessed by djinnies.

In their chapter on depression as seen in Tunisian children, Asma Bouden and Iméne Gasmi report a survey of children attending child psychiatric services. The main clinical features are clearly comparable to those described in the Western literature. Nevertheless, the chapter highlights the frequent comorbidity with somatic complaints and conversion features, together with the importance of ensuring that depressive disorders are not missed in children with somatic presentations of distress, as somatic complaints may be especially strongly correlated with emotional changes in certain cultures.

North-Asia is an area with comparatively high rates of suicide. Yoshiro Ono overviews global epidemiology and current knowledge on suicide and discusses suicidal behavior in Japanese children and adolescents. While earlier studies highlighted school difficulties as a main precipitating factor—which may reflect high levels of stress related to school in Japanese society—more recent work has identified family and interpersonal conflict. Nevertheless as in Western countries, the presence of psychiatric problems—especially mood disorders, though to a lesser extent perhaps also autistic spectrum disorders—is also highly relevant, as suicide may be the first indication of unrecognized depressive disorders.

The way in which parents cope with stressful situations has repeatedly been found to be of relevance for children's adjustment. P-A Rydelius and Atia Daud outline findings from projects carried out in Sweden within a program of research that addresses the effects of parental mental health on children, with special emphasis on the impact of traumatic experiences. This is of contemporary relevance given the marked growth in recent years of immigrant populations in Sweden as in other Western countries, and the stressful experiences that determine immigration for many families. The chapter describes earlier Swedish research into the mental health adjustment of children in contact with care services because of inadequate parenting, of those whose fathers have alcohol problems, and more recent work on children whose mothers were imprisoned in Greece because of their political beliefs, and on immigrant children from Middle Eastern extraction whose parents have experienced torture in their native countries. Results show that though mental health problems are increased in children who live under stress because of serious emotional disturbances in their homes, only some suffer deleterious effects—intrinsic child factors and care-giver support being linked to resilience and positive outcomes. The authors make a plea for mental health screening being added to the physical screening of families under stress and for the provision of the necessary mental health support.

The final group of chapters addresses training child psychiatrists and other mental health workers on transcultural issues and the setting up of interventions across the globe at times of political turmoil.

Anula Nikapota discusses the acquisition of knowledge and skills in child psychiatry in a transcultural context, with a special emphasis on the process of incorporating a transcultural perspective within the curriculum for training in child psychiatry, and with special reference to the international course at the Institute of Psychiatry in London. She points out that a primary challenge in developing content is achieving a balance between basic knowledge and skills that are applicable across cultures, and an acknowledgment of the role of sociocultural influences, thus ensuring that practice, service innovations, and research are culture and context appropriate or feasible in terms of context and resource availability. Where transcultural training takes place in a country other than the trainee's, nuances of language and culture need to be appreciated and incorporated into training as are specific issues such as those related to consent and confidentiality, which may be determined by social expectations about the role of children and adolescents within families in different countries. The international course at the Institute of Psychiatry is now well established and has been clearly successful in training young psychiatrists from many different countries, thus providing an excellent model for the expansion of training in transcultural child psychiatry.

Since 1989, Rose Marie Moro and colleagues, under the aegis of Medecins sans Frontieres, have been actively involved in setting up mental health programs in countries often suffering political or military turmoil, including not only Armenia, Palestine, Kosovo, Rwanda, Sierra Leone, Afghanistan, Guatemala, and Peru but also Columbia, Sudan, and Indonesia. They argue cogently for the relevance of child and adolescent mental health humanitarian programs of this kind for children in conditions of high environmental stress and they share the knowledge they have acquired through their implementation. Their five main aims are to console, provide care, provide training, witness, and evaluate input.

The final chapter by John Fayyad and colleagues describes ways of addressing the challenge of creating sustainable and long-term child mental health programs in Lebanon, with special emphasis on child abuse, pervasive developmental disorders, hyperkinetic and learning disorders, the development of evidence-base practice, and consideration of the impact of war on child and adolescent mental health service development. They highlight the need for collaboration by different governmental ministries when it comes to funding a national program, and the paramount importance of providing opportunities for professional training.

We trust that the chapters in this book will provide interesting and informative background reading for the Istanbul's 2008 World IACAPAP Congress.

I

CULTURAL ISSUES OF RELEVANCE TO CHILD MENTAL HEALTH

1

Developmental Challenges in Military Conflict

The Case of Palestinian Children

Raija-Leena Punamäki

THE TASK OF UNDERSTANDING

Turkish poet and political prisoner Nazim Hikmet wrote to his unborn child: "My little one, whether you are boy or girl, I hope you would not die in war, I hope you would not have to freeze in shelters. I wish you would not be imprisoned when defending the right of a human being to life and peace. And yet, my child, you are forced to fight, struggle until the morning light finally dawns. How difficult it is to be a father in our times." A Palestinian mother tells about visiting her fifteen- and sixteen-year-old sons in prison: "The youngest was crying, his stomach was aching, his pains were unbearable, and he could not walk or stand straight. He had been badly beaten by the interrogators. I had to carry him in my arms like a little baby. . . . I said to him: 'Prison is for men, you have to stand and be strong.' What else could I, as a Palestinian mother, have said to my son?" She cries silently and repeats: "What else?"

These glimpses reveal a deep pain, existential dilemma, and impossible equation of being a parent and a child in conditions of war, national conflict, and military violence. The parents' task is to safeguard their offspring from danger, humiliation, and human cruelty. Children's developmental tasks, in turn, involve building a sense of safety, becoming proud of human virtue, and gaining strength, mastery, and thrust. Military conflict and constant life threat mean unique emotional, social-relational, transgenerational, and ideological challenges for child development. This chapter analyzes these challenges using the Middle Eastern conflict and the Palestinian struggle for independence as a case.

A fundamental question is whether and how violent and life-endangering childhood environment makes us different from our peers who live in safe conditions, and which processes are crucial in underlying that impact. Four issues are worthy of examination in war conditions: (1) conflicts, dilemmas, discrepancies, and paradoxes embedded in child development; (2) the meaning of trauma and danger; (3) transgenerational dynamics and memory; and (4) unique versus universal survival strategies. Childhood and parenthood in life danger depicts a setting where cultural, social, psychological, and biological processes are all called up to serve survival, struggle, and even creation of new political realities.

THE MEANING OF CONFLICT, DILEMMA, AND DISCREPANCY

Today's Palestinian children face considerable conflicts, dilemmas, and discrepancies regarding their homeland, international image, identity, and history. They are the third generation engaged in the intensive political and military conflict over land and self-determination with the Israelis. These children belong to a dispersed, divided, and persecuted nation, a part of which is living in Jordan, Lebanon, and Syria as refugees since the establishment of the state of Israel in 1948, and a part in the West Bank and Gaza Strip occupied by Israel since 1967. This chapter focuses on children residing in the occupied land that is under acute dispute, fighting, and turmoil.

Palestinians regard the West Bank and Gaza as a part of the historical Palestine and as their future independent state, whereas Israelis consider these areas liberated, administrated, disputed, and a historical part of the biblical Jewish homeland. Despite this generalization, there are members on both sides with opposing views about the political and legal status of the West Bank and Gaza, ranging from compromising attitudes and efforts by the peace movement to ideas of transferring ownership to terrorizing the other nation. According to the UN resolutions and international law, the West Bank and Gaza are occupied lands with a disputed and temporary status that forbids any geographical and demographic changes such as land confiscation, building, and population transfer (Boyle, 2000). Figure 1.1 represents historical upheavals and major Middle Eastern wars and their impacts on Palestinians living in the occupied West Bank and Gaza.

There are antagonistic and conflicting images of Palestinian youth in the West. They are called terrorists and suicide bombers, or they are treated as heroic freedom fighters against new colonialists. The enemy sides, Israelis

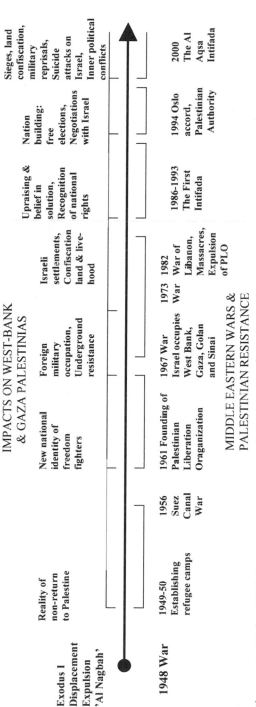

Figure 1.1. Major Middle Eastern wars and upheavals, and their impacts on Palestinians in the West Bank and Gaza

and Palestinians write their history differently; until the Oslo accords, the expulsion of Palestinians in 1948 as a consequence of the creation of the State of Israel was missing in Israeli school books, and Jewish Holocaust in Europe was absent from the Palestinian books.

Palestinian children meet severe conflicts and dilemmas in their everyday lives, which may be partly unique to the Middle East and partly universal among children living in unresolved military and national conflicts. Palestinian youth and children have taken an active role in their national struggle, and values of heroism, pride, and persistence (Al-Sumud) are highly appreciated. Simultaneously, shelling, destruction, and killing mean an acute life-danger and threats to their very existence, thus constituting a vital conflict between feelings of fear and horror and demands for heroism and invincibility. Children are forced, from a very early age, to choose between activism and withdrawal, social desirability and seeking a place of safety, pride and humiliation, and strength and weakness.

Similar to other children and adolescents in war zones, Palestinian children have to solve moral dilemmas between cherishing versus destroying life, helping others versus saving one's own life, and between joining a paramilitary group or a peace movement. In a military conflict, moral dilemmas emerge early in life and are urgent, constant, and highly concrete, whereas in peaceful societies moral choices actualize later in adolescence and remain more abstract. Moreover, Palestinian children and adolescents meet conflicting cultural demands of secular Western and religious Arab Islamic values, beliefs, and norms, and attempt to balance between their traditional society and technological global world.

Finally, the very activity of war and military violence is in contrast to the Middle Eastern religious, philosophical, and educational values and norms that encourage social equality, solidarity, and the cherishing of life. Children are taught to internalize social and moral rules of not harming human beings and nature that are the wonders and creations of God. Simultaneously they are encouraged to fight against and dehumanize the enemy, and forced to split between right and wrong and to defend their own fighters' acts of killing and destroying. Children struggle with the dilemma that while wars are generally bad, wrong, and immoral, their own defensive war is good, right, and benevolent (Punamäki, 1999). Seeking resolutions to moral dilemmas and antagonistic demands can be a question of life and death, rather than a hypothetical moral puzzle. This urgency of problems makes childhood socialization unique in war zones.

Optimum Level of Conflict and Dilemmas

Conflicts, dilemmas, and crises are sometimes conceptualized as beneficial for cognitive advancement, identity formation, innovative problem solving, and sophisticated moral development. Stage theorists call conflicts challenges and consider them preconditions for transition from an earlier developmental stage to the next (Piaget, 1962; Selman, 1980; Kohlberg, 1984; Erikson, 1968). Children realize discrepancies between their desire and reality, actual and potential, and between what they could or would like to do and what they actually perform. According to Vygotsky (1978) this potential, the zone of proximal development, is constructed in interaction with more competent persons, the parent or admired and envied elder siblings. The guidance of external experts for competences and achievements gradually diminish, and children need less and less prompting until they are able to perform themselves. Until, again, children face a new discrepancy between the actual and potential. Symbolic and sociodramatic play provides another example of the significance of discrepancies in child development. Play involves rehearsal of newly acquired skills, and training and trials for new ones. Toddlers solve conflicts and dilemmas first in play and then in reality, and train and achieve emotional and cognitive abilities first in "as if–activity" before engaging in real tasks and encounters (Bretherton, 1989; Bruner, 1986).

Erickson (1968) described personality and emotional development as proceeding across crises across the life span. Each developmental stage presents unique tasks and dilemmas that have to be resolved in order to achieve and maintain an integrated identity. Resolving discrepancies, for instance, between trust versus mistrust in the first year and between intimacy versus isolation in early adulthood provide a succession of potentials and new and more mature ways of interacting with other people and the society.

Both Middle Eastern and Western cultures implicitly emphasize the importance of conflict and struggle in facilitating maturation. The Middle Eastern cultures enhance symbolic narratives, fairytales, and myths, and allow blurred distinctions between reality and imagination. As a home of the three major religions and carrier of ancient mythological heritage, Middle Eastern discourses involve conflicts and struggles between extremes, good and bad, right and wrong, actual and potential, and possible and impossible. Wisdom, personal strength, and mature conduct are possible only after a person has struggled with difficult questions and antagonistic demands, and found compromise, balance, and a temporal solution.

Western cultures also recognize the important role of conflicts, but maybe more on individual levels. Conflicting parent-child relations are even seen as normative in adolescence, indicating healthy separation, independency, and moving ahead in life. Conflicts in safe human relations can provide training opportunities for complex human relations and allow multiple recognition of one's own and others' feelings. Through conflicting aspects, adolescents familiarize with people's different views and learn clear argumentation and sophisticated problem solving. There is some evidence suggesting that conflicts with parents predict good adjustment (Laursen, Coy, and Collins, 1998).

Moral development is suggested to proceed systematically from preconventional (avoiding punishment and restoring own interest) and conventional (following rules and being obedient) conduct into consideration of group welfare and universal moral principles (Kohlberg, 1984). Preconditions for sophisticated moral development are intriguing moral dilemmas that urge children and adolescents to solve them. Without dilemmas and antagonistic demands there is nothing to be challenged. Without struggling with impossible ethical equations, moral development may not proceed from concrete and instrumental stages into genuine respect for human life and universal rights. Relevant questions about right and wrong urge children and adolescents to evaluate the legitimacies of utilitarian, ego-centered concerns, social conventions, and universal human needs (Kohlberg, 1984; Eisenberg and Fabes, 1990). In conditions of war and destruction, the moral dilemmas between justice and caring, destroying versus saving life are highly elevated, relevant, and acute. The questions about compromising versus steadfastness and forgiveness versus revenge haunt adolescents.

The readers have apparently formed their own conclusions about the blessing versus cursing of conflicts, discrepancies, and dilemmas in child development. There is no empirical support for the idea that war-related experiences increase dilemmas between national obligations and human codes of right and wrong, which in turn would boost moral development. In a normal childhood in safer and peaceful societies, conflicts and discrepancies are inner and proximal in their nature, and do not constitute a life-threat. Apparently, preconditions for healthy child development involve, first, optimum or moderate levels of demands, problems, dilemmas, and discrepancies. Too few challenges result in underachievement, misused potentials, and passivity, whereas too intensive conflicts overwhelm children's cognitive-emotional processing capacities, and can result in developmental and mental health problems. Second, the adequate timing of moral and behavioral demands is essential for healthy development, in which the complexity of conflicts and dilemmas matches the cognitive-emotional capacity of the child. Third, balanced and integrated access to multiple levels of emotional and cognitive processing is important, as it prevents extremes of over- and underawareness and narrowed and biased views. The core tragedy of war is that all these preconditions are violated. Palestinian and other children in war zones are denied the optimum, flexible, multiple, and right timed developmental demands, which places high burdens on their well-being.

UNDERSTANDING TRAUMA IMPACT ON CHILDREN

The definition of trauma has evolved major changes in the past fifteen years. Meaning of traumatic events has moved from an objective and legally defined extraordinary event that is "happening to others," into a more subjective experience that evokes helplessness and horror in most of us and can happen to everybody (DSM-III and DSM-IV). Trauma is not considered something that is outside of normal people's imagination. We have realized that a great number of children in developing countries live in adverse conditions and frequently experience abuse, neglect, violence, and atrocities. The traditional safety of Western childhood is challenged by the global threat of terrorism and the war against it.

Similarly, posttraumatic stress disorders (PTSD) were judged as normal responses to abnormal events, involving an intuitive view that all who are exposed to horrors are also traumatized and at increased risk of developing psychopathology. Research shows, however, that a minority (about 17–25 percent) of children exposed to severe collective trauma (such as natural and technical disasters) and war and military violence (20–35 percent) develop PTSD (for reviews, see Salmon and Bryant, 2002; Perrin, Smith, and Yule, 2000). The majority of children thus recover from severe trauma without psychiatric problems, indicating that various social, psychological, and biological factors protect their intactness and resilience. Meta-analyses among adults have shown that trauma is a necessary but not sufficient precondition for PTSD or other mental health problems. Two issues are especially crucial in determining the risk of adult PTSD in traumatic conditions: sufficiency and adequacy of social support, family mental health, and past occurrence of mental illness (Ozer, Best, Lipsey, and Weiss, 2004).

Our studies in the Gaza Community Mental Health Program have focused on family, society, and trauma-related factors, and emotional-cognitive-social processes that can protect children's and adolescents' mental health in traumatic stress (for reviews, see Punamäki, 1998; 2002; Qouta, Punamäki, and El Sarraj, 2007). Good family relations involving loving and guiding parents, secure attachment, and cohesive and supportive atmosphere were effective in protecting children from developing PTSD, anxiety, and aggressive and antisocial symptoms when exposed to severe trauma. Resourceful and flexible coping responses that match the trauma characteristics could also protect children from psychological distress and facilitate their recovery. Finally, narrative, symbolic, and emotion-loaded nocturnal dreams could function as "self-healing" and prevent severe trauma resulting in psychological distress among Gaza children.

Research has shown, however, a considerable increase of PTSD and other psychiatric symptoms among Palestinian children during the Al Aqsa Intifada characterized by extreme life threats, systematic destruction, and killing (Thabet, Abed, and Vostanis, 2002, 2004; Thabet and Vostanis, 1999, 2000). Thabet and his group found that while 41 percent of children reported moderate to severe PTSD during the Palestinian Authority period (see figure 1.1), the level has increased to 58 percent during the Al Aqsa Intifada.

and disillusionment with national leaders. "I learned painfully that one cannot trust others, only oneself." Mothers of adolescents often worry about the possibility that exposure to military violence and posttraumatic symptoms will prevent girls from getting married.

The unexpectedness of traumatic events prevents material and mental preparation and evokes feelings of helplessness at all ages. Loss of control and submission to superior malevolent powers dramatically impacts the basic human illusion of invulnerability and security. Traumatic events that involve social humiliation and shame, such as sexual abuse and rape, are generally considered highly stressful (Foa and Hearst-Ikeda, 1996). Because the family symbolizes security and protection, witnessing humiliation and violence toward family members is distressing for children in all ages (Dybdahl, 2001). Yet, contemporary trauma research emphasizes that the sole occurrence and objective characteristics of trauma are not salient for mental health and psychopathology. The meaning attached to the trauma and subjective appraisal of the severity and consequences combined with one's own resources and supporting networks are decisive for mental health (Ozer et al., 2004).

TRANSGENERATIONAL TRANSMISSION OF TRAUMA

"When the soldiers are around in the camp, I feel as if it is the last night in our village," said a Palestinian grandmother. Ongoing sieges, curfews, and shelling evoke deep anxieties among the older generation who became refugees in the 1948 war. Sometimes, while telling about recent hardships, refugees mixed chronological events and lapsed into earlier states of mind, indicating blurred boundaries between current and past trauma. A woman told about the recent destruction of her house: "I was eight years old, when we had to leave our village in Palestine. I still remember the horror I felt, I couldn't understand, why everyone was running away, and why all were so speechless with pain. I only sensed that something terrible was happening. When the soldiers came last week, surrounded the house and blew up our home, the old memories came fresh, and so real. I felt only horrifying helplessness."

A unique aspect of the Israeli-Palestinian conflict is its sixty-year duration, involving low-intensity military violence with regular major wars. Palestinian experience of stateless people repeats the present history of Kurdish and the past history of Jewish people. Living dispersed and oppressed under hostile foreign military powers have resulted in massacres, ethnic removals, and persecution. Three generations have their own experiences and memories of expulsion, house demolition, night raids, and refugees (see figure 1.1), as well as hopes for conflict solution, dignity, peace, and recovery.

Our understanding of transgenerational transmission of hardships and psychopathology has increased due to research on depression (Goodman and Gotlib, 2002), childhood abuse (Egeland and Susman-Stillman, 1996), family dynamic patterns (Jacobvitz, Morgan, Kretchmar, and Morgan, 1991), and traumatic experiences (Yehuda, Halligan, and Bierer, 2001). Important questions are how commonly parental trauma and distress are transferred to the next generation, and through which mechanisms the transition happens.

Three explanation models illuminate mechanisms through which parents' traumatic experiences may be transferred to child development and mental health: (1) direct correlations between parents' and children's psychopathology such as PTSD and depression, possibly underlined by genetic and biological vulnerability; (2) parenting, especially early parent-child interaction and attachment relations, family dynamics, and communication patterns; and (3) epigenetic models stating that off-springs show early in their lives "dormant biases" that make them susceptible to potential negative effects, including dysfunctional cognitive and neuroregulatory processing.

Empirical evidence of transmission of severe trauma is available from families of Holocaust survivors, parents abused in their childhood, and, to some extent, from torture victims. Yehuda and her group (2001) have suggested a strong evidence of genetic and physiological vulnerability to PTSD in the sample of second-generation Holocaust survivors. Research is still scarce to confirm PTSD-related changes in brain architecture such as decrease in hippocampal volume and in dysfunctional connections between brain areas among trauma victims, indicating possible inherited pretrauma vulnerability (Nemerof et al., 2006; Sapolsky, 2002). Research shows that trauma victims with PTSD are about three times more likely to have family members with psychiatric disorders such as anxiety and depression (Davidson, Tupler, Wilson, and Connor, 1998; Yehuda, Schmeidler, Giller, Siever, and Binder-Brynes, 1998). Yehuda et al. (2001) specified that parental PTSD forms a risk for children to develop PTSD when they themselves are exposed to trauma. A study among Israeli soldiers provided evidence for that by showing that combat trauma made the offspring of Holocaust survivors especially vulnerable to PTSD (Solomon, Kotler, and Mikulincer, 1988). Single case analyses have suggested, however, that maternal untreated PTSD and especially dissociation symptoms can lead to PTSD among children without their own exposure to trauma (Schechter, Kaminer, Grienenberger, and Amet, 2003).

The question of the role of trauma in early parent-child interaction is vital among Palestinians, whose families continue to face traumatic stress. On the one hand, it has been popular to think that infants, the nonspeaking, are too unaware about the surrounding world to be affected by it. On the other hand, according to biblical prediction fathers' bad deeds affect their children until the third and forth generations (intergenerational transmission of persecution). Both extremes are ungrounded, and it is imperative to understand mechanisms through which psychological or relational inheritance functions, that is, what is transferred, and how and under which conditions. Parents are aware about transgenerational risks and are concerned about their children's healthy development. Witnessing their children falling victims of military violence is painful for parents who carry their inner promises "that the bad will not happen to my child as it happened to me" (Punamäki, 1986).

Attachment and Emotional Processing of Trauma

The transgenerational links in PTSD can be explained through early working models between traumatized parents and their offspring. According to attachment theory, in the early child-parent interaction children learn how to seek shelter and regulate and express emotions, and whether to trust themselves and others. Children differ in their abilities and willingness to explore environment and rely on adults when feeling threatened and distressed. Secure attachment relationship with a sensitively available caregiver provides the child a safe base from which to explore the environment. Insecure attachment relationships, in turn, force children to seek protection elsewhere by relying on themselves (insecure-avoidant) or clinging onto unpredictable parent care (insecure-ambivalent). About three-quarters of attachment style is transferred from mothers to their children (Bowlby, 1980; Bretherton, 1996; Crittenden, 1999).

Attachment behavior is normally activated in danger, and a caregiver's acts of soothing and reassuring the child overcome it. We have observed forty mothers with their one-year-olds in life-endangering conditions of the Al Aqsa Intifada. Children's attachment behavior tended to be constantly activated and mothers faced great difficulties to attenuate children's distress and provide a feeling of safety. The mothers told about their painful dilemma of knowing and feeling that a harmonious interaction is a precondition for the infant's survival and health, but the military situation made them unable to create a safe place for their children. There is a risk for the development of insecure attachment, as children either learned to deactivate and dismiss their adequate emotional needs (insecure-avoidant) or became overloaded with distress (insecure-ambivalent). Yet, the disorganized attachment pattern was not observed (Qouta, El Sarraj, Al Kassab, Abu-Shafief, and Punamäki, 2005).

It is essential to learn about preconditions that can break the potential transgenerational cycle of trauma, and research on child abuse may be informative. It shows that only about a third of the parents who were abused in their childhood continued to abuse their own children (Egeland and Susman-Stillman, 1996; Widom, 1989), meaning that a majority succeeded in breaking the transmission of that trauma to the next generation. Two issues characterized these parents. They lacked intrusive PTSD symptoms and dissociative states of mind, indicating that they had worked through their frightening and invasive memories, and did not deny or suppress them. Further, they enjoyed spousal and other social support that enabled them to distance and make sense of their traumatic past without projecting it into their children (Zenah, Boris, and Larrieu, 1997).

Parents' flashback-like states of mind are highly distressing to children, and therefore integrating traumatic memories into new narratives either through therapy or self-healing is decisive. Mothers and fathers living in life-endangering conditions should be helped to be aware of and work through their traumatic experiences. Startle responses, intrusive flashbacks, and dissociative states of mind frighten infants especially, who communicate predominantly through eye contact and are genetically tuned for human faces (Ekman, 1999; Keller, 2002). There is evidence that fear in the mother's eyes and her frozen emotions negatively affect early interaction and form a risk for insecure affect attachment (Carlson, 1998). Palestinians, while remembering painful events in their childhoods, referred to that by saying: "I saw fear in my mother's eyes." The national poet Ghassan Kanafani writes about the 1948 war: "Frightened I run towards my mother, but from her eyes I saw that I was not a child anymore."

Unprocessed traumatic memories are likely to negatively affect early interaction because parents either numb and deny their painful feelings or are overwhelmed by them. Recovery from trauma involves successful integration of fragmented, intrusive, and biased emotional experience (Foa, Rothbaum, and Steketee, 1993; Horowitz, 1979). Emotional communication of sharing and expressing mutual feelings is crucial for infant development, requiring mothers to be emotionally available, to recognize and understand the babies' needs, and to respond to them in a timely way. The optimal interaction culminates in children having access to both negative and positive feelings and learning a comprehensive repertoire of emotions typical of secure attachment. Insecure-avoidant children learn to overcontrol and insecure-ambivalent children learn to underregulate their distress (Crittenden, 1999).

Our earlier study confirmed that the ways in which trauma survivors think, act upon, and feel about their painful memories underlie their mental health. We identified three maladaptive emotional processing patterns that were associated with PTSD: (1) *ruminating alexithymic* and *depressively reactant*—emotional processing patterns were characterized by a predominance of behavioral readiness and intensive uncontrollable and alien feeling states; (2) *low intensity*—the pattern was excessive regulation of emotions in the form of repression, denial, and numbing; (3) *integrated*—involved synchronization between cognitive (appraisal), behavioral, and feeling states when remembering traumatic experiences, which was not related to PTSD (Näätänen, Kanninen, Qouta, and Punamäki, 2002). We may expect that

feel indebted to their parents who suffered and survived the trauma. Parents in their part may be overwhelmed by demands of balancing family life and national dignity, and transfer the burden to their children. Both hope that failures and humiliations will be healed in the future.

Similar to their "dear enemies, the Jews," the Palestinians highly appreciate education. They perceive schooling and knowledge as a compensation for the loss of land and military humiliation. "When the nation has lost her land, you need lots of books and wisdom to compensate the loss. Nobody can rob your mental and intellectual capital, as they have taken our homes. This is what you hear the older generation to say to the younger," commented a father.

We know, however, that exposure to trauma can severely burden cognitive capacity and information processing, and deteriorate concentration and memory functioning (Cicchetti, 2002; Yehuda and McEwen, 2004). There is evidence that Palestinian children who were exposed to severe traumatic events during the First Intifada showed low ability to concentrate, remember, and pay attention, and performed poorly in school. Further, cognitive information processing was less flexible and more rigid among severely traumatized children than less exposed ones (Qouta, Punamaki, and El Sarraj, 1995, 2001). Pupils who had been the targets of shooting, beating, and detention, and had witnessed killing and destruction had lower school scores (Miller, El Masri, Qouta, 2000) and performed below the standards in mathematics and language tasks (Diab, 2007). It is easy to imagine the despair of these underachieving children who nevertheless feel pressured to obtain good marks, both for national pride and parental consolation.

To Remember or Forget the Trauma—That is the Question

There is evidence that trauma victims who share their painful memories with others enjoy better mental health and balanced identity formation. The healing function of telling is based on the feeling of social affiliation, ventilation of agony and anger, and shared construction of a cohesive and meaningful narrative (Brewin and Holmes, 2003; Ehlers and Clark, 2000). Recalling, disclosing, and sharing memories integrate fragmented cues of traumatic scenes, console the victims, and help them to make sense of events. Clinical observations show, however, that trauma is striping children from the healing, identity-forming, and integrating function of memory. Trauma-related memories differ from neutral ones in encoding, retaining, and recall. Based on research among adults, table 1.1 illustrates characteristics of trauma-related and neutral memories and provides examples of Palestinian families' reports of their painful experiences.

Trauma impacts both the contents that victims remember and the process by which they encode and recall their experiences. The availability, access,

Table 1.1. Characteristics of traumatic and neutral memories and Palestinian illustrations

	Traumatic Memories	Neutral Memories	Illustrations
Encoding	• Implicit memory active and dominates over explicit memory • Automatized, unconscious, procedural, and situational • Dissociation; loss of sense of time, place, and body orientation	• Balance and interaction between implicit and explicit memory activation • New experiences associate with earlier experiences • Access to multiple memory types of semantic, procedural, and episodic	"I found myself running, cannot say what happened later." "I still can feel the blow of the bombs exploding in my skin. I did not see what happened around me ."
Recall	• Uncontrollable and involuntary • Memory content is unchanged, detailed and emotional • Intrusive, intensive, and vivid • Memory feels real as if the trauma would happen here and now • Sensory cues evoke memories without clear association	• Memories activate voluntarily and their intensity can be controlled • Clear association between cues and memories and between mood, thinking, and recall	"My youngest daughter saw the shooting and killing in the school. Any time she hears the jeep, she is panicking and tries to hide somewhere." "Soldiers raided our house and destroyed furniture, and mix flours and oil in the kitchen.
They			spit on my mother, and this is the scene I cannot get out of my mind. I am afraid it will follow me the whole life."

(continued)

Table 1.1. (*continued*)

	Traumatic Memories	Neutral Memories	Illustrations
Content and structure	• Frightening, persecuting, and shameful • Moment of realization of life-danger especially vivid • Nonverbal, sensomotor, and fragmented • Narrowed, biased toward negative issues and detailed	• Balance between negative and positive contents • Memory covers the whole progress of events with balanced level of details • Access to verbal, kinaesthetic, and sensomotor contents • Coherent and logically proceeding narratives	"The worst thing is when somebody you meet and communicate with every day, gets killed. That happened to me without me doing a thing to save her. Soldiers shot us while at school. I have dreams where I will be killed, too."
Communication	• Difficult to express verbally • Difficult to construct a narrative • Difficult to share with others • Attempt to protect others from the horrific scenes and humiliation	• Memories are shared and constructed together • Memories are constantly molded and re-remembered in interaction with others • Memories are not censored	"Those days are too painful to talk about." "Nobody likes to remember the humiliating scenes. So we do not talk about the prison."

and controllability of memories change as a consequence of trauma. Traumatic memories are encoded predominantly in implicit memory, are often automatized, semantic, and procedural (kinaesthetic), and lack narrative and episodic characteristics. They retain in memory strangely unchanged, vivid, and cemented images, and, subsequently, when recalled it feels as if the trauma is happening here and now. The trauma-related memories are detailed, shattering, and invasive. The moment of realizing the life-danger is, especially, very vivid and detailed, and stays unchanged in the memory (Söhnfeld and Ehlers, 2006).

While neutral and pleasant events can be consciously constructed and details can be invited accordingly, recall of traumatic events is involuntary and uncontrolled. Sensory cues such as smell, body positions, and movements typically evoke the memories. Children are often unaware of the connections between the reminders and the sudden terror they feel, which severely impacts their well-being. Neutral memories fade away with time and lose their significance, while traumatic memories can last from childhood to adulthood, as shown among sexual abuse victims and war veterans (Van der Kolk, 1996).

Trauma victims, both adults and children, tend to feel ashamed and are reluctant to communicate their experiences. They may also feel that nobody can understand what has happened to them. It is important to realize that it is not only a question about willingness to share the trauma, but that it may also be impossible to do so. Traumatic memories lack narrative and episodic characteristics, and emerge as fragmented and dissociated sensations, which interfere with narrating and sharing them. Victims often feel that they do not have succinct words to describe their experience, because looking death eye-to-eye is outside the normal vocabulary and story repertoires. They may also face difficulties in recognizing and comprehending their own feelings that the memories evoke, which further complicates communication.

In traumatic conditions memories and emotions are either strangely absent or overwhelmingly present. The numbing of feelings, avoidance of memories, and even lack of recall of trauma and obsession, and overinvolvement with trauma have been documented among children in war zones (Punamäki, 2002). Adults can believe that bad memories disappear when children do not speak about them. They can feel relieved when children are silent about adversities and seem not to remember the horrors, and parents may consciously and unconsciously encourage forgetting. Research shows, however, maybe counterintuitively, a beneficial impact of remembering, activating, and reprocessing traumatic events, and a harmful impact of forgetting and repressing them (Rothbaum, Meadows, Resick, and Foy, 2000). Effective therapies of healing PTSD (especially CBT—cognitive behavior therapy) involve techniques that focus on recalling, rehearsing, and reshaping traumatic memories, until trauma is integrated as a part of a normal processing of experiences, and it does not haunt survivors in nightmares, flashbacks, and human encounters (Ehlers and Clark, 2000; Herman, 1992). The underlying rationale of the healing function of intensive activation of traumatic experiences in a safe place includes the repetition principle of neutralization, integration of dual memory systems, and gaining control over and developing alternative feelings of trauma.

Both over- and under-remembering have been found among Palestinian children exposed to military violence involving death, wounding, destruction, and fighting. Overwhelming, vivid, detailed, and intensive recall of traumatic scenes were present in nocturnal dreaming, repetitive play themes among preschoolers, and acting out and risk-taking behavior among school-age children. Trauma-related dreams are very vivid, real, and threatening. Children often wake up in the middle of the dream and feel as if the actual trauma is happening again. Younger children have night terrors and contentless and sensomotor memories of trauma, and are highly bewildered and frightened of their state of mind. A six-year-old said, "The fighting in going on in my head in the night." In our collection of seven night dreams diaries among 295 Gaza Palestinian children, about 40 percent reported waking up in horror, shivering and screaming, indicating that the boundary between intensive dreaming of the trauma and reality was blurred (Punamäki, 1998). Two dreams of an eight-year-old girl illustrate the overflow of traumatic memory to waking-time reality.

> I dreamt that I was going to school. The soldiers faced me. So, I became frightened and woke up from my sleep. I woke up at night frightened from the soldiers.
> I dreamt last night that the masked persons killed a boy beside the school. I woke up at 5 o'clock still angry with the masked persons because they killed a man in front of my eyes.

A dream report by a fourteen-year-old boy further shows incorporation between dreaming and waking:

> I dreamt that I was in the wire stand and there were dogs around me and I could not escape. And the soldiers came and they shoot tear gas on me and they were screaming on me and I was unconscious. Suddenly I woke up and I realized that I was struggling in my breathing and furious and fierce and I woke up in the morning and I took stones and hurled them at the soldiers as a revenge for my dream.

Risk-taking behavior is relatively common in adolescents in Western societies involving drug abuse, self- and other-harming activity, and neglect of safety (Arnett, 1999). In the Palestinian case risk-taking behavior indicates a constant awareness of danger and direct acting out on it. A widely published scene of typical Palestinian risk taking is the confrontations of school children with the Israeli occupation soldiers, ending up in unequal skirmishs between stones and bullets. Our study during the First Intifada showed that 61 percent of boys and 43 percent of girls could be classified as risk-takers, and that personal exposure to military trauma was associated with increased risk taking activity (Qouta, Punamäki, and El Sarraj, 1995).

Avoidance, numbing, and lack of recall of traumatic scenes were evident among Palestinians in two settings. In a follow-up study, we asked Palestinian adolescents (N=195) to remember their most painful and happiest experiences in their lives. During the First Intifada about one-half of them had been exposed to severe traumatic events such as being detained and wounded, and losing their home in middle childhood. Strikingly few (12 percent) of those traumatized earlier recalled that event. Instead they reported proximal painful experiences, such as family conflicts, social humiliation, academic failures, and peer mistrust (Punamäki and Qouta, 2003). We analyzed the prevalence of denial, numbing, and avoidance as coping strategies with military violence in childhood reported retrospectively by 150 adolescents. The results show that 68 percent used denial and avoidance as coping (Punamäki et al., 2007).

Culture of Danger and Safety Seeking

Europa was a princess of Tyre whom Zeus seduced by disguising himself as a beautiful white bull. Tyre is a town in contemporary Lebanon, the land of Phoenicians. The myth reminds us of the shared roots and inheritance between the Western and Middle Eastern cultures, which are easily forgotten in times of wars and conflicts. Europe borrowed agricultural innovations from the Middle East and Anatolia around 6000 BC. Western culture benefited greatly from the Egyptian and Mesopotamian cultures (from 3000 BC) and was nourished by Assyrian and Persian influences, until it finally bloomed into the Hellenic Greek culture (around 500 BC). The Hellenic culture developed in the enriching interaction with other Mediterranean cultures, and influenced Middle Eastern cultures in turn through Alexander the Great around 300 BC. The Arabic Islamic culture had a strong influence on European science, world view, and literature between 600 and 1300 AD (Buckert, 2004; Parpola, 1993).

Emphasis on the shared genesis of cultures does not imply universality of psychosocial processes and child development. Rather a careful analysis is necessary to understand culture specific and universal influences on family relations and child development. War and military violence signify life threat, and therefore provide a fruitful setting to analyze universal (e.g., biological

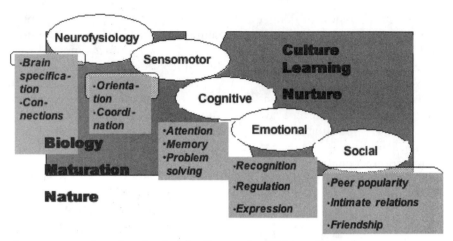

Figure 1.2.   Universal and Cultural Influences in Child Development

and evolutional) and cultural (wisdoms, values, norms, narratives) determinants of development. On the one hand, life threat activates evolutionary, ancestral, and biological survival strategies such as automatized attention, threat alarm, and fleeing. On the other hand, cultural traditions become especially important in frightening and traumatic conditions, because they provide guidance, consolation, and shared ways of expressing overwhelming emotions. Figure 1.2 provides a conceptual map to analyze the degree to which different domains in child development are relatively more biologically and culturally influenced.

As figure 1.2 shows, socioemotional development has been traditionally considered relatively culturally bound, while growth, sensomotor, and brain activity are determined by epigenetic rules and biological timing. Cognitive processes of memory, problem solving, and attention are considered equally influenced by both biology and culture. Other researchers have argued that the function and basic rules of emotional-cognitive processes are evolutionarily universal, but their contents and expressions vary greatly across cultures (Ekman, 1999). Novel findings emphasize the central role of environment in activating and modulation biological and genetic programming in child development. Research in behavioral genetics (Keltikangas-Järvinen et al., 2007; Plomin, Ashbury, and Dunn, 2001) and interpersonal neurobiology (Siegel, 1999) argues that interaction between culture (experience, learning, nurture) and biology (maturing, differentiation, nature) is a two-way process in which both influence each other. We have learned that the life-threatening environment of war brings an accumulation of specific experiences for both parents and children. These experiences, although culturally, historically, and politically determined, communicate with developmental psychophysiological and biological mechanisms such as elevated and diminished stress regulation, thus creating unique developmental paths.

Emotional development that is traditionally on the "environmental end," may provide an example of it belonging to the very "center," where gene-induced brain architecture and associative networks meet culturally mediated ways of expressing and communicating emotions, and vice versa. Middle Eastern cultures, including Palestinian, encourage intensive emotional communication and the expression of joy, grief, and anger are visible and often collectively shared. Marriage and childbirth are emotionally celebrated with singing, dancing, and women lamenting. According to ancient traditions, deceased persons are buried the same day before the sunset and grief is thus acute and despairing. During the Al Aqsa Intifada approximately 2,500 people have been killed in the occupied West Bank and Gaza (Palestinian Center for Human Rights [PCHR], 2006). Funerals are almost daily events and take place immediately after horrifying and violent scenes. According to contemporary understanding, the experiences of mourning and grief can shape neurobiological associations, especially in sensitive developmental periods, such as the first year and early adolescence (Schore, 2003; Spear, 2000).

Keller (2002) conceptualizes the early parent-child interaction as a meeting point of biology and culture, in which their mutual interaction explains individual, cultural, and sociohistorical varieties. What superficially seems to be either the most biologically or culturally determined developmental stage is embedding equally physiological and genetic (arousal, hormonal changes, growth spurts) and environmental (support networks, beliefs, norms) influences. For instance, the parent-child interaction is guided by epigenetic rules that direct infants' attention to their social world and allows them to learn about themselves and others in a specific context. These rules involve, namely, preference of a human face, interest in people, and early responsiveness to the mother tongue. Sociocultural rules involve culturally shared activity with explicit scripts about what is considered good and what harmful for child development. For instance, Middle Eastern and Western cultures enhance face-to-face messaging and emotional communication between mother and infant, implicitly aiming at children's autonomy and unique formation of personality. In many African societies parenting strategy is focused on sensomotor handling to enhance the speed of development and thus survival (Keller, 2003).

A constant presence of war and military conflict is molding older cultural scripts and possibly creating new ones to specify optimal mother-child and father-child relations in danger. Traditionally, lack of resources and life threat is understood as narrowing and one-sided parenting strategies. Parents are observed to invest only in primary care in order to reduce children's distress in extreme stress and poverty, and possibly to ease maternal agony in conditions of high infant mortality (De Vries, 1987). Contemporary Middle Eastern cultures such as Arab-Islamic, Jewish, and Christian derive from ancient Mesopotamian, Assyrian, and Egyptian wisdom and locate in the area that is a crossroad for Asian, European, and African influences. One may propose that surviving and blossoming in dangerous conditions requires a rich repertoire of strategies, multiple scripts, and a mix of influences rather than narrowing and allowing a predominance of one strategy.

We noted earlier that parenting behavior promotes proximity and comfort in families living in life-endangering conditions. Danger and threat activate attachment behavior in all ages, which thus serves a meaningful purpose and draws parents and children closer to each other. However, prolonged activation of security seeking and attachment behavior is counterproductive to children, and concern- and fear-induced behavior is burdening to their parents. Cultural resources serve their role in lightening this burden and preoccupation with threat by bringing wisdom, consolation, and meaningful ways of distraction.

Childhood of 1,001 Fairytales

Arab-Islamic and other Middle Eastern cultures appreciate stories, plays, wisdom, anecdotes, narratives, and jokes. The majority of universal fairytales originate from the Persian and Arabic collections, and Greek mythology has inherited themes from Mesopotamian and Egyptian epics (Graves, 1993; Opie, 1992). Fairytales, symbolic messages, and wise guidance are of utmost importance in life-endangering conditions. They provide multiple solutions, console children, and inoculate them against hardships. The ancient questions about strength, control, and self-worth, good and bad, and justice and injustice receive new meaning among children struggling for their developmental balance in life threat and danger.

A number of fairytales in the *Thousand Nights and a Night*–collection directly communicates stories about developmental problems that are fervent to Palestinian and other children and adolescents engaged in their national struggle. The introductory story of Scheherazade provides an example of collective and individual survival strategies. She is saving her nation through courage, wit, creativity, and sisterly help. In order not to be killed and to guarantee safety to other young ladies from the Sultan's bitter hatred, Scheherazade presented her last wish:

> I wish nothing more than that I could sit with You, My Excellent Spouse, these last moments of the night. I may dare to wish that I can tell you some stories? . . . And so the young wife of the Sultan started to tell about a wonderful and strange fairytale from Aladdin and his magic lamp. . . . The fairytale was in its

most exciting peak, when the firs rays of the day lingered between the curtains into the room. Simultaneously one could hear steps from the corridor. . . . A cruel prison ward was coming to take the spouse of the Sultan to the prison and execution. The Sultan jumped up: "No, No! The fairytale is in the middle. I order the imprisonment to be postponed until tomorrow." On the following night Scheherazade presented the story of Ali Baba and forty robbers . . . then next nights of Mountain of Magnets, Fisherman and the Spirit . . . Scheherazade organized her stories always so that in the morning the fairytale was interrupted in the most exciting event. And the guard who was sent for taking her into the prison gaol, was ordered to come back the next morning. . . . Like this the story telling lasted for a thousand and one nights.

Telling and sharing also tamed and neutralized the Sultan's traumatic memories of being betrayed and humiliated, and love between Scheherazade and the Sultan integrated the good and bad in human life span development.

REFERENCES

Abu Hein, F., S. Qouta, A.-A. Thabet, and E. El-Sarraj. (1993). Trauma and mental health of children in Gaza. *British Journal of Psychiatry* 306: 1129.

Arnett, J. J. (1999). Adolescent storm and stress. *American Psychologist* 54: 317–26.

Bowlby, J. (1980). *Attachment and Loss: Sadness and Depression.* New York: Basic Books.

Boyle, F. A. (2000). "A new direction for the Palestinian people." Media Monitors Network. http://www.medimonitors.net/francis3.html.

Bretherton, I. (1989). Pretense: The form and function of make-believe play. *Developmental Review* 9: 383–401.

——. (1996). Internal working models of attachment relationships as related to resilient coping, in G. G. Noam and K. W. Fischer (eds.), *Development and Vulnerability in Close Relationships* (pp. 3–27). Mahwah, NJ: Lawrence Erlbaum Associates.

Brewin, C. R., and E. A. Holmes. (2003). Psychological theories of posttraumatic stress disorder. *Clinical Psychology Review* 23: 339–76.

Bruner, J. S. (1986). *Actual Minds, Possible Worlds.* Cambridge, MA: Harvard University Press.

B'Tselem. (1998). *1987–1997 A Decade of Human Right Violations; Information Sheet: January 1998.* Jerusalem: B'Tselem—The Israeli Information Centre for Human Rights in the Occupied Territories.

——. (1999). "Detainees and prisoners." B'Tselem—The Israeli Information Centre for Human Rights in the Occupied Territories. http://www.btselem.org/English/statistics/Index.asp

Buckert, W. (2004). *Babylonian, Memphis, Persepolis. Eastern Contexts of Creek Culture.* Cambridge, MA: Harvard University Press.

Carlson, E. (1998). A prospective longitudinal study of attachment disorganization/disorientation. *Child Development* 69: 1107–28.

Cicchetti, D. (2002). The impact of social experience on neurobiological systems: Illustration from a constructivist view of child maltreatment. _Cognitive Development_ 17: 1407–28.

Crittenden, P. M. (1999). Danger and development: The organization of self-protective strategies. _Monographs of the Society for Research in Child Development_ 64: 145–71.

Davidson, J. R. T., L. A. Tupler, W. H. Wilson, and K. M. Connor. (1998). A family study of chronic post-traumatic stress disorder following rape trauma. _Journal of Psychiatric Research_ 32: 301–9.

De Vries, M. W. (1987). Cry babies, culture, and catastrophe: Infant temperament among the Masai, in N. Scheper-Hughes (ed.), _Child Survival: Anthropological Approaches to the Treatment and Maltreatment of Children_. Boston: Reidel.

Diab, S. (2007). _Underachievement among Palestinian Children: Child, Home, School and Society-related Determinants_. Manuscript, University of Oslo.

Dybdahl, R. (2001). Children and mothers in war: An outcome study of a psychosocial intervention program. _Child Development_ 72: 1214–30.

Egeland, B., and A. Susman-Stillman. (1996). Dissociation as a mediator of child abuse across generations. _Child Abuse & Neglect_ 20: 1123–32.

Ehlers, A., and D. M. Clark. (2000). A Cognitive model of posttraumatic stress disorder. _Behaviour Research and Therapy_ 38: 319–45.

Eisenberg, N., and R. A. Fabes. (1990). Empathy: Conceptualization, measurement, and relation to prosocial behavior. _Motivation and Emotion_ 14: 131–49.

Ekman, P. (1999). Facial expressions, in T. Dalgleish and M. J. Power (eds.), _Handbook of Cognition and Emotions_ (pp. 301–20). Chichester, England: Wiley & Sons.

Erikson, E. H. (1968). _Identity: Youth and Crisis_. New York: Norton.

Foa, E. B., and D. Hearst-Ikeda. (1996). Emotional dissociation in response to trauma, in L. K. Michelson and J. R. William (eds.), _Handbook of Dissociation: Theoretical, Empirical, and Clinical Perspectives_ (pp. 207–26). New York: Plenum Press.

Foa, E. B., B. O. Rothbaum, and G. S. Steketee. (1993). Treatment of rape victims. Special section: Rape. _Journal of Interpersonal Violence_ 8: 256–76.

Goodman, S. H., and I. H. Gotlib. (2002). Transmission of risk to children of depressed parents: Integration and conclusions, in S. H. Goodman and I. H. Gotlib (eds.), _Children of Depressed Parents: Mechanisms of Risk and Implications for Treatment_ (pp. 13–36). Washington, DC: American Psychological Association.

Graves, R. (1993). _The Greek Myths: Complete Edition_. London: Penguin Putnam.

Herman, J. L. (1992). _Trauma and recovery_. New York: Basic Books.

Horowitz, M. J. (1979). Psychological response to serious life events, in V. Hamilton and D. M. Warburton (eds.), _Human Stress and Cognition: An Information Processing Approach_ (pp. 235–63). Chichester, England: John Wiley & Sons.

Jacobvitz, D. B., E. Morgan, M. D. Kretchmar, and Y. Morgan. (1991). The transmission of mother-child boundary disturbances across three generations. _Development and Psychopathology_ 3: 513–27.

Keller, H. (2002). Development as the interface between biology and culture: A conceptualization of early ontogenetic experiences, in H. Keller, Y. H. Poortinga, and A. Scholmerich (eds.), _Between Culture and Biology: Perspectives on Ontogenetic Development_ (pp. 215–40). West Nyack, NY: Cambridge University Press.

———. (2003). Socialization for competence: Cultural models of infancy. *Child Development* 69: 817–32.

Keltikangas-Järvinen, L., S. Puttonen, M. Kivimaki, M. Elovainio, R. Rontu, and T. Lehtimaki. (2007). Tryptophan hydroxylase 1 gene hapolytes modify the effect of a hostile childhood environment on adulthood harm avoidance. *Genes, Brain and Behavior* 6: 305–13.

Kereste?, G. (2006). Children's aggressive and prosocial behavior in relation to war exposure: Testing the role of perceived parenting and child's gender. *International Journal of Behavioral Development* 30: 227–39.

Kohlberg, L. (1984). *Essays on Moral Development. Volume II. The Psychology of Moral Development.* San Francisco: Harper & Row.

Laursen, B., K. C. Coy, and W. A. Collins. (1998). Reconsidering changes in parent-child conflict across adolescence. *Child Development* 69: 817–32.

Lichtman, H. (1984). Parental communication of Holocaust experiences and personality characteristics among second-generation survivors. *Journal of Clinical Psychology* 40: 914–924.

Lieblich, A. (1976). *Tin Soldiers on Jerusalem Beach.* New York: Pantheon Books.

Miller, T., M. El Masri, and S. Qouta. (2000). *Health of Children in War Zones: Gaza Child Health Survey.* Hamilton, Ontario: McMaster University Press.

Montgomery, E. (2004). Tortured families: A coordinated management of meaning analysis. *Family Process* 43: 349–71.

Nemerof, C. B., J. D. Bremner, E. B. Foa, H. S. Mayberg, C. S. North, and M. B. Stein. (2006). Posttraumatic stress disorder. A state-of-the-science review. *Journal of Psychiatric Research* 40: 1–21.

Näätänen, P., K. Kanninen, S. Qouta, R. L. Punamäki. (2002). Trauma-related emotional patterns and their association with PTS and somatic symptoms. *Anxiety, Stress and Coping* 13: 1–17.

Opie, I. (1992). *The Classic Fairy Tales.* London: Oxford University Press.

Ozer, E. J., S. R. Best, T. L. Lipsey, and D. S. Weiss. (2004). Predictors of posttraumatic stress disorder and symptoms in adults. *Pschological Bulletin* 129: 52–73.

Parpola, S. (1993). The Assyrian three of life: Tracing the origins of Jewish monotheism and Greek philosophy. *Journal of Near Eastern Studies* 52: 161–208.

PCHR (2006). *Weekly Report on Israeli Human Rights Violations in the Occupied Palestinian Territory.* Ramallah: Palestinian Center for Human Rights.

Perrin, S., P. Smith, and W. Yule. (2000). The assessment and treatment of posttraumatic stress disorder in children and adolescents. *Journal of Child Psychology and Psychiatry* 41: 277–89.

Piaget, J. (1962). *Play, Dreams and Imitation in Childhood.* New York: Norton.

Plomin, R., K. Asbury, and J. Dunn. (2001). Why are children in the same family so different? Non-shared environment a decade later. *Canadian Journal of Psychiatry* 46: 225–33.

Punamäki, R. L. (1986). Stress among Palestinian women under military occupation: Women's appraisal of stressors, their coping modes, and their mental health. *International Journal of Psychology* 21: 445–62.

———. (1998). The role of dreams in protecting psychological well-being in traumatic conditions. *International Journal of Developmental Behaviour* 22: 559–88.

———. (1999). Concept formation of war and peace: A meeting point between child development and politically violent society, in A. Raviv, L. Oppenheimer, and D. Bar Tal (eds.), *Children and Adolescents' Understanding of War, Conflict and Peace: International Perspective* (pp. 127–44). San Francisco: Jossey-Bass.

———. (2002). The uninvited guest of war enters childhood: Developmental and personality aspects of war and military violence. *Traumatology* 8: 30–54.

Punamäki, R. L., and S. Qouta. (2003). *Memories of Childhood and Trauma.* Unpublished manuscript.

Punamäki, R. L., S. Qouta, and E. El Sarraj. (1997). Models of traumatic experiences and children's psychological adjustment: The role of perceived parenting, children's resources and activity. *Child Development* 68: 718–28.

Punamäki, R. L., S. Qouta, T. Miller, and E. El Sarraj. (2006). The determinants of resiliency among Palestinian children and adolescents: Family and child-related factors. Poster presented at the 2006 Biennial Conference of the Society for Research on Adolescence. San Francisco, CA.

Punamäki, R. L., J. Salo, S. Qouta, I. Komproe, M. El Masri, and J. T. V. M. De Jong. (In press). Coping styles and strategies, and psychological distress among Palestinian political ex-prisoners. *Anxiety, Stress, and Coping.*

Qouta, S., E. El Sarraj, A. Al Kassab, R. Abu-Shafief, and R. L. Punamäki. (2005). Mother-child interaction in military violence and life threat: Early attachment, maternal mental health and intervention. The 9th European Conference on Traumatic Stress (ECOTS), Stockholm, 18–21 June.

Qouta, S., R. L. Punamäki, and E. El Sarraj. (1995). Relations between traumatic experiences, activity and cognitive and emotional responses among Palestinian children. *International Journal of Psychology* 30: 289–304.

———. (2001). Mental flexibility as resiliency factor in traumatic stress. *International Journal of Psychology* 36: 1–7.

———. (In press). Child development and family mental health in war and military violence: The Palestinian experience. *International Journal of Developmental Behaviour* (in December).

Qouta, S., R. L. Punamäki, T. Miller, and E. El Sarraj. (In press). Does war beget child aggression? Military violence, child age and aggressive behavior in two Palestinian samples. *Aggressive Behavior.*

Rothbaum, B. O., E. A. Meadows, P. Resick, and D. W. Foy. (2000). Guidelines for treatment of PTSD: Cognitive-behavioral therapy. *Journal of Traumatic Stress* 13: 558–64.

Rousseau, C., A. Drapeau, and R. Platt. (1999). Family trauma and its association with emotional and behavioral problems and social adjustment in adolescent Cambodian refugees. *Child Abuse & Neglect* 23: 1263–73.

Salmon, K., and R. A. Bryant. (2002). Posttraumatic stress disorder in children—The influence of developmental factors. *Clinical Psychology Review* 22: 163–88.

Salo, J., S. Qouta, and R. L. Punamäki. (2003). Associations between self and other representations and posttraumatic adjustment among trauma victims. *Anxiety, Stress and Coping* 17: 421–40.

———. (2005). Adult attachment, posttraumatic growth and negative emotions among former political prisoners. *Anxiety, Stress, and Coping* 18: 361–78.

Sapolsky, R. M. (2002). Chickens, eggs and hippocampal atrophy. *Nature Neuroscience* 5: 1111–13.

Save the Children. (2006). *Mapping of Palestinian children's experiences and needs in West-Bank.* Unpublished report.

Schechter, D. S., T. Kaminer, J. F. Grienenberger, and J. Amet. (2003). Fits and starts: A mother-infant case-study involving intergenerational violent trauma and pseudoseizures across three generations. *Infant Mental Health Journal* 24: 510–28.

Schore, A. N. (2003). *Affect Regulation and the Repair of the Self.* New York: W. W. Norton.

Selman, R. (1980). *The Growth of Interpersonal Understanding Developmental and Clinical Studies.* New York: Academic.

Siegel, D. J. (1999). *The Developing Mind. How Relationships and the Brain Interact to Shape Who We Are.* New York: Guilford Press.

Solomon, Z., M. Kotler, and M. Mikulincer. (1988). Compact-related posttraumatic stress disorder among second generation Holocaust survivors: preliminary findings. *American Journal of Psychiatry* 145: 865–68.

Spear, L. P. (2000). The adolescent brain and age-related behavioral manifestations. *Neuroscience and Biobehavioral Reviews* 24: 417–63.

Söhnfeld, S., and A. Ehlers. (2006). Overgeneral memory extends to pictorial retrieval cues and correlates with cognitive features in posttraumatic stress disorder. *Emotion* 6: 611–21.

Thabet, A. A., Y. Abed, and P. Vostanis. (2002). Emotional problems in Palestinian children living in a war zone. *The Lancet* 359: 1801–4.

———. (2004). Comorbidity of post-traumatic stress disorder and depression among refugee children during war conflict. *Journal of Child Psychology and Psychiatry* 45: 533–42.

Thabet, A. A., and H. Abuateya. (2005). Palestinian refugee children and caregivers in the Gaza Strip, in D. Chatty and G. L. Hundt (eds.). *Children of Palestine. Experiencing Forced Migration in the Middle East* (pp. 149–72). New York & Oxford: Berghahn Books.

Thabet, A. A., and P. Vostanis. (1999). Post traumatic stress disorder reactions in children of war. *Journal of Child Psychology and Psychiatry* 40: 385–91.

———. (2000). Post traumatic stress disorder reactions in children of war: A longitudinal study. *Child Abuse and Neglect* 24: 291–98.

Van der Kolk, B. A. (1996). Trauma and memory, in B. A. Van der Kolk, A. C. McFarlane, and L. Weisaeth (eds.), *Traumatic Stress. The Effects of Overwhelming Experiences on Mind, Body and Society* (pp. 279–302). New York: Guildford Press.

Vygotsky, L. S. (1978). *Mind in Society.* Cambridge, MA: Harvard University Press.

Widom, C. S. (1989). Does violence beget violence? A critical examination of the literature. *Psychological Bulletin* 106: 3–28.

Yehuda, R., S. L. Halligan, and L. M. Bierer. (2001). Relationship of parental trauma exposure and PTSD to PTSD, depressive and anxiety disorders in offspring. *Journal of Psychiatric Research* 35: 261–70.

Yehuda, R., and B. S. McEwen. (2004). Protective and damaging effects of the biobehavioral stress response: Cognitive, systemic and clinical aspects: ISPNE XXXIV meeting summary. *Psychoneuroendocrinology* 29: 1212–22.

Yehuda, R., J. Schmeidler, E. L. Giller, L. J. Siever, and K. Binder-Brynes. (1998). Relationship between posttraumatic stress disorder characteristics of Holocaust survivors and their adult offspring. *American Journal of Psychiatry* 155: 841–43.

Zenah, C. H., N. Boris, and J. Larrieu. (1997). Infant development and developmental risk: A review of the past 10 years. *Journal of American Academy of Child and Adolescent Psychiatry* 36: 165–78.

2

The Effects of Stigma on Mental and Physical Health in Children with Special Reference to African Children

Cornelius Ani and Obeagaeli Ani

INTRODUCTION

The contribution of stigma to the burden of mental and physical disorders is increasingly being recognized worldwide (ILAE/IBE/WHO 2003). In Africa and other developing countries, limited medical and economic resources continue to create enormous disease burdens. Additional social and psychological distress engendered by stigma is likely to substantially increase associated disability and hardship.

In this chapter, we discuss the concept of stigma and the dimensions that determine the stigmatizing potentials of mental and physical conditions. We apply the stigma dimensions to specific disorders for which there is evidence of stigma in Africa. The chapter aims to address stigma as it relates to the mental and physical health of children in the African context. However, given the limited amount of empirical studies on the subject in this age group and context, where relevant, we supplement the discussion with additional data on adults and from other regions of the world. The chapter is not intended as an exhaustive sociological exploration of the concept of stigma. Instead, we have prioritized the examination of the impact of stigma with reference to common mental and physical disorders in Africa.

WHAT IS STIGMA?

Goffman's seminal work on stigma remains the benchmark for characteris-
ing the subject. He defined stigma as an attribute that is deeply discrediting
(Goffman 1963). Goffman described how possessing the stigmatizing attribute fundamentally intrudes on how others perceive the individual. In
the ensuing transaction, the person with the attribute subsequently inter-
nalizes the associated discredit thereby changing his or her own perception
of the attribute. For example, the person with the attribute may start to an-
ticipate discriminatory behavior from others. Goffman also described how
the stigma process could extend to other people without the attribute but
who are connected to the stigmatized person (e.g., relatives). He referred to
this as courtesy stigma.

Since Goffman's work, other sociologists have extended the characteriza-
tion of stigma. Jacoby (1994) elaborated on the concepts of *enacted* and *perceived* stigma. These latter concepts are particularly important in understanding the impact of stigma on affected individuals and in thinking of
appropriate interventions.

Enacted stigma describes the actual experience of negative and discriminatory behavior by others against the person with the stigmatizing attribute. The resulting distress in the affected individual is likely to be
valid. Thus, interventions to reduce enacted stigma would be more effective if directed at changing the negative and stereotypical attitudes of the
perpetrators.

On the contrary, perceived stigma is a subjective belief or anticipation
that having the stigmatizing condition will lead to discrimination by others (Scrambler 2004). The belief may be related to previous experiences of
enacted stigma or largely unfounded. Perceived stigma can have serious
disabling consequences due to the tendency by affected individuals to
take serious, sometimes extraordinary measures to conceal their attribute
(Scambler 2004; Scambler and Hopkins 1986). Typical consequences of
these efforts to avoid disclosure include isolation and loss of social and
economic opportunities (Leary et al. 1998). Even for life threatening diseases, perceived stigma and fear of enacted stigma could predispose affected individuals to make deliberate and seemingly irrational decisions
not to seek help. Consistent with Goffman's work, both enacted and perceived stigma can also apply to third parties with links to the stigmatized
individual (courtesy stigma).

Stigma is a ubiquitous and diffuse concept (Weiss et al. 2001), which is
now used to refer to a wide range of diverse processes that have in common
a sense of social rejection (Coker 2005). Related concepts, which are sometimes used loosely to infer stigma, include social rejection, negative attitude, prejudice, discrimination, and social embarrassment.

STIGMA DIMENSIONS

Stigma dimensions predict how others are likely to respond to the possession of a potentially stigmatizing attribute. Thus, these dimensions help us understand why certain attributes and not others become stigmatizing. Katz (1981) and Jones et al. (1984) described several interrelated stigma dimensions including: visibility, threat or peril, chronicity, responsibility, and disruptiveness.

The dimension *visibility* refers to the extent the attribute is obvious, concealable, or aesthetically challenging to others. In general, stigma theory predicts that the more visible and disfiguring an attribute (e.g., skin disorders), the more stigmatizing it is likely to be.

Threat or *peril* is to do with the perceived danger posed to others by virtue of a person possessing the attribute. Consistent with this dimension, it is well recognized that having a potentially fatal infectious disease such as tuberculosis is stigmatizing.

The dimension of *chronicity* predicts that long-lasting conditions would be more stigmatizing than acute short-lived disorders that leave no permanent marks.

The dimension of *responsibility* refers to the assumption that people are more likely to experience stigma if they are considered in some way personally responsible for acquiring the negative attribute.

Disruptiveness describes the extent to which possessing the attribute interferes with interpersonal relationships. Disruptiveness is also related to other dimensions such as chronicity, since more severe and long-standing disorders tend to also be more disruptive.

STIGMA AND MENTAL AND
PHYSICAL DISORDERS IN CHILDREN IN AFRICA

Although Goffman's seminal work on stigma was based on mental disorders, the dimensions and characterizations of stigma have been successfully applied to a wide range of physical disorders. To explore the extent to which stigma applies to the mental and physical health of children in Africa, we searched the major electronic databases from inception to April 2007 using broad terms *stigma* and *Africa*. We also used individual African countries as additional search terms. We found that the vast majority of studies of stigma were in relation to HIV-AIDS. We also found a few studies on mental disorders, epilepsy, tuberculosis, onchocerciasis, sickle cell disease, and teenage pregnancy. In the sections that follow, we discuss the evidence of stigma and its impact with respect to these disorders. We start with an extended discussion of HIV-AIDS to reflect the more extensive data available on the subject. We follow this with a summary of the other disorders. We highlight where there is data in relation to children and supplement the discussion with studies of adults. Most of the studies reviewed defined stigma in terms of negative public attitudes and unfavorable perceptions. These definitions of stigma are usually assessed with measures of self-reported attitudes (e.g., perceived social distance or tolerance toward affected individuals) or behavioral rejection. Other studies examined self-perceived stigma by people affected by stigmatizing conditions. Self-perceived stigma is typically assessed by disclosure management and self-perception of social distancing by nonaffected persons. A few studies examined both aspects.

HIV-AIDS and Stigma

The devastating impact of HIV-AIDS in sub-Saharan Africa is well known (UNAIDS 2006). Although the pandemic appears to have reached a plateau in parts of the region, prevalence rates are still as high as 24 percent in some countries (UNAIDS 2006). Even if the increasing availability of highly active antiretroviral therapy (HAART) in Africa slows the mortality rate from HIV-AIDS, the pandemic has already produced millions of orphans who are living with enormous social and psychological burdens worsened by stigma. HIV-AIDS–related stigma has a powerful wide-ranging influence, including the accuracy of the epidemiological data on which service planning and resources are based (Gouws 2005).

HIV-AIDS and Stigma Dimensions

To understand why HIV-AIDS is highly stigmatizing, it is necessary to explore how the disease relates to stigma dimensions. The biomedical and psychosocial aspects of HIV-AIDS closely fit with all the stigma dimensions discussed earlier (visibility, threat, chronicity, and disruptiveness). This close fit makes HIV-AIDS an archetype of a stigmatizing attribute.

Impact of HIV-AIDS Related Stigma

Stigma has wide-ranging impact on all aspects of HIV-AIDS including individual decisions about service access (e.g., voluntary testing and treatment) and even palliative care. The impact extends to carers and orphans through courtesy stigma.

Impact of Stigma on Voluntary Counseling and Testing (VCT)

Several studies from different parts of Africa have shown a close association between HIV-AIDS–related stigma (measured by desire for social distance) and reduced utilization of voluntary counseling and testing (VCT) services. In South Africa, Hutchinson and Mahlalela (2006) found that HIV-AIDS stigma was one of several determinants of the utilization of VCT, especially among women. Two other studies in Northern Nigeria (Iliyasu et al. 2006; Babalola 2006) also found fear of stigma as a major determinant of rejection of VCT. Significantly, the uptake of VCT in these studies was low (e.g., 9 percent for women in rural areas in the South African study) (Hutchinson and Mahlalela 2006). Also in the latter study, women who strongly endorsed increased social distance from people affected by HIV-AIDS were much less likely to have used VCT compared with women who had more favorable perceptions (14.35 vs. 23.7 percent). Thus, the impact of stigma on decisions on voluntary testing has overarching implications for HIV-AIDS control strategies. Other important transmission control strategies such as infant feeding decisions are also negatively affected by HIV-AIDS related stigma (Thairu et al. 2005). For example, despite professional advice, HIV-AIDS–affected mothers may persist with breast-feeding their newborn babies to avoid the suspicion that alternative feeding practices may raise about their HIV-AIDS status.

Impact of Stigma on Disclosure

HIV-AIDS–related stigma influences decisions about disclosure of HIV status. This has important implications for limiting transmission and access to treatment and support for affected individuals. In a study of HIV-infected Ugandan children aged seven to seventeen years, Bikaako and colleagues found that stigma militated against treatment adherence (Bikaako et al. 2006). For example, some of the children had to go into hiding in order to take their lunchtime dose of medication in school. Only 29 percent of the caregivers in this study had fully disclosed the reasons for medication to the affected children. Significantly, treatment adherence and motivation were much higher among the children who had had full disclosure compared with those who were unaware of their HIV-AIDS infection (Bikaako et al. 2006). As in Uganda, a study of HIV-infected children in South Africa found that due to fear of the children publicizing their diagnosis and attracting social rejection to themselves and their families, most caregivers did not disclose the children's HIV status to them despite the children wanting to know (Kouyoumdjian et al. 2005).

In a study of pregnant women in Tanzania, only 17 percent of HIV-seropositive women disclosed their HIV status to their partners. The main reason given for nondisclosure was fear of stigma and divorce (Kilewo et al. 1999). Another study of HIV-infected adults in Nigeria found that due to fear of stigma, only 23 percent disclosed their HIV status to their sexual partners and even fewer to family members (10 percent). Unfortunately, limited disclosure in these contexts has obvious adverse implications for controlling HIV transmission.

Kalichman and colleagues have shown that respondents who stated that HIV-infected persons should conceal their HIV status scored higher on a new scale they developed to measure AIDS-related stigma. Similarly, respondents who declined to state whether they had had a HIV test scored higher on the scale. Incidentally, this new 9-item scale showed good psychometric properties and construct validity (Kalichman et al. 2005).

To the contrary, an in-depth interview with HIV-positive speakers from several African and Asian countries found that public disclosure of their HIV-status resulted in reduced discrimination, a less stressful and more productive life, and an improved sense of well-being (Paxton 2002a). However, while these findings are encouraging, the overwhelming positive outcome of disclosure for these individuals cannot be guaranteed in different contexts. These speakers might have been a self-select group whose contexts favored a positive experience from public disclosure. It is likely that in less protected contexts, such as women in rural areas of sub-Saharan Africa, public disclosure is more likely to engender a negative outcome.

Impact of Stigma on Perceived Risk of HIV Infection

Understanding the determinants of people's perception of personal risk is important in designing effective HIV-AIDS preventative strategies. Studies show that personal perception of HIV-AIDS risk interacts with stigma. In a study of HIV-AIDS stigmatizing attitude among young people in Swaziland, Buseh and others found that young people who perceived themselves as susceptible to HIV-AIDS infection had increased stigma toward people with HIV-AIDS (Buseh et al. 2006). Thus, despite perceiving a higher personal risk, the associated negative attitudes toward affected persons could make it less likely for these individuals to access VCT. On the other hand, another study from Namibia found that people who had more HIV stigmatizing attitude perceived less personal risk of HIV-AIDS infection (Smith and Morrison 2006). Such a low perception of personal risk in a country with very high HIV-AIDS seropositivity rate is a concern.

Impact of Stigma on Palliative Care and Grieving

Uys (2003) explored palliative and terminal care for people dying from HIV-AIDS in South Africa. She found that health workers were often unable to provide relatives with optimum emotional support because most terminally ill patients had refused permission to discuss their HIV-AIDS.

The stigma of HIV-AIDS continues to have impact even after death. Frohlich (2005) has noted that AIDS-related courtesy stigma in South Africa prevents relatives from grieving openly and from following traditional rituals associated with death. Given the importance of acknowledgment and expression in the recovery of children bereaved traumatically, for example by HIV-AIDS, stigma-related interference with normal open grieving could lead to locking of grief in "frozen blocks of time" (Goldman 1996). Also, the reluctance by others to openly acknowledge the disease even after the affected person's death suggests a significant level of collective community denial driven by stigma. This has serious implications for preventative strategies.

Impact of Stigma on Orphans and Informal Caregivers

UNAIDS estimates that the HIV-AIDS pandemic had produced 12 million orphans in sub-Saharan Africa by 2005 (UNAIDS 2006). Children orphaned by HIV-AIDS have significant psychosocial vulnerabilities. For example, a study exploring the psychosocial adjustment of orphans (aged ten to fourteen years) in Tanzania found high levels of internalizing problems with one-third of the children having contemplated suicide in the past year (Makame et al. 2002). In addition to lack of basic physical care needs, studies suggest that AIDS-related stigma is a major contributing factor to psychological maladjustment in orphans. For example, in a recent qualitative study in South Africa, Cluver and Gardner (2007) found that in addition to other stressors like bereavement, physical abuse, poverty, and loss of contact with remaining family members, more than one-fifth of the orphans identified instances of enacted stigma as contributing to their distress.

Given limited health and formal support services in most African countries, informal caregivers take prime roles in supporting people living with HIV-AIDS. Unfortunately, AIDS-related stigma multiplies the already high physical and psychosocial burden on informal caregivers. In a study of informal caregivers of HIV-AIDS patients in Ghana, Mwinituo and Mill (2006) found that many caregivers were living in secrecy. They avoided disclosing their care-giving role resulting in isolation of both patients and their caregivers. Many had not shared their relative's diagnosis even with members of the extended family. The authors noted that AIDS-related stigma exposed affected patients and their caregivers to negative attitudes by neighbors, other relatives, and even some health workers (Mwinituo and Mill 2006). The resulting isolation means patients and their carers are unable to access much needed emotional and psychosocial support at a time they need it most.

Implications of HIV-AIDS–Related Stigma and Strategies for Intervention

Awareness of the contributing factors and impact of HIV-AIDS–related stigma is essential for the development of stigma reduction strategies. This in turn has important implications for HIV-AIDS control strategies.

Antiretroviral Treatment

The availability of highly active antiretroviral therapy (HAART) has dramatically changed the outlook of HIV-AIDS from a painfully wasting and invariably fatal disease to a manageable chronic disease consistent with a good quality of life. Thus, HAART has successfully challenged the therapeutic nihilism, which has been one of the primary drivers of HIV-AIDS–related stigma. HAART also changes some of the stigma dimensions related to HIV-AIDS, especially *visibility* and *peril*. Thus, ensuring widespread availability of antiretroviral treatment is one of the most powerful strategies for reducing HIV-AIDS–related stigma (Abadia and Castro 2006).

Education and Information

Misinformation is a well-recognized predictor of HIV-AIDS–related stigma. Despite the high prevalence of HIV-AIDS in sub-Saharan African countries, widespread misinformation remains a major problem. For example, in a recent study of teachers and students in Mali (Castle 2004), the most frequently stated mode of HIV transmission was urinating in the same place as an affected person. Most respondents believed that HIV could be transmitted by sharing clothes, food, and water, or by talking with an affected person. Not surprising, most endorsed isolating people living with HIV-AIDS (Castle 2004).

Although education and availability of accurate information alone may not reduce stigma, there is good evidence that this is an important starting point. Stigler and her colleagues demonstrated the antistigma effect of HIV-AIDS education program in a study of Tanzanian school children (Stigler et al. 2006). The authors found that increasing exposure to knowledge of HIV-AIDS transmission and prevention helped to significantly reduce the children's stigma toward people living with HIV-AIDS.

In a study of young people in Swaziland, Buseh and colleagues found that greater HIV-AIDS knowledge was associated with a less stigmatizing attitude toward people living with HIV-AIDS (Buseh 2006).

Utilizing speakers affected by the condition is effective in providing young people with HIV-AIDS–related information and education (Paxton 2002b). In a study utilizing this strategy, Paxton (2002b) found that young people who met the HIV-affected speakers had a sustained reduction in fear and prejudice. As previously mentioned, the speakers also found that the self-disclosure involved in their work was rewarding in terms of improving social support and reducing discrimination (Paxton 2002a).

Legislation and Statutory Support

People at increased risk of HIV-AIDS, including sex workers, intravenous drug users, and people in homosexual relationships, tend to have pre-existing vulnerabilities to stigmatization and discrimination. Acquiring HIV-AIDS amplifies these vulnerabilities. Reducing HIV-AIDS stigma therefore requires a high profile political endorsement of antidiscriminatory ethos in the society backed, where appropriate, by legislative frameworks (Campbell et al. 2005).

Summary of HIV-AIDS Related Stigma

Sub-Saharan Africa is the region most affected by HIV-AIDS in the world (UNAIDS 2006). The burden and suffering engendered by HIV-AIDS is worsened in several ways by stigma. HIV-AIDS–related stigma adversely affects voluntary testing, disclosure practices, and self-perceived risk of infection, all of which hamper strategies to minimize spread of the disease. Courtesy stigma on orphans and caregivers complicate their already fragile psychosocial adjustments. Thus, tackling stigma should be a critical component of HIV-AIDS programs. Making highly active antiretroviral therapy (HAART) widely available to affected people in Africa is probably the single most effective strategy against HIV-AIDS–related stigma. By favorably changing the course of the disease from a fatal to a chronic one compatible with good quality of life, availability of antiretroviral treatment, and appropriate education should also encourage more people to accept voluntary testing, which is an important element in HIV-AIDS control strategy. International and local political leadership are required to raise the profile and guarantee resources for supporting HIV-AIDS programs, including treatment and protection from discrimination for people living with the disease.

EPILEPSY-RELATED STIGMA IN AFRICA

Eighty-five percent of the estimated 50 million people affected by epilepsy live in developing countries, where the medical resources for assessment and effective treatments are very limited (WHO 2005). The burden of epilepsy in Africa is likely to continue to be high, as many preventable risk factors for the disease remain relatively common (WHO 2005).

A huge evidence base, mainly from developed countries, indicates that epilepsy is a highly stigmatizing condition. Studies in children and adolescents with epilepsy in developed countries show increased association between self-perceived stigma (measured as perceived social distance and concealment practices) and adverse psychological outcomes including low self-esteem and depression (Westbrook et al. 1992; Austin et al. 2004). In 1997, increasing recognition of the adverse impact of stigma on people with epilepsy prompted the start of an international campaign "Out of the shadows" by the World Health Organization, International League Against Epilepsy, and International Bureau for Epilepsy (ILAE/IBE/WHO 2003).

This campaign aims to increase public and professional awareness of epilepsy as a treatable condition and to improve the public acceptability of the condition. This is achieved though publicity, training, identifying the needs of people with epilepsy, and encouraging those in authority to address these.

Epilepsy and Stigma Dimensions

The stigmatizing potential of epilepsy is shown by its close fit with many stigma dimensions. Epilepsy is a chronic, disruptive, and visible disorder. A generalized tonic clonic seizure event is usually very dramatic and highly visible, especially when it occurs in a public place. Restrictions on work and driving could be disruptive and the lack of curative treatment in most cases makes epilepsy a life-long condition even though actual seizure events may be infrequent.

Epilepsy Related Stigma

Despite the huge burden of epilepsy in Africa, we found only few studies of epilepsy-related stigma. Baskind and Birbeck (2005) recently reviewed epidemiological, anthropologic, and sociologic studies of epilepsy in sub-Saharan Africa and found that epilepsy attracts a very negative public perception in the region. This negative attitude is also associated with constrained social and economic opportunities. Bearing this review in mind, we concentrate on more recent and salient data in the sections that follow.

The mystery associated with the dramatic presentation of epileptic seizures in many societies has historically led affected individuals to seek spiritual remedies. This places religious leaders in a powerful and influential position in such communities. In recognition of this, Atadzhanov and colleagues surveyed the attitude of religious leaders in Zambia toward epilepsy (Atadzhanov et al. 2006). Most of the religious leaders knew someone with epilepsy and 40 percent had an affected family member. However, this high level of exposure was not associated with a better attitude toward epilepsy. Younger and more educated religious leaders and those who practiced in urban areas were more tolerant. For the cohort, the experience of formal education was the most important predictor of tolerance toward epilepsy. This finding emphasizes the importance of education and opportunity to correct misinformation and improve attitudes toward epilepsy.

Teachers are in a unique position to support young people with epilepsy, given the opportunity of almost daily contact with them. In recognition of this, Sanya and colleagues surveyed the attitude of teachers in Nigeria to epilepsy (Sanya et al. 2005). This study found a surprisingly high level of misinformation in the group. Although all the teachers knew about epilepsy, 30 percent believed it could be acquired through the saliva of an affected person, 27 percent considered epilepsy a possession by an evil spirit, and 10 percent believed epilepsy was the same as insanity. This study demonstrates that in addition to general education, more specific targeted health education is required to improve teachers' understanding and attitudes toward children with epilepsy. The association between epilepsy and spirit possession highlighted by this study is significant. Historically, such demonologic attributions are highly stigmatizing and tend to attract punitive attitudes (Hinshaw 2005).

In a recent study of the relationship between parental psychopathology and quality of life in adolescents with epilepsy in Nigeria, Adewuya (2006) found an association between parental psychopathology and a wide range of adolescent-perceived quality of life measures including epilepsy-related stigma. This finding highlights the complex interaction between caregivers' well-being and young people's adjustment to chronic physical conditions such as epilepsy. The interaction, however, is reciprocal as the level of disability or complexity of the young person's health needs can also directly affect the caregiver's mental health status.

Studies of young people in developed countries consistently find adverse impact of epilepsy-related stigma on young people's psychological and emotional adjustment (Westbrook et al. 1992; Austin et al. 2004). A recent study in Nigeria found a negative association between self-perceived stigma and the school achievement of adolescents affected by epilepsy (Adewuya et al. 2006). However, as the study was cross-sectional, it is also plausible that the poor school achievement was the cause of these adolescent's self-perceived stigma.

Summary and Implications

The burden of epilepsy is high in African countries. Stigma can limit the psychosocial adjustment and opportunities for people affected by epilepsy in the region. Influential groups such as religious leaders and teachers still have significant gaps in their knowledge and attitude toward epilepsy. Epilepsy-specific education delivered in a targeted and accessible format could help to improve knowledge and attitude of the general public and key community stakeholders. For example, a survey of one thousand Hungarians in 1994 and 2000 (Mirnics et al. 2001) showed a significant reduction in public prejudice against people with epilepsy following the country's participation in the "Out of the shadows" campaign by the World Health Organization, International League Against Epilepsy, and International Bureau for Epilepsy (ILAE/IBE/WHO 2003). Reducing seizure frequency and improving the physical well-being of people living with epilepsy through effective medical care could also significantly reduce associated stigma by attenuating the saliency and disruptiveness associated with the condition.

MENTAL ILLNESS–RELATED STIGMA IN AFRICA

Mental disorders are common worldwide, with 25 percent lifetime prevalence (WHO 2001). Epidemiological studies in Africa continue to show significant burdens of mental disorders among children and young people. Fekadu and colleagues recently found a 20 percent prevalence of mental disorder among Ethiopian child laborers. In Guinea Bissau, de Jong (1996) found a 12 percent prevalence of mental disorders among children in the community.

Mental Illness and Stigma Dimensions

Of all health conditions, mental disorders have had the closest historical association with stigma. Indeed, Goffman's pioneering work was based on mental disorders (Goffman 1963). Severe mental illnesses such as psychotic disorders possess many attributes consistent with stigma dimensions. When acutely ill, the behavior of mentally disordered patients can easily be recognized by others as unusual, thus making the disorder visible. Additionally, severe mental disorders such as schizophrenia are chronic and disruptive. Historically, mental disorders have attracted demonologic attributions, which, as previously highlighted, are associated with heightened stigma and punitive responses (Hinshaw 2005).

Mental Illness Stigma in Africa

It is sometimes suggested that mental illness is less stigmatizing in Africa and this is occasionally supported by empirical evidence (Makanjuola 2006). However, when stigma is investigated with less direct measures (e.g., desire for social distance), the evidence points to high levels of negative attitude by the public. For example, in a study of Nigerian University students, 65 percent of the respondents were classified as having high social distance toward people with mental illness (Adewuya and Makanjuola 2005). Seventy-nine percent of the students would not consider marrying someone with a history of mental illness and 64 percent would have difficulty sharing a room with the afflicted person.

In a study comparing the care-giving experiences of relatives of people with schizophrenia, major affective disorders, cancer, infertility, and sickle cell disease in Nigeria, Ohaeri and Fido (2001) found that, compared with other groups, relatives of people with severe mental disorders perceived more social embarrassment. A similar study of relatives of patients with schizophrenia and major affective psychosis in Ethiopia (Shibre et al. 2001) also found high levels of self-perceived stigma; 42 percent of the respondents worried they would be treated differently and 37 percent wanted to conceal their relative's mental illness. Significantly, both the Nigerian and Ethiopian studies elicited demonologic attributions for mental disorders, which, as already noted, is associated with increased public perceptions of stigma (Hinshaw 2005). Other studies in Egypt (Coker 2005) and South Africa (Hugo et al. 2003) point to significant levels of negative attitudes toward psychiatric disorders in different parts of Africa.

Summary and Implications

Childhood mental illnesses are common in African countries and mental illness continues to attract significant stigmatizing attitudes in the region. Stigma is likely to worsen the already high psychosocial burden of mental disorders on affected individuals and their families. Although mental health provision is limited in most parts of Africa, where services exist, stigma could militate against access. High levels of stigmatizing attitude even among highly educated groups suggest that mental health–specific public education is required to tackle stigma in this context. As already highlighted, effective treatment for stigmatizing disorders like mental illness is in itself a potent antistigma strategy. Successful treatment attenuates associated stigma dimensions (e.g., visibility) and challenges the therapeutic hopelessness that fuels stigma and misinformation.

OTHER STIGMATIZING CONDITIONS IN AFRICA

Stigma is a ubiquitous and diffuse concept (Weiss et al. 2001), which makes it easily applicable to a range of conditions. Our literature search elicited some evidence of stigma in relation to several physical disorders in Africa that are relevant to children and young people including tuberculosis, onchocerciasis, sickle cell disease, and teenage pregnancy. In the sections that follow, we briefly review the evidence and impact of stigma in relation to these disorders.

Tuberculosis

The prevalence of tuberculosis (TB) in Africa has substantially increased in the last few years due to its close association with HIV-AIDS (Corbett et al. 2007). The treatment has also become complicated with the emergence of multidrug resistance.

Active TB infection is consistent with many stigma dimensions. The chronic productive cough and wasting associated with pulmonary TB make the infection highly visible. Skin lesions and lymphadenopathy make other forms of TB also highly visible. The stigma dimensions of "threat and lethality" have a close fit with TB, which is a highly contagious and potentially lethal infection. In a review of TB in developing countries, Cassie (2002) identified perceived stigma as a major contributing factor to both delayed presentation and noncompletion of treatment.

In a study of patients with TB and unaffected members of their community in a rural district of South Africa, Edginton and colleagues found evidence of both misinformation and stigma (2002). Many of the respondents believed that TB results from breaking cultural taboos related to sex and that only traditional healers can treat it. The authors identified negative public attitudes, including those of health workers, as a barrier to treatment access and adherence. Another study from Gambia involving both patients with TB and health workers found high levels of negative perceptions about TB, especially among women (Eastwood and Hill 2004). As in South Africa, the Gambian study highlighted stigma as a barrier to treatment access. Other studies in Kenya (Liefooghe et al. 1997) and South Africa (Westaway and Wolmarans 1994) all support the importance of TB-related stigma in treatment access and adjustment of affected individuals.

It is evident that addressing TB-related stigma is an essential element in successful TB treatment and control strategies. A study from Ethiopia illustrates one successful strategy using "TB clubs" (Getahun 1998). The author described the introduction of TB clubs consisting of affected persons from the same family and neighborhoods. Each club consisted of three to ten members and an elected leader. The leader monitored treatment adherence and side effects. The clubs disseminated TB information in their communities, resulting in reduced stigma and social isolation for members. The clubs also increased clinic attendance from 68 percent to 98 percent.

Onchocerciasis

Skin disorders are classically stigmatizing because of their association with the stigma dimension of visibility. For example, studies of psoriasis (Leary et al. 1998) and vitiligo (Kent 2000) in developed countries consistently show high levels of perceived stigma by affected persons. The associated stigma tends to be closely related to the extent and location of the skin lesions with more visible lesions linked with higher levels of stigma.

Onchocerciasis is a filarial worm infestation affecting millions of people in Africa (Brieger et al. 1998). The worms typically cause skin or eye lesions. The skin lesions cause widespread itchy and unsightly rashes, which with prolonged scratching make the skin rough and leathery. The unsightly nature of the skin lesions makes them easily visible. The associated stigma can have serious consequences for affected individuals including difficulty finding marriage partners (Brieger et al. 1998).

In a study of self-perceived stigma among people with onchocercal skin lesions in Nigeria, Brieger and colleagues found that more than two-thirds felt ashamed and embarrassed and 33 percent perceived being avoided by others. Of those that were married, 33 percent were having marital difficulties related to onchocercal skin lesions. Twelve percent reported that their unaffected relatives were also having difficulty getting married due to courtesy stigma. Interestingly, the study also found that in the community's hierarchy of disfiguring skin conditions, leprosy and chicken pox were rated worse than onchocercal skin lesions (Brieger et al. 1998).

The Brieger and colleagues study also illustrated how having accurate information can positively attenuate perceived stigma in people with stigmatizing conditions. The study found that those who correctly labeled their lesions as being secondary to onchocerciasis had lower scores on a measure of self-perceived stigma than those who did not (Brieger et al. 1998).

In addition to accurate information, medical treatment of the onchocercal lesions (e.g., with ivermectin) is a potent strategy for reducing associated stigma. In a placebo-controlled trial in Nigeria, Brieger and colleagues showed that ivermectin was more effective than the placebo in reducing the occurrence of new onchocercial lesions (Brieger et al. 2001). Thus, the importance of active interventions to reduce the visibility and saliency of stigmatizing conditions cannot be overemphasised.

Sickle Cell Disease

Sickle cell disease (SCD) is a blood disorder that affects millions of people of African origin (Sergeant 1992). The condition is associated with serious physical and psychosocial complications (Anie 2005) and attenuated life expectancy (Sergeant 2005).

The biomedical and socioanthropological aspects of SCD show consistency with several stigma dimensions including visibility, chronicity, and disruptiveness. SCD is associated with highly visible signs such as jaundice and chronic leg ulcers. By definition, the condition is chronic and life-long. Also, the associated medical complications and frequent hospital admissions are disruptive to schooling, employment, and peer relationships.

Although empirical studies of stigma in SCD are extremely limited, anecdotal and socioanthropological evidence points to SCD as a stigmatizing disorder. In general, it is well recognized that genetic disorders like SCD are stigmatizing (Sankar et al. 2006). People with SCD are often referred to as "sicklers." Slovenko (2001) has highlighted that such descriptions that personify the individual with their disorder increase stigma by implying that

Implicit Association Test) (Teachman et al. 2006). The latter are less prone to eliciting socially desirable responses.

Once the prevalence and determinants of stigma are better understood, intervention studies targeting the full range of potential determinants will become appropriate. It would be helpful to explore different strategies for improving public knowledge and attitudes to specific stigmatizing conditions. It is important to identify helpful strategies for improving the resilience of stigmatized persons and for reducing the personal distress engendered by perceived stigma. Studies need to examine both the content and the process of delivering effective interventions against stigma in order to facilitate their replication and scale up into programs.

CONCLUDING REMARKS

In this chapter, we have reviewed evidence relating to the application of the concept of stigma to many disorders and other conditions affecting children and people of other age groups in Africa. There is evidence that stigma adversely affects the life of people living with HIV-AIDS, tuberculosis, onchocerciasis, and sickle cell disease as well as those living with mental disorders. In these contexts, stigma has the potency to worsen already high medical and psychosocial burdens and in some cases predispose vulnerable young people to avoidable premature mortality. Thus, addressing stigma will benefit not only the affected individual but could have overarching public health benefits, for example, in limiting spread of HIV and TB infections.

We have argued that at the individual level, effective treatment of stigmatizing conditions is one of the most powerful strategies for combating associated stigma. Effective treatment challenges the therapeutic nihilism that commonly underlies stigmatizing attitudes. Also, effective treatment typically reduces the visibility of the condition, which is one of the key measures of the stigmatization potential of common disorders.

Stigma is often driven by misinformation; hence, providing accurate information is an important antistigma strategy. This is helpful for both the public in general and the specific people with a stigmatizing condition.

Concerted and effective large-scale antistigma strategies are important. However, they are unlikely to succeed without the resources and political support of influential stakeholders. Working with this group is more likely to ensure that not only individual stigmatized persons are supported but also whole communities are carried along, where appropriate, with the support of legal frameworks. The success of the "Out of the shadows" campaign in reducing epilepsy-related prejudice (Mirnics et al. 2001) supports this strategy.

For many children in Africa, the medical and psychosocial burden of physical and mental disorders is hard to bear; tackling the additional burden due to stigma could make their conditions more bearable.

REFERENCES

Abadia, B., and Castro, A. (2006). Experiences of stigma and access to HAART in children and adolescents living with HIV/AIDS in Brazil. *Social Science and Medicine* 62: 1219–28.

Adedoyin, M. (1992). Psychosocial effects of sickle cell disease among adolescents. *East African Medical Journal* 69: 370–2.

Adewuya, A., and Makanjuola, R. (2005). Social distance towards people with mental illness amongst Nigerian University students. *Social Psychiatry and Psychiatric Epidemiology* 40: 865–68.

Adewuya, A. (2006). Parental psychopathology and self-rated quality of life in adolescents with epilepsy in Nigeria. *Developmental Medicine and Child Neurology* 48: 600–3.

Adewuya, A., Oseni, S., and Okeniyi, J. (2006). School performance of Nigerian adolescents with epilepsy. *Epilepsia* 47: 415–20.

Anie, K. (2005). Psychological complications in sickle cell disease. *British Journal of Haematology* 129: 723–29.

Atadzhanov, M., Chomba, E., Haworth, A., Mbewe, E., and Birbeck, G. (2006). Knowledge, attitudes, behaviors and practices regarding epilepsy among Zambian clerics. *Epilepsy and Behavior* 9: 83–88.

Atuyambe, L., Mirembe, F., Johansson, A., Kirumira, E., and Faxelid, E. (2005). Experiences of pregnant adolescents—voices from Wakiso district, Uganda. *African Health Sciences* 5: 304–9.

Austin, J., MacLeod, J., Dunn, D., Shen, J., and Perkins, S. (2004). Measuring stigma in children with epilepsy and their parents: instrument development and testing. *Epilepsy and Behavior* 5: 472–82.

Babalola S. (2007). Readiness for HIV testing among young people in Northern Nigeria: The roles of social norm and perceived stigma. *AIDS and Behavior* 11 (5): 759–69.

Baskind, R., and Birbeck, G. (2005). Epilepsy-associated stigma in sub-Saharan Africa: The social landscape of a disease. *Epilepsy and Behavior* 7: 68–73.

Bikaako, K., Luyirika, E., Purcell, D., Downing, J., Kaharuza, F., Mermin, J., Malamba, S., and Bunnell, R. (2006). Disclosure of HIV status and adherence to daily drug regimes among HIV-infected children in Uganda. *AIDS and Behavior* 10: S85–93.

Brieger, W., Oshiname, F., and Ososanya, O. (1998). Stigma associated with onchocercal skin disease among those affected near the Ofiki and Oyan Rivers in Western Nigeria. *Social Science and Medicine* 47: 841–52.

Brieger, W., Kale, O., Ososanya, O. (2001). Development of reactive onchocercal skin lesions during a placebo-controlled trial with ivermectin among persons without lesions at baseline. *Tropical Doctor* 31: 96–98.

Buseh, A., Park, C., Stevens, P., McElmurry, B., and Kelber, S. (2006). HIV/AIDS stig-matizing attitudes among young people in Swaziland: Individual and environ-mental factors. *Journal of HIV/AIDS Prevention in Children and Youth* 7: 97–120.

Campbell, C., Foulis, C., Maimane, S., and Sibiya, Z. (2005). "I have an evil child in my house": Stigma and HIV/AIDS management in a South African Community. *American Journal of Public Health* 95: 808–15.

Cassie, T. (2002). A literature review of the problems of delayed presentation for treatment and non-completion of treatment for tuberculosis in less developed countries and ways of addressing these problems using particular implementa-tions of the DOTS strategy. *Journal of Management in Medicine* 16: 371–400.

Castle, S. (2004). Rural children's attitudes to people with HIV/AIDS in Mali: The causes of stigma. *Culture, Health and Sexuality* 6: 1–18.

Cluver, L., and Gardner, F. (2007). Risk and protective factors for psychological well-being of children orphaned by AIDS in Cape Town: A qualitative study of children and caregivers' perspectives. *AIDS Care* 19: 318–25.

Coker, E. M. (2005). Selfhood and social distance: Toward a cultural understanding of psychiatric stigma in Egypt. *Social Science and Medicine* 61: 920–30.

Corbett, E., Bandason, T., Cheung, Y., Munyati, S., Godfrey, F., Hayes, R., Churchyard, G., Butterworth, A., and Mason, P. (2007). Epidemiology of tuberculosis in a high HIV prevalence population provided with enhanced diagnosis of symptomatic dis-ease. *PLoS Medicine*, January 2, 2007, vol. 4(1): doi:10.1371/journal.pmed.0040022

de Jong, J. (1996). A comprehensive public mental health programme in Guinea Bissau: A useful model for African, Asian and Latin American countries. *Psycho-logical Medicine* 26: 97–108.

Eastwood, S., and Hill, P. (2004). A gender-focused qualitative study of barriers to accessing tuberculosis treatment in The Gambia, West Africa. *The International Journal of Tuberculosis and Lung Disease* 8: 70–75.

Edginton, M., Sekatane, C., and Goldstein, S. (2002). Patients' beliefs: Do they af-fect Tuberculosis control? A study in a rural district of South Africa. *The Interna-tional Journal of Tuberculosis and Lung Disease* 6: 1075–82.

Frohlich, J. (2005). The impact of AIDS on the community. Pp. 351–70 in K. S. Ab-dool and K. Q. Abdool, eds., *HIV/AIDS in South Africa*. New York: Cambridge Uni-versity Press.

Getahun, H. (1998). Partners against tuberculosis: Ethiopia's TB clubs. *Africa Health* 21: 20.

Goffman, E. (1963). *Notes on the Management of Spoiled Identity*. Englewood Cliffs, NJ: Prentice-Hall.

Goldman, L. (1996). *Breaking the Silence: A Guide to Helping Children With Compli-cated Grief*. Washington, DC: Accelerated Development.

Gouws, E. (2005). HIV incidence rates in South Africa. Pp. 67–76 in K. S. Abdool and K. Q. Abdool, eds., *HIV/AIDS in South Africa*. New York: Cambridge University Press.

Hinshaw, S. (2005). The stigmatization of mental illness in children and parents: Developmental issues, family concerns, and research needs. *Journal of Child Psy-chology and Psychiatry* 46: 714–34.

Hugo, C., Boshoff, D., Traut, A., Zungu, D., and Stein, D. (2003). Community atti-tudes toward and knowledge of mental illness in South Africa. *Social Psychiatry and Psychiatric Epidemiology* 38: 715–19.

Hutchinson, P., and Mahlalela, X. (2006). Utilisation of voluntary counselling and testing services in the Eastern Cape, South Africa. *AIDS Care* 18: 446–55.

ILAE/IBE/WHO. (2003). *Global Campaign against Epilepsy*. Heemstede, Netherlands: International Bureau for Epilepsy.

Iliyasu, Z., Abubakar, I., Kabir, M., and Aliyu, M. (2006). Knowledge of HIV/AIDS and attitude towards voluntary counselling and testing among adults. *Journal of the National Medical Association* 98: 1917–22.

Jacoby, A. (1994). Felt versus enacted stigma: A concept revisited: Evidence from a study of people with epilepsy in remission. *Social Science and Medicine* 38: 269–74.

Jones, E., Farina, A., Hastorf, A., Markus, H., Miller, D., and Scott, R. (1984). *Social Stigma: The Psychology of Marked Relationships*. New York: Freeman.

Kalichman, S., Simbayi, L., Jooste, S., Toefy, Y., Cain, D., Cherry, C., and Kagee, A. (2005). Development of a brief scale to measure AIDS-related stigma in South Africa. *AIDS and Behavior* 9: 135–43.

Katz, I. (1981). *Stigma: A Social Psychological Analysis*. Mahwah, NJ: Lawrence Erlbaum.

Kent, G. (2000). Understanding the experiences of people with disfigurements: An integration of four models of social and psychological functioning. *Psychology, Health, and Medicine* 5: 117–29.

Kilewo, C., Massawe, A., Lyamuya, E., Semali, I., Kalokola, F., Urassa, E., Giattas, M., Temu, F., Karlsson, K., Mhalu, F., and Biberfeld, G. (1999). HIV counselling and testing of pregnant women in sub-Saharan Africa: Experiences from a study on prevention of mother-to-child HIV-1 transmission in Da es Salaam, Tanzania. *Journal of Acquired Immune Deficiency Syndromes* 28: 458–62.

Kouyoumdjian, F., Meyers, T., Mtshizana, S. (2005). Barriers to disclosure to children with HIV. *Journal of Tropical Pediatrics* 51: 285–87.

Leary, M., Rapp, S., Herbst, K., Exum, M., and Feldman, S. (1998). Interpersonal concerns and psychological difficulties of psoriasis patients: Effects of disease severity and fear of negative evaluation. *Health Psychology* 17: 530–36.

Liefooghe, R., Baliddawa, J., Kipruto, E., Vermeire, C., and De-Munynck, A. (1997). From their own perspective. A Kenyan community's perception of tuberculosis. *Tropical Medicine and International Health* 2: 809–21.

Makame, V., Ani, C., and Grantham-McGregor, S. (2002). Psychosocial functions of orphans in Tanzania. *Acta Paediatrica* 91: 459–65.

Makanjuola, A. B. (2006). Public stigma towards psychiatric patients in a South-Western Nigerian Town. *The Nigerian Postgraduate Medical Journal* 13: 210–15.

Mirnics, Z., Czikora, G., Zavecz, T., Halasz, P. (2001). Changes in public attitudes toward epilepsy in Hungary: Results of surveys conducted in 1994 and 2000. *Epilepsia* 42: 86–93.

Mwinituo, P., and Mill, J. (2006). Stigma associated with Ghanaian caregivers of AIDS patients. *Western Journal of Nursing Research* 28: 369–82.

Nzewi, E. (2001). Malevolent Ogbanje: Recurrent reincarnation or sickle cell disease? *Social Science and Medicine* 52: 1403–16.

Ohaeri, J., and Fido, A. (2001). The opinion of caregivers on aspects of schizophrenia and major affective disorders in a Nigerian setting. *Social Psychiatry and psychiatric Epidemiology* 36: 493–99.

Onwubalili, J. (1983). Sickle-cell anaemia: An explanation for the ancient myth of reincarnation in Nigeria. *Lancet* 2: 503–5.

Parker, R., and Aggleton, P. (2003). HIV and AIDS-related stigma and discrimination: A conceptual framework and implications for action. *Social Science and Medicine* 57: 13–24.

Paxton, S. (2002a). The paradox of public HIV disclosure. *AIDS Care* 14: 559–67.

———. (2002b). The impact of utilizing HIV-positive speakers in AIDS education. *AIDS Education and Prevention* 14: 282–94.

Sankar, P., Cho, M., Wolpe, P., and Schairer, C. (2006). What is in a cause? Exploring the relationship between genetic cause and felt stigma. *Genetics in Medicine* 8: 33–42.

Sanya, E., Salami, T., Goodman, O., Buhari, O., and Araoye, M. (2005). Perception and attitude to epilepsy among teachers in primary, secondary and tertiary educational institutions in middle belt Nigeria. *Tropical Doctor* 35: 153–56.

Scambler, G. (2004). Re-framing stigma: Felt and enacted stigma and challenges to the sociology of chronic and disabling conditions. *Social Theory and Health* 2: 29–46.

Scambler, G., and Hopkins, A. (1986). Being epileptic: coming to terms with stigma. *Sociology of Health and Illness* 8: 26–43.

Sergeant, G. R. (1992). *Sickle Cell Disease*, 2nd ed. New York: Oxford University Press.

———. (2005). Mortality from sickle cell disease in Africa. *British Medical Journal* 330: 432–33.

Shibre, T., Negash, A., Kullgren, G., Kebede, D., Alem, A., Fekadu, A., Fekadu, D., Madhin, G., Jacobsson, L. (2001). Perception of stigma among family members of individuals with schizophrenia and major affective disorders in rural Ethiopia. *Social Psychiatry and Psychiatric Epidemiology* 36: 299–303.

Singh, S. (2006). Hospital admissions resulting from unsafe abortion: Estimates from 13 developing countries. *Lancet* 368: 1887–92.

Slovenko, R. (2001). The stigma of psychiatric discourse. *Journal of Psychiatry & Law* 29: 5–29.

Smith, R., and Morrison, D. (2006). The impact of stigma, experience, and group referent on HIV risk assessment and HIV testing intentions in Namibia. *Social Science and Medicine* 63: 2649–60.

Stigler, M., Kugler, K., Komro, K., Leshabari, M., and Klepp, K. (2006). AIDS education for Tanzanian Youth: A mediation analysis. *Health Education Research* 21: 441–51.

Teachman, B., Wilson, J., and Komarovskaya, I. (2006). Implicit and explicit stigma of mental illness in diagnosed and healthy samples. *Journal of Social & Clinical Psychology* 25: 75–95.

Thairu, L., Pelto, G., Rollins, N., Bland, R., and Ntshangase, N. (2005). Sociocultural influences on infant feeding decisions among HIV-infected women in rural KwaZulu Natal, South Africa. *Maternal and Child Nutrition* 1: 2–10.

UNAIDS. (2006). Report on the global AIDS epidemic 2006. http://data.unaids.org/pub/GlobalReport/2006/2006_GR_CH02_en.pdf (accessed May 29, 2007).

Uys, L. R. (2003). Aspects of the care of people with HIV/AIDS in South Africa. *Public Health Nursing* 20: 271–80.

Varga, C. A. (2002). Pregnancy termination among South African adolescents. *Studies in Family Planning* 33: 283–98.

Weiss, M., Jadhav, S., Raguram, R., Vounatsou, P., and Littlewood, R. (2001). Psychiatric stigma across cultures: Local validation in Bangalore and London. *Anthropology and Medicine* 8: 71–87.

Westaway, M., and Wolmarans, L. (1994). Cognitive and affective reactions of black urban South Africans towards tuberculosis. *Tubercle and Lung Disease* 75: 447–53.

Westbrook, L. E., Bauman, L., and Shinnar, S. (1992). Applying stigma theory to epilepsy: A test of a conceptual model. *Journal of Pediatric Psychology* 17: 633–49.

WHO. (2005). Atlas: Epilepsy care in the World. Geneva: World Health Organization.

WHO. (2001). World Mental Health Report. Geneva: World Health Organization.

3

Anthropology and Child Psychiatry— The Cambodian Case

Maurice Eisenbruch

ETHNOGRAPHY AND CHILD PSYCHIATRY

Child psychiatrists in a global world must practice with "cultural competence." Culture exerts a profound influence on the diagnosis of emotional disturbances affecting children (Berganza et al. 2001; Harper 2001). Despite the calls for cultural competence in child psychiatry (Pumariega and Cross 1997), the evidence base in child psychiatry remains firmly built on Western studies in Western settings using Western instruments. A culturally competent framework for child psychiatry, based on sound anthropological foundations and appropriate for resource-poor as well as resource-rich countries, while sorely needed, has not been developed.

The growth of anthropological studies of child development (LeVine and LeVine 1981; LeVine and New 2007) has also led to an interest in the anthropology of childhood behavioral disturbances and illness (Ensink and Robertson 1996; Nichter 1994; Nichter 1985; Reynolds 1996; Swartz 1996). The need is great to learn how children in different cultures get sick and, even more so, to learn through this about the society itself—its rules of logic, its mythology, its views of gender, parenthood, and death.

An area of inquiry termed "ethnography of childhood" provides valuable insights into child development, social relations, and acculturation (Behera 2005; Bourdillon 1989; James 1998; Kapavalu 1993; Morton and Lee 1996;

Stephens 1998) as well as into childhood illness (Christensen 1999). This chapter aims to show how an ethnographic approach can provide insight into the local constructions of child development, psychopathology, and illness.

The material in this chapter is derived from ethnographic work carried out with children in Cambodia (see the report of an earlier stage in Eisenbruch 1998). In this Theravadin Buddhist society there are few psychiatrists, virtually none of whom are trained to manage children, but there are thousands others including Buddhist monks, professional healers *kruu*, mediums, and traditional birth attendants who minister traditional healing (Eisenbruch 2004a; Eisenbruch, de Jong, and van de Put 2004; van de Put and Eisenbruch 2004).

Although one might start with the "great tradition" (what does the formal religion say about child behavior?), a more powerful entry point is the popular beliefs as reflected for example on folk tales such as "The child who lied to eat" cited by Thierry (1994, 251–65).

Long ago there lived a boy with his mother, who took care of a pig. The child desperately wanted to eat this pig, but his mother wouldn't allow it as she needed to take it to market. The boy created this ruse. He told his mother that angels in a dream had revealed the location of a golden treasure. He told his mother to accompany him there. Off they went with a pannier, to the heart of the forest. They set down the pannier and the boy exclaimed that this was the location of the treasure. Then he ordered her to wait there with the empty pannier until he returned. The boy returned home, killed and devoured the pig. Meanwhile, the exhausted mother realised that her son was a swindler. Returning home, she discovered him finishing the remains of her pig and drinking liquor. Enraged, she told her younger brother that she didn't need such a son and asked him to thrust him into a sack and throw him into the water.

As the uncle was on the verge of throwing him in, the boy continued his ruse, and begged his uncle to spare him. He said that as he was on the verge of dying, and he had forgotten his 'Lying manuals' at home, could his uncle please retrieve them for him. Without these, he added, he would have no way after his imminent death to stop the ghosts from devouring him. Off went his uncle.

The boy, alone in his sack on the river bank, peered through a space in the sack and saw an approaching leper. The boy exclaimed loudly that he had contracted leprosy and had crawled into this sack in order to be healed, but at this stage he didn't know if his lesions were cured. When the leper heard this story, he ripped open the sack so that he could hop inside. At this, the boy ran off.

Meanwhile, the uncle had asked the boy's mother for his "Lying manual," to be told that this boy needed no such thing. There were no manuals. The enraged uncle returned to the sack and flung it into the water. The leper drowned.

This child used his talents to violate all but one of the Five Buddhist Precepts (do not kill, do not steal, do not indulge in sexual misconduct, do not make false speech, do not take intoxicants). Had he had a bad character from birth, by now his mother would have had her fingers burned and wouldn't have gone along so readily with his story. The child's character is believed to be set from birth but modified according to how children are handled. A child born with special attributes (such as the umbilical cord draped across its neck) that signify an endowment of intelligence and power, could develop in either direction: in the service of high morality (as in becoming a healer) or to aid the development of "creative" psychopathic tendencies.

After more than twenty years of the autogenocidal Khmer Rouge regime, disintegration of the health infrastructure, an ensuing civil war, famines, wholesale posttraumatic psychiatric morbidity, and now social chaos and the specter of childhood HIV, children in Cambodia face among the worst prospects of any in the world. According to the Demographic and Health Survey 2005 (National Institute of Public Health and National Institute of Statistics [Cambodia] and ORC Macro 2006, 2005), one in every fifteen babies born in Cambodia does not survive to his or her first birthday. No less than 65,000 Cambodian children die every year before they reach their fifth birthday. Abnormal parenting, child abuse, trafficking, and other gross behavioral disorders are rife.

The focus of this chapter is on illnesses affecting infants and young children, examined through an ethnographic lens.

METHOD

Breadth or Depth?

Cambodians have emerged from decades of civil war to seek a future but three scourges hinder the building of a sustainable peace: (1) the consequences of the Khmer Rouge cultural ethnocide and further threats to tradition; (2) the epidemic of HIV/AIDS adding to the collapse of communities, with deep questions about intergenerational relations and cultural transmission; and (3) new incarnations of social upheaval marking the coming of age of youth born in the wake of the Khmer Rouge who faced this future unprotected by cultural codes. The complex data can more easily be generated and analysed from an in-depth study in one setting (Institute of Medicine Committee on Communication for Behavior Change in the 21st Century 2002). Table 3.1 shows criteria for choice of study population and why Cambodians are an appropriate group.

Setting

The ethnography was carried out between 1990 and 2007 with a network of 1,300 traditional healers (monks, *kruu*, traditional birth attendants,

Table 3.1. Criteria for Choosing the Study Population and Why Cambodians Are an Appropriate Group

Criteria for Group	Rationale for Cambodian Target Group
Feasibility	Access to the groups in-country, permission, cooperation, and human resources.
Salience of issues	Recovery from thirty years of civil war and Khmer Rouge (Chandler 1999). "Bottom heavy" age pyramid, with *high rates of childbearing*; growth of social problems, for instance, domestic violence (Zimmerman 1994); sexual abuse, with HIV-AIDS depicted as "Cambodia's new killing fields" (Faulder 2001). Notions of what constituted "Khmerness" changing (Ebihara, Mortland, and Ledgerwood 1994).
Culturally distinct group	(1) Cambodia is fairly homogenous ethnically. (2) Even after some years postconflict, culture is still a salient force—80 percent of people are rural and culture powerfully shapes belief and behavior.
Culturally distinct family patterns	Traditional Cambodian *notions of family conduct*—for instance, in relation to childhood—health care decision making and prevention of social problems disorders are clear (Ang 1986).
Organizational culture for problem solving	Postconflict Cambodian community has re-established its healing organization (monks, healers who advise and treat) (Harris 2005; Marston and Guthrie 2004) outside that of the dominant culture
Responses to education	Cultural issues affect responses to health education; calls for understanding traditional practices (beyond "health education" about "facts") (van de Put and Eisenbruch 2002a; van de Put and Eisenbruch 2002b, 93–156)
Mental health of families	Can examine how cultural styles are affected by mental health issues. Cambodians exhibit high rates of childhood behavioral disturbances (van de Put and Eisenbruch 2002a; van de Put and Eisenbruch 2002b, 93–156)
Conflict experiences	Cambodians bring an experience of childhood abuse, wholesale *trauma* and loss. There is a Cambodian semiotics of violence (Hinton 1998; Locard 2003).
Intergenerational influences	Can examine repetition of problems into next generation. War *adversely affected parenting*, for instance, sexual abuse; experiencing childhood violence may create risk in next generation.
Geography	There is little work on childhood ethnography in mainland Southeast Asia.

mediums, and lay healers) in several hundred villages across Cambodia. On arrival in an area, we found each practicing traditional healer. By snowball sampling, we observed the traditional healers and the families who sought treatment. We observed in detail how the healers made objects such as amulets, applied them to the patient, and helped the patient's integration back into the village. After the treatment, we clarified the healer's rationale and choice in examining, diagnosing, and treating the woman or child; and how the "illness" mirrors problems in social and economic development.

I found a subgroup of healers who were particularly adept in the treatment of children and became a sometime apprentice to them. Every effort was made to observe healers while engaged in treatment of children and thereby snowball to meet their patients, families, and neighbors. In this way, I followed the trail of opinions and practices of those in the community who, as indicated by their help-seeking behavior and by follow-up discussions, had a shared belief system about illnesses affecting children. The Cambodian research assistants engaged in autoethnography (Tedlock 2000, 455–86). I gained a better understanding not only of the healers' general vocabulary and ways of healing such as their pharmacopoeia but, more important, I learned something of their codes of conduct.

In exploring family narratives about childhood health and illness, we (1) focused on nonthreatening aspects and moved to more evocative problems, (2) explored indigenous terminologies, (3) explored traditional codes of conduct governing family life, their modification in response to globalization, and the perceived consequences for health (e.g., mediated through descent from mother or father, combinations of biological and nonbiological), (4) explored attributions for childhood illness (natural/supernatural; mystical-animistic-magical) guided by the Explanatory Model Schedule, a 45-item tool validated in Khmer (Eisenbruch and Handelman 1989), and (5) mapped concepts that are evocative but do not challenge (e.g., nonverbal techniques such as outline diagrams of children onto which parents "draw" the problem and its cause-and-effects). A female assistant spent time with female devotees, mediums, and patients.

Intergenerational and Gender Dynamics

We observed how the original code of conduct concerning children has changed. Were current codes different from what family members remembered of past values and codes? What was the place occupied by new forms of violence (e.g., children murdering their parents)?

Cultural Attributions About the Legacy of Survival and Memory

We explored ideas that children were affected from their previous life— for instance, a mark on the child's skin signaling that it had been reborn from the Pol Pot time with the mark indicating that it had been bound or tortured. We probed what parents thought this might do to their child's behavior; for instance, would children killed during 1975–1979 be reborn and, coming of age, savagely seek revenge? And, we observed parents' responses; for instance, did they pity their child, seek help from a healer, or were they unconcerned?

FINDINGS

Young Children Who Fail to Thrive

Crucial questions involve learning how parents come to terms with the illnesses of young children. How does culture shape parental attitudes to their babies' vulnerability and risks? And how might culture protect parents or, at the very least, reduce their sense of powerlessness and guilt? Indigenous notions of neonatal illnesses and their traditional treatments reveal cultural ideas about the origin of life and about genetics.

Causes

Healers tried to work out *who* did what (parents, infant, and traditional birth attendant); the effects *before* the birth (mother's anatomy) and *after* it (disposal of the placenta); and the force of events during the parents' and child's *present* lives (violations of moral codes by the parents, or the infant's inability to suckle) and as legacies of their *previous* incarnations (ignoble feelings by the parents in their previous existence and the reactions of the child's "preceding mother" from its earlier incarnation).

Breasts and Milk

Abnormal breasts signaled evil, misfortune, and danger. Any abnormality could disrupt infant feeding. The breasts could have the wrong form or the wrong size.

Or the milk was hot, bad, or sour. Bad blood could rise from the mother's uterus and lodge in her breasts—blood was believed to be the forerunner of milk, so the suckling baby absorbed the bad blood and became ill. A Khmer proverb was "the pike fish (*cdao*) eats its own child." The pike doesn't eat its eggs, but its baseball-shaped form was likened to that of a man.

"Child Not Harmonious"

The term *kAAp* means "to be agreeable," or "to be in harmony," or "to be effective, successful or propitious." It depicted the state in which domestic animals—or their animal husbandry masters—raised healthy offspring. It also depicted how a person nurtured his business, but was not usually applied to raising children. If there had been, for example, a genetic incompatibility between mother and newborn, this condition was known as "child not in harmony" (*koon m?n kAAp?*). The child might also be out of harmony with its mother, in which case bad blood, retained after childbirth, would enter the breast milk.

The view was expressed that "child not in harmony" was caused when parents had not taken enough care of their infant. Perhaps they had returned from the rice field and hadn't cleaned the mother's breast before allowing the infant to suckle. Or the parents, taking their child to the rice fields, placed it under a tree, or on the dike or levee bordering the paddy field, where spirits—like the ants, centipedes, or other insects—stung and poisoned the lone infant. The fault lay on the shoulders of the parents and had nothing to do with mismatched predestiny. This was the most extreme case of parental culpability, but even this had to do with pressures and ignorance (the Khmer term implied neglect and carelessness rather than deliberate malice, for which the phrase "hate the child" is used even when the abusing parent generally loved the infant).

The parents of a prospective couple had first checked their children's compatibility with the religious assistant at the Buddhist pagoda. Even though they were both born in the Year of the Tiger—in theory, not compatible with one another, as leading to the lineage of the female giant ogre—he had assured them there was no incompatibility and they had gone ahead with the wedding. In 1982, after three years of marriage, the first child was born. Given the parental incompatibility, he would have died but, ironically, he survived because his father was press-ganged into the military.

By the time the father was demobilized and allowed to return, their child was nine, old enough to be immune to the incompatibility between his parents. The family reunited, the mother became pregnant but the infant died within weeks of the birth. The couple realized something was wrong between them, and returned to ask the assistant what had gone wrong with his prenuptial prediction. He replied that he had predicted the marital compatibility and, in this, he had been proved right, for they were a happy couple. Their incompatibility with their offspring was into the future and irrelevant to the prenuptial diagnosis. Now, he examined their fortune as parents, using the combination of calendrical year, name of animal, and the element giving rise to the lineage. The explanation did nothing to reassure the parents, and when the mother became pregnant for the third time, they took great care. Sadly, this infant died too. The mother understood that the children suffered because she and her husband were born in the Year of the Tiger.

One night the mother saw a large black figure descending onto her chest and face and screamed in terror. She ran to her sister-in-law's house and stayed there. The couple had not broken up, but the wife knew that it was too dangerous for her to stay in the marital home, where her husband stayed, taking care of their fourteen-year-old daughter, the first-born and only living child.

This is an all too common story, with versions told in the voices of the mother, the monk, and the *kruu*. It was obvious to the mothers that poverty led to malnutrition but they also believed that their astrological destiny was the key. The monk, in explaining the link between the infant's life in this world and in that of its preceding mother, described a widely known belief in "being born with incomplete life span." A person who died and was reincarnated, for example as an animal, in his haste to be reincarnated once more as a human might strive to cut short his life span in the "other world," that is, his nonhuman state. Monks, influenced by Buddhist metaphysics, would define two universes, the orb of humans and that of nonhumans. It was no use trying to speed up the lifespan in the other world because there was a shortfall in the number of years required to assemble the necessary life span so that, on seeking entrance to the human world, he was refused and told to return and make up the shortfall of years. A person who had died shortly before their generational years had been lived out on this earth would go to the other orb; on arrival, he would not be received by the Death Committee, whose membership, under its chairman, the Deity *macco?riec* or Yama, included all the preceding mothers of the world. The committee ordered him back to live out the necessary generational cycle in the human world before admission to the other world. Returning, he would start out again as an infant—but with a life span preset to be short. A person short by a year or so of the required cycle would serve out that time in the world of humans—and fall ill and probably die with "child of *?aarih.*"

CHARACTERISTICS

The healers, using evocative terms such as "peacock spur" breasts, conveyed the image of the infant shaking its head like a calf massaging its mother's teats to stimulate the let-down reflex. In one curious symptom, the child was unable to look directly at his parents' faces, but looked at them out of the corner of his eye or quickly averted his gaze. True or not, this sidelong glance perceived by the adults reflects the belief that the child felt resentment, for it had done nothing to warrant illness. There was a perceived breakdown of trust from child to mother who, for whatever reason, had withheld good milk.

TREATING THE MOTHER

In the "puppy dog substitution ritual," the mother had to find a puppy and take it to the *kruu* to be looked after. The healer took it to a nice place and said to the puppy, "I want to have a baby puppy, you go back to your mother and tell your mother to send me another baby from your litter." Sometimes the healer took the puppy back to its mother, or he took it to his house. After that, the mother could safely have a healthy child, as if the bitch had donated one of her litter to the human mother and, in return, one of the puppies, instead of her child, fell ill.

As the breasts were often to blame, it was no surprise that *kruu* used rituals to ritually transform and "substitute the breast." The Tiger Deity spirit can be stopped in its path if destroyed metaphorically, as the substitution ritual does, by burning a lump of clay, for example, which represented the breasts. The Tiger Deity spirits and "misfortune" lurked in only one particular breast, as shown by the presumed asymmetry. Most spirits can readily switch location in the victim's body, but these Tiger Deity spirits, less crafty than the normal sort of spirits that caused illness, seemed to be pegged within one breast and didn't readily cross to the other to evade the healer. This belief gave rise to the practice of aiming the ritual spraying onto the breast inhabited by the spirit, the one on which the suckling infant failed to thrive whereas, fed exclusively on the other, he did well.

A monk performed this metaphoric surgery in four stages, illustrated by the following case of a woman who had been diagnosed as having asymmetric breasts. He fashioned a miniature earthen or clay image of the child, placed it on top of the mother's chest, and placed two uneven ends of banana, one big, one small, on top of the earth figurine. Second, he performed substitution on the breast. The husband draped a betel leaf on top of the bigger breast, and he cut off a bit of the leaf. Third, the monk sought a woman who had had many living children. He took two uneven lengths of incense sticks, and symbolically evened up the uneven clavicles.

The fecund woman laid a stick of incense on each side of her, each running from the breast upward and outward to the clavicle; or she laid two sticks along the lengths of each clavicle. Then she cut a segment off the longer incense stick that represented the bigger breast, making the two sticks of even length.

The monk made a three-sided "pig's snout" (pDD), on which he placed the clay figure that had been placed on the mother's chest, and added the bits of leaf and wood that had been left over. He placed it in the center of the threshold of the doorway. The mother stood in the doorway and squashed it with her foot. The monk instructed the family to boil a goose egg for the woman to eat.

In the first step, the monk, in fashioning the images with the bananas and the earthen figurines, defines the inequality between the mother's two breasts. In the second stage, the father, as metaphorical surgeon, "amputates" the bigger breast to equalize the size of the pair. In the third stage, the spotlight shifts to the mother, who by her own hand kills the substitute *?aar?h koon*—as, it was believed, she would have been fated to do to her real child, by giving it her bad breast, were it not for this substitution. Finally, the family shares in the symbolic celebration of their fertility. Geese are said to be better than ducks or chickens in taking care of their babies. The goose egg had to have been fertilized but spoiled and destined never to hatch to produce a live chick, which is why it was called literally "waiting in the nest." If the woman ingested this blighted egg, the evil was displaced onto the egg, sparing her baby.

TREATING THE BABY

The baby is like a little bird, such as a turtledove. To ensnare one, people ventured to the forest where the birds lived. They placed a cage containing a captured *decoy* male turtledove (*lClCCk tneak*), on an elevated platform, in front of which the trap was set, and it sang its song. Other male turtledoves approached in anger, female ones in response to the mating call, and the trap was sprung. This decoy principle was also applied to help call future children to live. If a woman had a history of losing babies because of "child not in harmony," she and her husband could set the decoy to call the not-yet-conceived child to come to her womb and to stay with her (that is, to live). It was best to get the help of a fecund family member, who "gave" one of their young children, not more then two years old, to be fostered with the childless family for some time. It was hoped that this child, designated as "decoy child" (*koon tneak*), would act like the turtledove in drawing the child into the family's net. The childless family cared for it for years and during this time the woman became pregnant and gave birth, it was hoped, to a child who would be healthy. After that the fostered child could return to its parents. Misfortune was not a one-way street: in one example a childless family took in a decoy child, but the plan backfired as the misfortune was transmitted to the decoy child, who fell ill in their home.

TREATING THE YOUNG CHILD

To Throw Off the Scent

The healer tried to change the child—its name, gender, or place. Changing its name was of such urgency that parents would bestow a decoy name before the real name. Healers also ritually transformed the gender of male infants by piercing the ear and inserting an earring. A third option, for either gender, was to transform by disguise, to dispossess the parents of the child, giving the child to the monk who receives it and then returns it to the parents. He gives the child a yellow robe and says, "Take the child from me, and look after him on my behalf." The parents cut up the robe to make into clothes for the child. At the same time, the name is chosen carefully; the child is often called something like Aruh (the one who is alive) or Achie (the one who is healthy).

Pseudoabandonment, Lease-Back Monk's Child

Some substitution rituals aimed to split the bond between the child and its biological parents as a sort of pseudoabandonment. This ritual could not be performed for a child born after a family history in which the first few infants had died after birth.

A month or so after the child's birth, the ritual assistant put it into a two-handled straw basket and abandoned it at a crossroads outside the village. The parents stood some distance away, waiting. Meanwhile, the ritual assistant returned to his pagoda and, without explanation, invited his monk to set out along the road. When the monk saw the abandoned child, he asked to whom it belonged and, of course, no one replied, so the monk said he would take this child as his own. Everybody went back to the pagoda.

The parents were received by that monk, who said, "Oh, by the way, I was walking along the road, and happened upon this infant. I have no idea whose it is. Now, it's mine. But, as I am a monk, I can't take care of it. I need to find someone to help me." The parents offered and the monk appointed them. They requested an old saffron robe of this monk, to cut up into clothes for the infant; after three months, it could wear normal clothing. As a code of conduct, they were forbidden to announce that the child was theirs.

Ritually "Cutting" and Repelling Preceding Mother

In a mirror image of the pseudoabandonment ritual, "dead things" were placed around the child's neck, repelling the agents of death. The rotten smell would repel the preceding mother. A favorite were the talons of the night bird *Strix flammea*, believed to give its mournful cry at night in the vicinity of a sick person, to call the soul of the person. Also included were the proboscises of seven small stingless bees, insects renowned for having millions of "babies." The nectar, eggs, and larvae go in and out of the insect's proboscis, and if the woman eats this stuff she too will have lots of viable babies slide out of her tube. In another example, one could use the fur of a kind of "Brahma" monkey and a "white" monkey, which happily make offspring in the forest.

The Preceding Mother

Chea, a young Cambodian mother, was startled one night by the chilling sound of the night bird. She rushed down the ladder of her hut and shrieked a retort as if it was a spirit: "Robber bitch! Slut! Get out of here! What are you looking for, you lowly unworthy nothing! There are no kids here for you! Get lost!" She went inside and, grasping a handful of unhusked rice, with which she encircled her child, said, "Please, you fourteen souls, station yourselves once more in my child." In an effort to lure the ravenous evils spirits from her child, she hurled the unhusked rice to the earth saying, "One, two, three, ciiik" (the word people called out to put the shoulder to the wheel to get something heavy moving). She returned inside, and fell asleep calmly next to her baby.

BREAKING THE LINK WITH THE PAST

From the moment of its first breath, all residual links between the infant and its previous life must be severed, in particular its links with its mother in its previous incarnation. The preceding mother, like her human counterpart, could not shake off the attachment and the hunger, for up to a year after birth. Such behavior by a preceding mother smacks of what Western grief therapists have called grief reactions. We know that it takes roughly a year for grief to subside, but that nothing parallels the intensity and duration of that experienced by a parent for a lost child—and which may never end. If it seems strange that the preceding mother's grief should be so malignant, consider any mother in a developing country facing the ever-present threat of her child's death. She cannot shake off the threat. She certainly cannot start up an anticipatory grief reaction for a living child, but in a way she really does. It is as if she projects the constant fear of her child's death onto the mythical preceding mother.

How fascinating that the Cambodian word for attachment and nostalgia is *ʔaalay*, which means "the abode"—the Pali word *alayo* denotes a dwelling, desire, attachment, and lust. It is another suggestion of the link between homesickness and the house as symbolized by the burial of the placenta close to the ritual fire lit after the birth; but that is for several hours later. For now, within minutes of the birth, the traditional birth attendant hastens to place the newborn on the mat near its mother, with objects above its head such as betel, white cotton cord, wax, a bottle of medicine, and a pair of scissors.

The healers helped to cut the links by wiping the newborn's meconium onto a cloth that they wound around the index finger of the mother, and then wiped it around its mouth. The newborn brought the meconium from its previous life, a trace of its dreaded preceding mother, as indicated by the Khmer term for meconium, "feces of the enemy." Khmer has a way of grouping "inaugural" products, such as the placenta of a first delivery or a virgin's first menstrual period that have special magical properties, and the meconium, which is the infant's "first" bowel action. In emerging from the baby's lower orifice, it stood for the baby emerged from its mother's lower orifice. In the substitution ritual, the healer put the meconium as emblem of the *preceding* mother, something that emerged from the lower orifice, back into the mouth, the upper orifice. The anus signified dirty feces = morally bad end = the last tangible product of life nourished by the preceding mother, in opposition to the child's mouth, which signified upper end = clean food = morally good end = the first tangible site of nutrition from the new mother in the present life.

Birth is the transition between the newborn's two mothers. The cry of the night birds—a portent that their child will develop *skAn* and die—also strikes fear into the hearts of parents and has to be dealt with. If, for whatever reason, the preceding mother can't cut her ties with the child being born into this world, she will come after him. In one illustration of this drama, I saw a child who was suffering from "child of the deity" (*koon preah*).

An eleven-year-old boy, named Blue Soviet because he had been born in the Soviet hospital, had had a history of convulsions since birth. In the course of the delivery, there had been "a problem between mother and child"—the doctor had pulled the umbilical cord and broken the placenta. The mother bled furiously, and everyone had concentrated on saving her, to the neglect of her baby. The staff, thinking him dead, threw him into the trash, but someone noticed that the little body was convulsing and that he was alive. From that day, he had seizures said by the hospital to be due to damaged nerves. This boy had lost an essential part of his mental faculties (v?ññien) which "they" had taken from him "to study." This child had a voracious appetite but remained thin. He wandered impulsively, hitting and biting. The father's phrase for his son's behavior (leh-lAh), is used to describe those who interfere with others like monkeys—climbing, biting, and hyperactive from morning till night. He seemed not to have developed further than a monkey.

The mother's recollection was different. Just before she learned that she had become pregnant, she had a dream. Two children, a boy and girl, had approached her to request that they live with her. She noticed that the male child was beating a turtledove to death. The female child took the dead bird to her bosom and wandered far away. The boy stood alone, blinking in apparent bewilderment as to why his female counterpart had left. The mother woke and was certain that she was pregnant with a boy. The pregnancy was normal, but when she entered labor, the waters refused to break and the midwife had to break them. Then the infant refused to be born and the labor remained obstructed, with the mother in severe pain, for twenty-four hours.

The birth took place in the commune clinic. The mother's life being in danger, the midwife (not a TBA) had yanked the umbilical cord, but this caused problems for the infant, who became chronically sick. They took the child to seek help from all possible avenues: doctors, kruu, Christian missionaries. Nothing helped.

His father, a Party official, sought the best available treatment for his son, at the Central Party hospital, but nothing helped. In desperation he came to a particular healer, who said that this was a spirit rather than a medical problem. By pulling the umbilicus, the doctor had sped up the child's egress not only from its mother but also from its previous life, where it had been a "child of the deity," and it was dangerous to pull it too fast from that realm. He forecast that the child would not recover until, at the age of twenty-four years, "they" would give his faculties back.

Four years later, we visited this family. The child, now sixteen, seemed like other children, except that he was impervious to danger and played with knives and fire. The kruu *had declared he was a "child of the Deity" and in four years he would regain his normal faculties. The child liked to light incense sticks and pour water onto his head—perhaps in mimicry of the* kruu, *perhaps because he was a "child of the deity." The mother concluded, on the basis of her presaging dream, that her son's illness was the result of his bad action in his previous life.*

The dream is not unusual as a presage. This mother apparently believed she was destined to have twins but that the bad action of the male in its previous life drove away its female twin and she was left with just the male. Her dream showed another popular symbol: the normal turtledove is an innocent harmless bird, easy to keep in its hutch—the image of an ideal infant. By killing this form of bird, the boy in its previous life set the scene for the turtledove to avenge the wrong by attacking him in his new incarnation: this time the turtledove itself incarnated as the dangerous "ghost turtledove," the deadly symbol of *skAn* which Khmer mothers dread. In this case, the healer elevated the "preceding mother" to an exalted rank and therefore the wretched child, son of a moderately important Communist Party official, is not stigmatized as ill because of its mother; his preceding mother ranks on a par with his father. As for the symptoms, intellectually slow children like this one are commonly labelled as "child that the lunar eclipse stepped over" (*krieh kAnlAAE*)—eclipses are linked with a mentally deficient child.

Cambodian legend is rich in accounts of *riehu?* (Sanskrit *Rahu*, the seizer, the mythological demon who swallows the sun and moon and causes eclipse). In one legend, for example, *riehu?* would "see" the fetus in the mother's womb and would "pass over" it and make it mentally defective. During eclipses of the moon, pregnant mothers customarily secured a container of quicklime under their sarong over the belly to confuse the moon into attacking the quicklime rather than her fetus. I mention this condition (which in itself Cambodians don't necessarily consider an illness) because frequently such backward children develop seizures and then they are said to have *skAn*. Intellectual backwardness—which can often accompany neurological disorders—is seen as a temporary state of laziness, rather than as a ceiling on the intellect.

Causes

The Preceding Mother Enters Her Child's Body

Each of the twelve varieties of *skAn* is depicted in a specific drawing of the sick child being attacked by the pathogen (preceding mother or metaphoric animals believed to cause the localized symptoms). The healer, in drawing his homunculus—the three maternal ancestors with long tresses flowing into the child's brain—shows the shared beliefs of patient and healer about how the preceding mother enters her child's body.

Biting or Clawing of Metaphorical Animals

If the child with *skAn* had been born in the Year of the Ox, the second year of the lunar cycle, he suffered from *skan* of the dog (*skAn ckae*). It was symbolically caused by the dog, or wolf, biting the child's right torso or foot. If the child was born in the sixth year of the lunar cycle, the Year of the Snake, he might develop Crocodile *skAn* (*krApBB*). Malnourished infants were said to be prone to it. It affected only children under the age of three.

Parenting

The attitude of the caregivers to the baby could also lead to *skAn*. Parents "thinking too much" about their insoluble misfortunes could cause the baby to develop "*skAn* madness" or "madness of shaking body elements." Negligent parents, for example, might warm a child with a fever, rather than cooling it. Even the mood of the TBA during birth could transfer to the infant; if she had been angry, for instance, the child would absorb this mood and cry angrily at night.

Characteristics

Most cases of *skAn* developed when the child was a few months to twelve years old, and usually the variants caused by the preceding mother struck younger infants. Sometimes the illness was exacerbated each month on the days that people observed the Eight Precepts. The child knew first because, being so young, it retained the ability to "see" by night the exact form of the attacker, but few were capable of telling what they had seen. It was believed that the child dreamed, for example, of its preceding mother coming to embrace him. In "dog or wolf *skAn*," he dreamt of a dog or wolf with bared fangs about to pounce, and he woke in a rage. In "cartwheel *skAn*," he saw the mythical form of Indra's rainbow or bow, waxing and waning. In "crocodile *skAn*," he saw the crocodile approach, ready to bite his legs and, in a reflex to escape, he violently contracted them. In "monkey *skAn*," he dreamed of a monkey. In "owl *skAn*," he heard the owl hooting in the night, and later he fell so severely ill that, if he recovered, he could infect other children, or even domestic animals, who happened to cross his path. No wonder that the classic feature of any sort of *skAn* was crying a lot at night, sometimes at a fixed time.

Treatment

There were six methods of treating, and then preventing, recurrence of *skAn*: (1) substitution rituals; (2) expulsion; (3) unblocking; (4) cooling; (5) repulsion of the preceding mother's return; and (6) the use of special magical formulae specific to *skAn*.

The preceding mother had to be entreated with rice, soup, dessert, or money to allow the child to suckle its current mother and to sleep peacefully, because the former mother already had lots of other children and this particular child now lived in this world, not hers. The healer and parents implored her to take their offering to nourish her own spirit children in the other world. The healer organizing this ceremony made a libation of the food, which he placed in a tiny woven basket (*pee*). He fashioned a clay image of the sick child and inserted it into the first basket. He prepared a second image of the preceding mother carrying her child in her arms and told it, "The first image is your child. Now don't come any longer for your child. Come and compete for this one." The *kruu* pointed to the sick child and asked the real mother of the sick child, "Is this your child?" and when she replied in the affirmative he asked, "And what about the child in the woven basket?" and she said, "That is not my child." The ritual reinforced the mother's confidence that the child was safely hers.

I have mentioned that "normal mouth blisters," if not treated, can develop into "mouth blisters of the preceding mother.'" To prevent such a disastrous complication, the healer burned a small species of house lizard, *Hemidactylus maculatus*, ground it to a powder, and mixed it with coconut oil to make a puree. He or the parent wrapped a white cloth around the index finger, dipped it in the medicament, and smeared it around the blistered mouth of the child. I was reminded of a story of the house lizard as the *kruu*, that is, the teacher, of the crocodile. They shared a number of attributes, such as the way they seize their prey. But the crocodile couldn't scale walls, and the lizard could. The savage crocodile asked the lizard how it was done, but the prudent lizard didn't tell. Angered, the crocodile wanted to devour its master, but the lizard escaped up the wall. The legend, translated to the clinical situation, is about the preceding mother who, like the crocodile, approaches from the underworld to seize her "prey," her former child. Crocodile and lizard, of the same appearance, are of one family. In the treatment ritual, the child's mouth—that is, snout—is changed. The slippery coconut oil, smeared in the child's mouth, deters the preceding mother from her purchase on her former child. In another reversal, lizard and preceding mother are "teachers" of the crocodile and the child and, as such, share a hierarchical position. Whereas in the illness the "respected" mother turns on her former child, in the legend it is the student who turns on the teacher. In the treatment ritual, the lizard is literally put into the mouth of the child and cancels out the attack.

The *kruu* in drawing his homunculus—the three preceding mothers, with long tresses flowing into the child's brain—shows the shared beliefs of patient and healer about the maternal ancestor entering the child's body through the brain. The first of the three subtypes of preceding mother *skAn*, associated with the Year of the Tiger, has power beyond the other two. When the child saw its preceding mother approach, it was like looking in the mirror at a part of himself. And she recognized him too and embraced him. But the child saw a female who was not his regular mother and, instead, had the staring eyes of a ghost. His terrified scream resembled that of the spirit, not his regular cry.

Each type of *skAn* had characteristics that determined the direction along the axis of the child's body in which the healer performed ritual spraying. When the metaphorical animal was perched on the child's head, the healer sprayed from the feet, which induced a bowel action; when it devoured the child from its feet, he sprayed from the head, which induced vomiting. But sometimes the devious adversary, to evade expulsion, migrated around the child's body, and the healers had to spray in several directions in succession until they triggered a bowel action, the sign that the cause of *skAn* had been evacuated.

Repulsion of the Preceding Mother's Return

Some healers knew that the old hag of a preceding mother could be driven off by symbols of fresh fertility. They gave expression to this by including in the ingredients woodchips taken from the inner edge of the planks on both sides of a latrine over which one squats. These they mixed with a virgin's menstrual blood, which was wrapped in a piece of cloth and rubbed to make the solution for the child to drink.

Pharmacological

The ingredients in the medicaments stank and, in this way, would repel the preceding mother. The ingredients included, for example, a variety of lemon grass that stank like foul urine; a small thorny shrub known as "rotten stink *Mimosa fera*"; an acrid resin; a spoiled egg that never hatched, literally "egg that waited in the nest"; and a broom used to sweep the ground.

The medicaments, like a symbolic broom, swept away all unwanted dirt (illness) that might contaminate the body once more. In another example, the ingredients included wood shavings from the surface of the two blocks of wood on which one balances when squatting on the toilet, mixed with water that the child drank. With good reason, the preceding mother was afraid of this water. Then the healer dipped a shirt in the menstrual blood of a virgin and wrapped it around some bits of wood gathered from the remains of the water used in the first stage and the child drank again.

DISCUSSION

The naming of a vulnerable child, a substitution ritual to ward off misfortune, is a well-known technique in other societies. Among the Gusii, when a woman has lost a number of children in succession, she may call the next one Makori or Nyabara, references to wide paths or roads, and put the neonate in a basket, take it to a cowpath or road, sit at a junction with some old women and ask passersby to look after the baby, and give it to them for a token (LeVine et al. 1994). The Gusii and Cambodian rituals are remarkably identical.

The most tangible link between baby and its past is the placenta. The placenta is similarly significant, and its ritual burial is widely practiced in Southeast Asia (Laderman 1983); it gives expression to the local belief that a person is safe at home and enters a state of danger on journeying from it. If the placenta is safe, so is the child—provided it does not stray too far. If the placenta is disturbed, so is the child, who may develop *skAn* (Eisenbruch 1992a). The location is crucial as the placenta is the "globe of the origin of the soul" of the child. The site is covered with cactus or spiny plants to protect it from interference by dogs or spirits. People fear that a violation of this code may cause harm to the mother or to the baby. A similar metaphorical continuity between placenta and house as protective structures is found among the Gusii of Kenya—the Gusii word for placenta literally refers to the bark strips that kept together the frame of a house before the advent of nails (LeVine et. al. 1994). The placenta is like a "tree of life" and even after resettlement, the Hmong refugees, for example, want the placenta buried in the hospital, as the person upon death must collect it in order to enter the next life (Rice 1994).

Of what use are such rituals? We may say that when a healer, trying to expel an angered spirit from a possessed patient, goes into mortal combat with it—he or she ties it, threatens it, and finally expels it; the patient may relapse in a year or two but for now the incident is closed. In a substitution ritual, on the other hand, the healer can't go into mortal combat with the preceding mother who, in any case, has not yet made the child ill. Instead, he or she *pretends* that the preceding mother has been engaged. This has the advantage that the make-believe outcome is always as expected, with victory to the living. The down side is that a substitution ritual is a "soft" protection that does not deter the preceding mother, at some time in the future, from attacking the child. The purpose of the ritual is to help families deal with loss and the threat of loss.

Childhood illnesses confront the ambiguity between the world of the adult and the child. It straddles the period when the child is not yet born and the months after birth when the child is gradually defined as separate from its previous life. The danger subsides with the developmental milestones and the associated rites of passage—such as the naming ceremony, closure of the fontanelles, cutting the hair, and weaning. At each point along this developmental road, the child forgets a bit more of its preceding life and in so doing becomes progressively more safely embedded in this life.

Postulates About Time, Epigenesis, and Child Development

- The child's development is seen as nonlinear. This is explored by examining the progression of indigenous categories of illness, from the time an infant becomes ill. It is anticipated that certain illnesses will switch abruptly at different developmental stages (for example, an infant may contract furuncles from his syphilitic father; these become redefined as mental retardation at early adolescence and as another illness in early adulthood). This has implications for anthropological aspects of genetics, microbiology, and theories of contagion.
- A child is seen as having circular, rather than linear, development. This is explored by examining the notions of the child's links to its past life—as shown by the capacity of its preceding mother to cause illness. Special cases, such as twins, help to better understand the process of a child having two or more mothers and a kind of "spliced" epigenetic development.

Postulates About Cause-and-Effect

- The state of a child's health is not an absolute, but is seen as though it can be "rewound" rather like a tape recorder. This is explored by examining the use by traditional healers of substitution rituals to metaphorically change the child's identity, or that of its mother, in an effort to displace an illness from the child's body. This has implications for anthropological aspects of pediatrics and genetics.

Postulates About Gender, Guilt, and Responsibility

- Theories of inheritance are shaped by gender and astrology, resulting in an asymmetric theory of inheritance from the parents. This is explored by examining the taxonomies and explanations among families with serial illnesses and deaths of infants, in which, it is anticipated, the mother is held accountable according to her astrological configuration. This will have implications for anthropological aspects of embryology and genetics.
- There is a nonlinear view of responsibility for a child's ill health, in which a child may fall ill because of the bad actions of its parents or other relations. This is addressed by exploring the natural history of failure to thrive in relation to the view that ancestral spirits of the parents are punishing them by inflicting illness on their child. This has implications for anthropological aspects of child and family psychiatry.

General

The infrastructure in some countries postconflict may have decimated the child mental health workforce—in Cambodia, for example, where the country's entire infrastructure, including the health system, was destroyed during the Khmer Rouge regime—and in 1979 none of the forty-three surviving medical doctors in Cambodia were psychiatrists (Savin, 2000). Child and adolescent psychiatrists coming to resource-poor countries may play a vital role in educating others but must be willing to increase their cultural competence and self-reflection, increase their mindfulness of the local cultural context and understanding of the inherent capacity of the existing systems, carefully ensuring the provision of appropriate education.

Horacio Fabrega Jr. (1994) argued, on the basis of his fieldwork conducted in Tlaxcala, Mexico, that "infant deaths should be examined within a framework of meaning that has spiritual and existential connection to everyday affairs, and that this approach would provide the mourner with a meaningful cultural rationale that can facilitate emotional release and spiritual significance." Convulsions in childhood, whatever the underlying cause, are terrifying and sometimes life threatening, and, as shown in Benin (Obi, Ejeheri, and Alakija, 1994) cultural beliefs do not always lead parents to seek appropriate medical care. The Cambodian tradition sees the episode as an expression of the child's unsevered link with its previous life and its preceding mother. She is the embodiment of feelings of jealousy, giving expression to what in other societies is the "evil eye." In the Cambodian case, instead of locating the enemy women in this world, as a neighbor, the enemy is in the "previous world." This would be a benefit for social cohesion.

It seems that "substitution rituals" play a key role in enabling the family and community to overcome their helplessness in the face of their sick children. Such rituals were noted in ancient history, for example, the Hittite ritual performed by the midwife for the newborn (Berman, 1972; Goedegebuure, 2002) and in South Asia (Doniger, 1994; Smith, 1991).

Child psychiatry needs to be informed by an understanding of local cultures, including cultural survival and transformation, the way people construct for themselves multiple cultural identities, and the role of traditional healers in development (Bichmann, 1986). "Healing" is not just about individual children; it repairs the community's social and moral fabric. It makes use of and enhances "cultural capital"—the shared sense of meaning that determines the group's way of life and invested in families by their forebears (Bourdieu, 1973). Cultural capital, in turn, draws from the "intangible cultural heritage—the representations, expressions, knowledge, and skills transmitted from generation to generation, is constantly re-created by communities, and provides them with a sense of identity and continuity" (UNESCO, 2002).

Traditional healers can act as "trauma therapists" helping children in countries recovering from war and function as a link with the past. Responses to conflict and trauma are dictated by local history and culture, and an understanding of local idioms of distress helps us to understand how (Eisenbruch, 1992b). Recovery may depend on an understanding of how societies remember (Connerton, 1989), with culture as the context for memory in the healing of trauma (Antze and Lambek, 1996). Healers have helped to understand the responses to violence among young people (Reynolds, 1990). Combining local resources such as traditional healers with external relief workers can help to assess psychosocial problems of large groups, not just individuals, and inform health programs to alleviate suffering (de Jong, 2002) and build the social conditions for peace. Moreover, a culture-sensitive *emic* approach is essential in order to avoid perpetuating the "category fallacy" in which indigenous subjective understandings of violence are overlooked and Western categories imposed where they have no local validity (Kleinman, Das, and Lock, 1997).

The evidence base about child behavior and illness in resource-poor settings such as Cambodia needs to be built using a culturally competent research design and procedure—and anthropology provides a key ingredient. Eisenbruch (2004b) has defined a template for the steps needed to ensure cultural competence in research, namely in community engagement, communicating with research subjects, design, cross-cultural validation of research instruments, sampling, calibrating diversity variables, demographic variables measured in data sets, research ethics, data collection techniques, data processing and analysis, and dissemination and action. International

Maurice Eisenbruch

child psychiatry research should pay attention to participation from the
perspective of community members (Lindenberg et al., 2001; Lindgren and
Lipson, 2004; Penrod et al., 2003).

ACKNOWLEDGMENTS

Mr. Chou Sam Ath assisted with the fieldwork and Mr. Thong Thel provided
much scholarship on the texts and rituals.

REFERENCES

Ang, C. (1986) *Les êtres surnaturels dans la religion populaire khmère*. Paris: Cedoreck.

Antze, P. and M. Lambek. (1996) *Tense Past—Cultural Essays in Trauma and Memory*.
New York: Routledge.

Behera, D. K. (2005) "Ethnography of Childhood Revisited Workshop: National
University of Singapore 9–11 July 2005 Participants."

Berganza, C. E., J. E. Mezzich, A. A. Otero-Ojeda, M. R. Jorge, S. J. Villasenor-
Bayardo, and C. Rojas-Malpica. (2001) "The Latin American guide for psychiatric
diagnosis. A cultural overview," *The Psychiatric Clinics of North America* 24, no. 3,
pp. 433–46.

Berman, H. (1972) "A Hittite Ritual for the Newborn," *Journal of the American Ori-
ental Society* 92, no. 3, pp. 466–68.

Bichmann, W. (1986) "The role of traditional medicine in African development,"
Schriftenreihe der Deutschen Stiftung fur Internationale Entwicklung 1238 B/a, 175–92;
OQEH., pp. 175–92.

Bourdieu, P. (1973) "Cultural reproduction and social reproduction," in R. Brown,
ed., *Knowledge, Education and Social Change*. London: Tavistock.

Bourdillon, M. F. C. (1989) "Fourth International Ethnography of Childhood Workshop," *Anthropology Today* 5, no. 6, p. 20.

Chandler, D. P. (1999) *Voices from S-21 Terror and History in Pol Pot's Secret Prison*.
Berkeley: University of California Press.

Christensen, P. H. (1999) *Towards an Anthropology of Childhood Sickness: An Ethnographic Study of Danish Schoolchildren*. Hull: University of Hull.

Connerton, P. (1989) *How Societies Remember*. Cambridge, UK: Cambridge University Press.

de Jong, J. T. V. M. (2002) *Trauma, War, and Violence: Public Mental Health in Socio-
Cultural Context*. New York: Plenum/Kluwer.

Doniger, W. (1994) "Speaking in tongues: Deceptive stories about sexual decep-
tion," *The Journal of Religion* 74, no. 3, pp. 320–37.

Ebihara, M. M., C. A. Mortland, and J. Ledgerwood. (1994) *Cambodian Culture Since
1975: Homeland and Exile*. Ithaca, NY: Cornell University Press.

Eisenbruch, M. (1998) "Cambodian techniques to prevent failure to thrive, childhood epilepsy, and STD/AIDS in childhood," *Clinical Child Psychology and Psychiatry* 3, no. 4, pp. 503–15.

———. (1992a) The use of traditional healing for treating children of war: The case of *skan* in Cambodia. Refugee Studies Programme (Oxford), 3.

———. (1992b) "Toward a culturally sensitive DSM: Cultural bereavement in Cambodian refugees and the traditional healer as taxonomist," *Journal of Nervous and Mental Disease* 180, no. 1, pp. 8–10.

———. (2004a) "Khmer Rouge architects of mass crime and traditional healers as post-conflict peacebuilders in Cambodia," in B. Pouligny, A. Schnabel, and S. Chesterman, eds., *Mass Crime and Post-Conflict Peacebuilding*. Tokyo and New York: United Nations University Press.

———. (2004b) "The lens of culture, the lens of health: Toward a framework and toolkit for cultural competence," in *Resource Document for UNESCO Asia-Pacific Regional Training Workshop on Cultural Mapping and Cultural Diversity Programming Lens to Safeguard Tangible and Intangible Cultural Expressions and Protect Cultural Diversity, Bangkok, 15–19 December 2004*, pp. 1–248.

Eisenbruch, M., J. T. V. M. de Jong, and W. van de Put. (2004), "Bringing order out of chaos—A culturally competent approach to managing the problems of refugees and victims of organized violence," *Journal of Traumatic Stress* 17, no. 2, pp. 123–31.

Eisenbruch, M. and L. Handelman. (1989) "Development of an Explanatory Model of Illness Schedule for Cambodian Refugee Patients," *Journal of Refugee Studies* 2, no. 2, pp. 243–56.

Ensink, K. and B. Robertson. (1996) "Culture and mental health in the Rainbow Nation: Transcultural psychiatry in a changing South Africa," *Transcultural Psychiatric Research Review* 33, no. 2, pp. 137–72.

Fabrega, H. i. J. and H. Nutini. (1994) "Sudden infant and child death as a cultural phenomenon: A Tlaxcalan case study," *Psychiatry* 57, no. 3, pp. 225–43.

Faulder, D. AIDS is carrying on the work of Pol Pot. Asiaweek.com, November 28, 2001.

Goedegebuure, P. M. (2002) "KBo 17.17+: Remarks on an old Hittite royal substitution ritual," *Journal of Ancient Near Eastern Religions* 2, no. 1, pp. 61–73.

Harper, G. (2001) "Cultural influences on diagnosis," *Child and Adolescent Psychiatric Clinics of North America* 10, no. 4, p. 711.

Harris, I. C. (2005) *Cambodian Buddhism—History and Practice*. Honolulu: University of Hawai'i Press.

Hinton, A. L. (1998) "Why did you kill? The Cambodian genocide and the dark side of face and honor," *Journal of Asian Studies* 57, no. 1, pp. 93–122.

Institute of Medicine Committee on Communication for Behavior Change in the 21st Century (2002) *Speaking of Health—Assessing Health Communication Strategies for Diverse Populations*. Washington, DC: National Academies Press.

James, K. (1998) "Becoming Tongan: An ethnography of childhood," *The Australian Journal of Anthropology* 9, no. 2.

Kapavalu, H. (1993) "Dealing with the dark side in the ethnography of childhood: Child punishment in Tonga," *Oceania* 63, no. 4: 313–329.

Kleinman, A., V. Das, and M. M. Lock. (1997) *Social Suffering*. Berkeley: University of California Press.

Laderman, C. (1983) "Wives and midwives: Childbirth and nutrition in rural Malaysia." Comparative Studies of Health Systems and Medical Care, Volume 7. Berkeley: University of California Press.

LeVine, R. A., S. Dixon, S. LeVine, A. Richman, P. H. Leiderman, C. H. Keefer, and T. B. Brazelton. (1994) *Child Care and Culture: Lessons from Africa*, 20th ed. New York: Cambridge University Press.

LeVine, S. and R. A. LeVine. (1981) "Child abuse and neglect in sub-Saharan Africa," in *Child Abuse and Neglect: Cross-Cultural Perspectives*. Berkeley: University of California Press, pp. 35–55.

LeVine, R. A. and R. S. New. (2007) *Anthropology of Childhood: A Cross-Cultural Reader*. Oxford: Blackwell.

Lindenberg, C. S., R. M. Solorzano, F. M. Vilaro, and L. O. Westbrook. (2001) "Challenges and strategies for conducting intervention research with culturally diverse populations. [Review] [30 refs]," *Journal of Transcultural Nursing* 12, no. 2, pp. 132–39.

Lindgren, T. and L. G. Lipson. (2004) "Finding a way: Afghan women's experience in community participation," *Journal of Transcultural Nursing* 15, no. 2, pp. 122–30.

Locard, H. (2003) "State sponsored crimes against humanity and 'genocide' in Cambodia (1975–1979)," in *Learning and Remembering: The Holocaust, Genocide and State Organized Crime in the Twentieth Century. International Committee of Memorial Museums for the Remembrance of Victims of Public Crimes—Topography of Terror Foundation (Berlin)*, Georg Eckert Institut für Internationala Schulbuchforschung, Braunschweig.

Marston, J. A. and E. Guthrie. (2004) *History, Buddhism, and New Religious Movements in Cambodia*. Honolulu: University of Hawai'i Press.

Morton, H. and H. M. Lee. (1996) *Becoming Tongan: An Ethnography of Childhood*. Honolulu: University of Hawai'i Press.

National Institute of Public Health and National Institute of Statistics [Cambodia] and ORC Macro. 2006 2005, *Cambodia Demographic and Health Survey*, National Institute of Public Health, National Institute of Statistics, and ORC Macro, Phnom Penh, Cambodia and Calverton, Maryland, USA.

Nichter, M. (1985) "Cultural interpretations of states of malnutrition among children: A South Indian case study," *Medical Anthropology* 9, no. 1, pp. 25–48. Special Issue: The Client's Perspective in Primary Health Care.

———. (1994) "Acute respiratory illness: Popular health culture and mother's knowledge in the Philippines," *Medical Anthropology* 15, no. 4, pp. 353–75.

Obi, J. O., N. A. Ejeheri, and W. Alakija. (1994) "Childhood febrile seizures (Benin City experience)," *Ann. Trop. Paediatr.* 14, no. 3, pp. 211–14.

Penrod, J., D. B. Preston, R. E. Cain, and M. T. Starks. (2003) "A discussion of chain referral as a method of sampling hard-to-reach populations," *Journal of Transcultural Nursing* 14, no. 2, pp. 100–7.

Pumariega, A. and T. Cross. (1997) "Cultural competence in child psychiatry," *Basic Handbook of Child and Adolescent Psychiatry* 4, pp. 473–84.

Reynolds, P. (1990) "Zezuru turn of the screw: On children's exposure to evil," *Culture, Medicine and Psychiatry* 14, no. 3, pp. 313–37.

———. (1996) *Traditional Healers and Childhood in Zimbabwe*. Athens: Ohio University Press.

Rice, F. (1994) "Folk medicine: Observations and examples," *Journal of Cult. Divers.* 1, no. 1, pp. 26–27.

Savin, D. (2000) "Developing psychiatric training and services in Cambodia," *Psychiatric Services: A Journal of the American Psychiatric Association* 51, no. 7, p. 935.

Smith, B. K. (1991) "Classifying animals and humans in ancient India," *Man* 26, no. 3, pp. 527–48.

Stephens, S. (1998) "Challenges of Developing an Ethnography of Children and Childhood," *American Anthropologist* 100, no. 2, pp. 530–31.

Swartz, L. (1996) "Culture and mental health in the Rainbow Nation: Transcultural psychiatry in a changing South Africa," *Transcultural Psychiatric Research Review* 33, no. 2, pp. 119–36.

Tedlock, B. (2000) "Ethnography and ethnographic representation," in N. K. Denzin and Y. S. Lincoln, eds., *Handbook of Qualitative Research*. Thousand Oaks, CA: Sage Publications Inc., pp. 455–486.

Thierry, S. (1994) "A propos de l'enfant dans la littérature khmère," in J. Koubi and J. Massard, eds., *Enfants et sociétés d'Asie du Sud-Est*. Paris: L'Harmattan, pp. 251–65.

UNESCO (2002) *Convention for the Safeguarding of the Intangible Cultural Heritage.*

van de Put, W. and M. Eisenbruch. (2002a) "Health in context: Or in convenient conventionalism?" *International Health Exchange* 10, pp. 12–15.

———. (2002b) "The Cambodian experience," in J. T. V. M. de Jong, ed., *Trauma, War, and Violence: Public Mental Health in Socio-Cultural Context*, New York: Plenum/Kluwer, pp. 93–156.

———. (2004) "Healing trauma in Cambodian communities," in K. Miller and L. Rasco, eds., *From Clinic to Community—Ecological Approaches to Refugee Mental Health*. Mahwah, NJ: Lawrence Erlbaum.

Zimmerman, C. (1994) *Plates in a basket will rattle: Domestic violence in Cambodia, Phnom Penh, December 1994 s.n,* Phnom Penh, Cambodia.

4

International Adoption and Mental Health

Long-Term Behavioral Outcome

Frank C. Verhulst

INTRODUCTION

Adoption is the permanent, legal placement of an abandoned, relinquished, or orphaned child within a family. Adoption can occur into a family of relatives (kinship adoption) or into an unrelated family (nonkinship adoption), and adoption can occur within the country of birth of the child (domestic adoption) or across the borders of countries (international adoption). Of course, most international adoptions are nonkinship adoptions.

Over the years, an increasing number of children have been adopted across countries, from 17,538 per year in the 1980s to at least 40,000 per year in 2003 (Selman, 2000, 2005). International adoptions largely pertain to a move of children from poor to rich countries, although the poorest countries are not always the major sources. In absolute terms, the United States is the leading country of destination, with 21,000 adoptees who came from other countries, mainly China, Russia, Guatemala, and South Korea in 2003 (Selman, 2005). In terms of the number of international adoptions per 1,000 births, Norway and Sweden have had the highest rates with over 10 adoptees per 1,000 births, whereas the United States and The Netherlands had medium rates (around 5 per 1,000 births) and Germany and the United Kingdom had the lowest rates (Selman, 2000). Additionally, the sending countries show large variations in number of children who are

PROBLEMS IN CHILDHOOD AND ADOLESCENCE

Problem behavior was another area in which internationally adopted children did somewhat worse than nonadopted children. In a convincing meta-analysis of studies comparing 15,790 internationally adopted children and 30,450 nonadopted controls, it was concluded that international adoptees showed more behavior problems, although the effect sizes could be regarded as small (Juffer and Van IJzendoorn, 2005). International adoptees showed more total, externalizing, and internalizing problems than their nonadopted peers and they are overrepresented in mental health services. Somewhat surprisingly, in their meta-analysis, age at adoption does not appear to be important for the development of behavior problems. This meta-analysis provided evidence that children with backgrounds of extreme adversity are at risk for more behavior problems, especially externalizing problems, compared with international adoptees without such preadoption adversities.

PROBLEMS IN ADULTHOOD

The meta-analysis by Juffer and Van IJzendoorn (2005) pertained to studies that compared adopted versus nonadopted children's behavioral functioning at ages between four and eighteen years. Based on these findings we do not know how internationally adopted children fare once they reach adulthood. Also, as already mentioned, despite the catch-up compared to their past peers, internationally adopted children had slightly higher levels of problem behaviors, showed more often insecure attachments and school problems than their nonadopted peers, and they were overrepresented in mental health care referrals. These findings also make it necessary to study the long-term adjustment of internationally adopted children into adulthood.

Few studies provided information on the developmental course of problems in internationally adopted children based on multiple assessments, and to our knowledge no studies have been published that followed internationally adopted children's problem behaviors longitudinally into adulthood. This is especially important since our own study on the developmental course of internationally adopted children in The Netherlands, The Sophia Longitudinal Adoption Study, indicated that the level of parent-reported problems increased over a three-year period from ages ten to fifteen years to ages thirteen to eighteen years (Verhulst and Versluis-Den Bieman, 1995). It was also found that the difference in level of problems between adopted versus nonadopted children clearly increased with increasing age, both cross-sectionally and longitudinally. The increase in the level of problems, along with the growing disparity between adopted and nonadopted children in adolescence, stressed the importance of obtaining information on long-term adult functioning of international adoptees.

There are only three studies that focused on the behavioral adjustment of internationally adopted children who reached adulthood. Hjern et al. (2002) and Lindblad et al. (2003) studied a national database of clinical records from all Swedish hospitals. This national cohort study involved more than 11,000 international adoptees, including young adults. Their conclusion was that internationally adopted children run a significantly higher risk of suicide, psychiatric illness, and social maladjustment compared to nonadopted controls. However, a limitation of this study was that no standardized diagnostic procedures were used. They based their diagnostic findings on unstandardized information from clinicians. A second limitation of this study was that the authors only had information on adoptees who were admitted to a hospital. Those with problems who were not admitted to a hospital were ignored in this study. Cederblad et al. (1999) studied the adult outcome of a small and selected sample of internationally adopted children in Sweden and concluded that they were well adjusted.

The lack of information on the functioning of international adoptees in adulthood inspired us to follow up a large sample of by now young-adult children who were borne outside The Netherlands and adopted by Dutch parents.

THE SOPHIA LONGITUDINAL ADOPTION STUDY

The Sophia Longitudinal Adoption Study, launched in 1986, was originally inspired by the increasing concern of adoptive parents and mental health professionals about the overrepresentation of adopted children in residential treatment. We studied the behavioral development of a large sample of internationally adopted children. The ages of the children at assessment were ten to fifteen, thirteen to eighteen, and at the last assessment twenty-four to thirty years. The results of this longitudinal study enabled us to look at the development of children who were often born and raised under adverse conditions and who, after being adopted, had to cope with the adaptation to a new environment and with successive developmental tasks. More specifically, we studied to what extent deficits in behavioral functioning persisted and to what extent recovery was possible. The change in life pattern through adoption provided a natural experiment through which it was possible to study the environmentally mediated effects of adverse rearing circumstances, and similarly the effects of a major change of environment to above-average adopting families in The Netherlands. In most studies on the effects of adverse rearing circumstances, it is not possible to disentangle the effects of early versus later environmental influences since most non-adopted children who grow up with problematic parents remain in the same family and thus experience the effects of chronic adversity.

The target sample consisted of all children (n = 3,519) legally adopted by nonrelatives in The Netherlands and born outside The Netherlands between January 1, 1972, and December 31, 1975. Children were selected from the national adoption register of the Dutch Ministry of Justice. Of the 3,309 parents reached, 2,148 participated (64.9 percent). The distribution across native countries was: Korea 32.0 percent; Colombia 14.6 percent; India 9.5 percent; Indonesia 7.9 percent; Bangladesh 6.7 percent; Lebanon 4.9 percent; Austria 5.0 percent; other European countries 4.2 percent; other non-European countries 15.2 percent. The mean occupational level of parents in the adoption sample was much higher than in the general population (Verhulst et al., 1990a).

Three years after the initial data collection, we approached the sample again. This time we not only obtained information from parents but also self-reports. Usable information was obtained on 1,538 adoptees, which was 74.3 percent of the original sample after correction for deceased subjects, those who moved abroad, those who were untraceable, and a small group who participated in another study (Verhulst and Versluis-den Bieman, 1995).

Eleven years after the second (and fourteen years after the first) assessment, we approached the sample of now adult international adoptees. We obtained information from parents and from the adoptees themselves. Not only did we request the participants to complete questionnaires, we also asked each adoptee to be interviewed with a standardized psychiatric interview. We obtained usable information on 1,521 adoptees which was 74.3 percent of the original sample after correction for those who had died, emigrated, and who had intellectual disabilities (Tieman et al., 2005).

Table 4.1 shows the instruments used to assess psychopathology at the three times of assessment of this fourteen-year longitudinal project. Because we conducted a parallel fourteen-year longitudinal study of children from the general population using the same assessment procedures, we were able to compare the developmental course in adopted with that in nonadopted children over a long period.

Ages of the adopted children at the first assessment were between ten and fifteen years. We had no standardized information on the children's functioning shortly after arrival in The Netherlands. Therefore we were not able to study the short-term recovery from the effects of early adverse rearing circumstances. The results of our measurements thus reflect a mix of effects of early adversities and the environmental influences after placement in the adoptive family.

Table 4.1. Instruments used to assess psychopathology in the Sophia Longitudinal Adoption Study

	Time 1	Time 2	Time 3
Age (years)	10–15	13–18	24–30
	CBCL	CBCL	YABCL
		YSR	YASR
			CIDI

CBCL = Child Behavior Checklist (Achenbach, 1991a)
YSR = Youth-Self-Report (Achenbach, 1991b)
YABCL = Young Adult Behavior Checklist (Achenbach, 1997)
YASR = Young Adult Self-Report (Achenbach, 1997)
CIDI = Composite International Diagnostic Interview (World Health Organization, 1992)

PROBLEM BEHAVIOR IN CHILDHOOD AND ADOLESCENCE

Comparisons of CBCL parent ratings between adopted versus nonadopted children at ages ten to fifteen years showed that, in general, adopted children were at increased risk of showing parent-reported problems, especially externalizing problems (Verhulst et al., 1990a). The CBCL mean total problems score showed a significant but small difference of only 2.32 points on a scale theoretically ranging from 0 to 240, with adopted children obtaining less favorable scores. However, this difference in mean total problems scores could largely be attributed to the extremely high scores obtained by a few adopted boys aged ten to fifteen years. Applying a clinical cutoff score revealed that more problems were reported for boys than for girls, and for twelve- to fifteen-year-olds than for ten- to eleven-year-olds. The largest proportion of children that could be regarded as deviant was found among twelve- to fifteen-year-olds, with more than twice as many boys with considerable problems in the adopted versus the nonadopted sample. At the level of specific problems, the largest differences between adopted versus nonadopted children were found for the CBCL scales Delinquent Behavior and Attention Problems in twelve- to fifteen-year-old adopted boys.

Based on these findings it was concluded that although a substantial proportion of adopted boys showed problem behaviors, the majority of adopted children did not show more problems than nonadopted children despite the adopted children's unfavorable experiences early in their lives.

A worrying finding was, however, that the level of parent-reported problems tended to increase over the three-year follow-up period, with the largest increase for the CBCL syndrome scales designated as Withdrawn and Delinquent Behavior (Verhulst and Versluis-den Bieman, 1995). Apparently, withdrawal from contact and covert antisocial behaviors are of increasing concern to parents of adopted children when they move into adolescence. The

Fifty percent of the children who experienced five or more changes in the caretaking environment showed later maladjustment. Problem behavior was also found in 24 percent of the children who had been severely neglected and 31 percent of the severely abused children. It was clear that in our study children who had experienced early negative environmental influences run a greater risk of developing problem behaviors than children who grew up under relatively favorable circumstances despite the fact that these children had also experienced separations and adaptation to a totally new environment.

The early adverse factors that we studied were all strongly associated with the age of the child at placement. This association was so strong that age at placement did not add to the contribution of early risk variables to the probability that the child could be regarded as deviant. In other words, it was not the child's age at placement per se, but the fact that later placement increased the risk of having been subjected to early adverse circumstances, which increased the risk of developing later problem behaviors. In particular, evidence that a child had been abused was a potent predictor of later maladjustment. When these early influences were taken into account, the age of the child at placement as such is of lesser significance.

It is possible that this finding may explain the discrepancy between our finding that age at placement was associated with later maladjustment whereas Juffer and Van IJzendoorn (2005) did not find such an association. It may be that other studies looking at the effect of age at placement did not pertain to children who had been so severely deprived as many of the children in our sample. Even in our sample, taking account of the effects of deprivation removed the effect of age at placement. It was hypothesized that raising a child from his or her first months onward is easier than raising an older child who speaks a foreign language and has already acquired skills and habits and has a history of his or her own. However, the findings of our study could not confirm this hypothesis, and as such corroborates the findings by Juffer and Van IJzendoorn (2005). Children adopted at a relatively old age did not seem to run a greater risk of later maladjustment because they were adopted when they were older, but because they had been subjected to early adverse experiences.

Of the risk factors studied, we found that abuse contributed most strongly to the prediction of later maladjustment. The effect of abuse was so strongly associated with later functioning that the other factors of neglect and number of changes in the caretaking environment had no significant additional value in predicting later problems. In other words if it was known that a child had been abused, this was sufficient information to expect greater likelihood for later maladjustment.

It is known that boys run a greater risk than girls for developmental problems such as ADHD and pervasive developmental disorders. Although developmental disorders are highly genetically determined, it may be that children genetically differ in their susceptibility to environmental influences. We were therefore interested whether the sex difference in adopted children's levels of problems could be attributed to differences in susceptibility to environmental adversities for boys versus girls. However, the greater risk for maladjustment in adopted boys versus girls could not be attributed to sex differences in vulnerability to early adverse factors.

Earlier we discussed that age at placement was associated with a higher risk of developing antisocial and depressive problems. The strong association between age at placement and the early adverse factors indicate that early adversities put children at greater risk of developing conduct problems and depression. This finding is informative with respect to the links between depression and early loss and other environmental adversities.

We can of course also look at the results from a more positive side and focus on the fact that it is remarkable that the majority of children who had backgrounds known to be very damaging functioned well! Apparently, the negative effects of early adverse influences can fade away under the positive influence of the adoptive family. Some children escaped the influences of early adversities and showed remarkable catch-up in the behavioral domain.

Early Adversity and the Increase of Problem Behavior in Childhood and Early Adolescence

As we have described above, adopted children showed an increase in problems from early into later adolescence across the three-year follow-up period in our study. We wanted to know if early adversities were responsible for this increase by making adolescents more vulnerable to the developmental strains of adolescence. The results showed that early environmental factors that were responsible for increased risk for maladjustment at ages ten to fifteen years were still responsible for maladjustment three years later. However, the early negative environmental influences were *not* responsible for the *increase* in problems across the three adolescent years of our follow-up. Factors other than early risks, possibly those that characterize adolescence such as the developmental increase in cognitive abilities, independence from the family, identity formation, and sexual maturation may be more stressful for adopted adolescents than for nonadopted adolescents.

It is possible that with increasing age, adolescent adoptees become more and more prone to develop problem behaviors as a result of their increasing concerns over their biological parentage. Their increased cognitive abilities may enable them to reflect on the meaning of being adopted. They are increasingly able to evaluate the lack of connectedness with their adoptive parents as well as with their biological parents. Their sense of loss of having

once been abandoned and their awareness of the lack of genealogical connectedness are evaluated in adolescence in terms of their developing identity.
Emotional and behavioral reactions may result from this sense of loss, which
is exacerbated by a loosening of the ties between the adolescent and his or
her adoptive family and by the adolescent's striving toward independence.

Ethnicity and the Increase of Problem Behavior in Childhood and Early Adolescence

Our sample of internationally adopted children mainly consisted of children whose parents had a different ethnic background. However, there were
also internationally adopted children who had been born in other European
countries such as Austria and Greece. Therefore we could divide our sample
into children who had been transracially adopted versus those who had
been intraracially adopted. Ethnic differences both within or outside the
family may put adopted children under extra stress, for example through discrimination. Especially in adolescence when children increasingly lack the
protection of the family and operate more independently, transracially
adopted children in a predominantly white population in The Netherlands
may meet more stressful situations than intraracially adopted and nonadopted children. However, we could not conclude that differences in ethnicity between parent and their adopted child were responsible for the longitudinal increase in problems in adolescence.

Internationally Adopted Children on the Threshold to Adulthood

International adoption seems to be in the best interest of the child (Van
IJzendoorn and Juffer, 2006), because internationally adopted children
show dramatic developmental catch-up in various domains of physical,
cognitive, and behavioral functioning. However, it is largely unknown how
well these children adapt to adult life with its new occupational and social
challenges, including relationships. Especially because still a large minority
of internationally adopted children have serious adjustment, behavioral, or
learning problems, it is important to know how they make the transition
into adulthood. Knowledge about internationally adopted children's adjustment problems in adulthood may help to identify ways to support this
transition and prevent or treat problems.

PROBLEM BEHAVIOR IN ADULTHOOD

Fourteen years after the first assessment, we approached the adopted sample, now aged between twenty-four and thirty years, again. Given the higher

levels of problems in childhood and early adolescence and the increase of problems during the following three-year follow-up into adolescence, we had expected high levels of problems in adulthood. We will present here the findings with respect to psychopathology and social functioning.

All participants were interviewed with the CIDI (World Health Organization, 1993), a standardized psychiatric interview to derive DSM-IV diagnoses. Because we used the same assessment procedures in a longitudinal study of a general population sample, also across a fourteen-year interval, we could compare the findings for the adoption sample with those for the general population sample (Hofstra et al., 2000).

Figure 4.2 shows the percentages of adopted and nonadopted individuals who met criteria for DSM-IV diagnoses based on the CIDI interview (Tieman et al., 2005). The odds ratio (OR) for anxiety disorder was 1.52, and the OR for substance use disorder was 2.05 with adoptees having higher probabilities for having a disorder than nonadoptees. We also looked at interactions between adoption status and gender, and adoption status and socioeconomic status. Adopted men were 3.76 times more likely to have a mood disorder than nonadopted men, whereas for women no significant difference between adoptees and nonadoptees in their likelihood to have a mood disorder was found. For all diagnoses together, adoptees with low and middle parental socioeconomic status in childhood did not differ from the comparison subjects, while adoptees with high parental

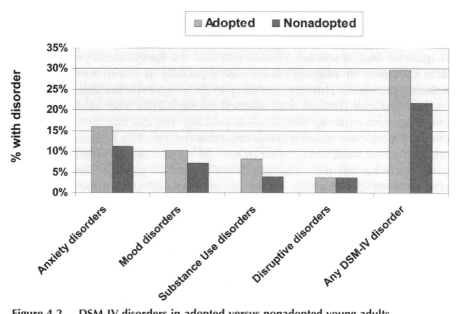

Figure 4.2.   DSM-IV disorders in adopted versus nonadopted young adults

that variations in maternal behavior serve as a mechanism for the nongenomic transmission of individual transmission of individual differences in
stress reactivity across generations.

Social, Educational, and Professional Functioning in Adulthood

People who meet criteria for a DSM disorder can still vary in the degree
to which the disorder affects their everyday functioning. Especially since
we found that the prevalence of substance use disorders in internationally
adopted males and females and of depression in internationally adopted
males was higher than in their nonadopted comparisons, it was important to obtain insight in their everyday social functioning. The only study
of the social functioning of internationally adopted individuals that to
our knowledge was available is the study by Lindblad et al. (2003) who
reported that international adoptees were long-time recipients of social
welfare and that their level of education was comparable to that in the
general population. We therefore compared sociodemographic factors
and social functioning measures of young-adult international adoptees
versus same-aged young adults from the general population (Tieman et
al., 2006).

Figure 4.3 shows the percentages of adopted and nonadopted subjects
who, at the time of assessment, were married, had had a relationship which
lasted more than one year, were living with a partner, or who were living
alone. The results indicated that significantly more nonadopted than
adopted individuals were married, had had a relationship which lasted more
than one year, or were living with a partner. Significantly more adopted than
nonadopted individuals were living alone. Thus, the results showed that
young-adult adoptees were less likely to commit themselves to a partner. It

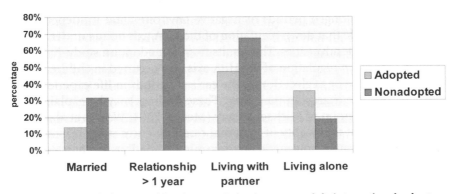

**Figure 4.3. Sociodemographic characteristics in young-adult international adoptees
and comparisons from the general population**

may be that early adversities including separations resulting in attachment problems have rendered adopted individuals less capable of forming lasting intimate relationships. Of course, it is also possible that international adoptees are less in need of close relationships and find living alone less stressful or problematic than nonadoptees.

In this light, the findings by O'Connor et al. (2003) who studied attachment problems in Romanian-adopted children are relevant. The authors studied child-parent attachment quality with an adoptive caregiver at age four years in a sample of 111 children adopted into the United Kingdom following early severe deprivation in Romania and a comparison group of fifty-two nondeprived adoptees. Findings indicated that, compared with nondeprived adoptees, children who experienced early, severe deprivation were less likely to be securely attached and more likely to show atypical patterns of attachment behavior. Within the sample of deprived adoptees, there was a dose-response association between duration of deprivation and disturbances in attachment behavior. The children in this sample were only four years of age and it is not known what the impact of attachment problems will be in the long run, especially in dealing with developmental tasks of adulthood such as forming and maintaining intimate relationships and child bearing.

Preliminary findings from the Sophia Longitudinal Adoption Study showed that internationally adopted women in our sample who were pregnant and who had been subjected to severe adverse environmental influences early in life had much higher levels of salivary cortisol than internationally adopted women who were pregnant but who had not been severely deprived (Van der Vegt et al., submitted c). High levels of cortisol reflect high levels of stress and it is known that stress during pregnancy increases the risk of psychopathology in the offspring (Huizink et al., 2004). It is not known what psychological or biological mechanisms are responsible for the high levels of cortisol in pregnant internationally adopted women who had been subjected to severe adverse environmental influences early in life. However, these findings show that the exposure of the fetus to high levels of cortisol due to environmental factors involves a nongenomic transmission of risk across generations. The permanently altered HPA axis functioning of the deprived mother has now even become responsible for exposure to risk in the next generation. This is especially worrying since these severely deprived internationally adopted women may have more difficulties establishing or maintaining a healthy relationship with their child, who, as a result of prenatal exposure to high levels of stress, may have early signs of behavioral difficulties such as regulatory problems.

Although internationally adopted children as young adults show slight signs of problems in their social functioning as far as the establishment of

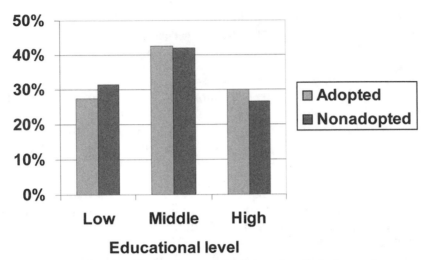

Figure 4.4.　Educational level of young adult international adoptees and comparisons from the general population

intimate relationships is concerned, they do remarkably well in other domains of social functioning. Measures of social functioning including the areas of leisure time activities, self-care, civic sense, parental functioning, family functioning, functioning without partner, relationship with partner, relationship with parents, relationship with siblings, relationship with friends, education, employment, and housekeeping indicated that international adoptees functioned just as good as nonadopted individuals of the same age.

Adoptees reached the same educational and professional level as nonadoptees, even after correction for socioeconomic status, since more adoptees came from high SES families than nonadoptees. Figures 4.4 and 4.5 show the percentages of adopted versus nonadopted individuals with low, middle, or high educational and occupational level respectively. The differences between adopted and nonadopted individuals are small and statistically nonsignificant. Comparing the adopted and nonadopted samples by gender, we found that only male adoptees reached a slightly lower educational level than nonadopted males. These positive findings are remarkable since the young adult adoptees in our sample were much less competent in academic functioning than nonadopted individuals in early adolescence (Verhulst et al., 1990a). Evidently internationally adopted children do not only show catch-up growth in childhood in areas such as physical growth, cognitive functioning, and self-esteem, catch-up during the transition from adolescence to adulthood is also present in many areas of social, educational, and professional functioning.

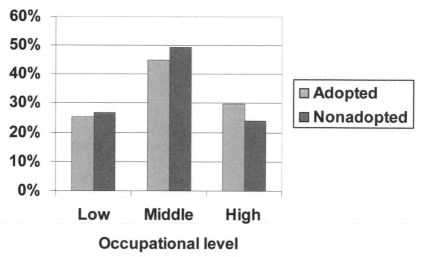

Figure 4.5. Occupational level of young adult international adoptees and comparisons from the general population

CONCLUSIONS

International adoption of children who have been abandoned or relinquished can ethically be justified if structural efforts to enable poor birth parents to rear their own birth children are inherent to the adoption process, and if adoption is successful in creating the conditions for basic trust, self-esteem, and healthy psychological adjustment (Van IJzendoorn and Juffer, 2006). Abandoned or relinquished children who have been subjected to adverse early circumstances such as institutional deprivation often suffer from biological and psychological damage resulting in delays in physical, cognitive, behavioral/emotional, and social development. Adoption offers a second chance to these children in a warm and protective family. Despite their deprived backgrounds these children show a remarkable catch-up after adoption. Compared to their past peers left behind in the institution or family of origin, adoption can be regarded a highly effective intervention. However, compared to their current, nonadopted peers who are reared in regular families, internationally adopted children still lag behind in a number of areas, including physical growth, attachment, and school achievement and to lesser extent behavioral and emotional problems. It is also clear that adoption which takes place before the age of twelve months is more successful in terms of a more complete catch-up than adoption after the age of twelve months.

Most studies up to this date on the outcomes of internationally adopted children pertain to children and adolescents. However, it is largely unknown how these children fare once they are faced with the challenges of adult-hood. The Sophia Longitudinal Adoption Study offered the opportunity to look at the long-term outcome of internationally adopted children who were between ten and fifteen years at the first assessment and twenty-four to thirty years at the last assessment, which was fourteen years later. We were espe-cially interested in the young-adult outcomes of the international adoptees in our sample since the level of problems tended to increase quite strongly across adolescence. It was therefore hypothesized that if these negative de-velopments continued into adulthood, a large proportion of the interna-tional adoptees would have significant problems.

The main conclusion that we can draw from standardized diagnostic in-formation is that overall there is considerable catch-up in the functioning of the internationally adopted children once they reach adulthood and that the dramatic increase in problems across adolescence has been stopped and turned into a more positive development. Despite this overall favorable de-velopment, there were negative aspects too. Internationally adopted men and women ran a higher risk for having an anxiety disorder or substance use disorder than nonadoptees. Adopted men were more likely to have a mood disorder than nonadopted men, whereas this was not true for adopted women. We have no data to answer the question why adopted men were especially vulnerable to develop a mood disorder. Whereas the risk for mood disorders in adopted women was nonsignificantly elevated com-pared with nonadopted women, adopted men nearly had the same level of mood disorders as nonadopted women.

In contrast to the elevated risk of psychiatric disorders, the adoptees' so-cial functioning, including educational and professional level was not dif-ferent from nonadoptees except that young adult adoptees were less likely to commit themselves to a partner. Significantly more nonadopted than adopted individuals were married, had had a relationship which lasted more than one year, or were living with a partner, and significantly more adopted than nonadopted individuals were living alone. We speculate that this apparent lack of (need for) intimate relationships may reflect adoptees' problems in forming secure attachment relationships (Van IJzendoorn and Juffer, 2006). Rutter et al. (2007) found that in their study of children who were initially reared in profoundly depriving institutions in Romania and subsequently adopted into UK families, more of these children showed disinhibited attachment than children who had not ex-perienced institutional deprivation and who had been adopted within the United Kingdom. Moreover this disinhibited attachment style was per-sistent from ages six to eleven years. The authors concluded from their study that disinhibited attachment formed a handicapping clinical pat-tern that is strongly associated with institutional rearing. We have to await further results from this study to know what becomes of these children who show relationship styles that may be adaptive in an environment with instable attachment figures, if any, but that are maladaptive in an environment in which overall functioning heavily relies on stable social relationships.

There are many factors why adopted children are at higher risk for developing problems than nonadopted children. Irrespective of the negative effects of institutional rearing, all adopted children have to deal with the knowledge that they have once been abandoned. Especially in adolescence and young adulthood when they become more independent, adopted individuals tend to reflect on the meaning of being adopted. They are increasingly able to evaluate the lack of connectedness with their adoptive parents as well as with their biological parents. We do not know how this affects the choices they have to make, for example, with respect to education, profession, relationships, and later their own parenthood.

A solid finding from our own studies was that early deprivation asserts its damaging effects even into adulthood. Multiple early adversities rendered adopted young adults at increased risk of showing DSM-IV psychiatric disorders, especially anxiety disorders, mood disorders, and substance abuse/dependence. It was also found that at a biological level the traces of early deprivation were still to be found. Early adversities were associated with HPA-axis (hypothalamic-pituitary-adrenocortisol axis) dysfunction, which reflects problems in the individual's stress regulation. The so-called downregulation of the HPA-axis that we found among adopted young adults who had been severely abused or neglected during the earliest periods in life, may have made them vulnerable to develop psychiatric problems. It should be noted that these effects were still present in adoptees even after experiencing a dramatic positive change in their lives. The negative effects of early adversities may even be transmitted to the next generation through biological mediation. Pregnant adopted mothers who had been severely abused or neglected during the earliest periods in life exposed their fetuses to high levels of the stress hormone cortisol, which is known to exert a negative influence on the unborn child. In this way, risk is transmitted across generations, even in a nongenomic way.

Despite the fact that there is some evidence that the most deprived adopted children are caught in a situation in which the early influences persistently exert their negative effects, there is also evidence that many international adoptees function well in young adult life. Looking at the picture from the positive side, the majority does not have a psychiatric disorder, shows adequate social functioning, finished education, and has jobs of the same level as nonadopted individuals. We do not know for sure but it seems likely that despite the problems in some, internationally adopted individuals are much better off than their past peers left behind in the institution or family of origin.

REFERENCES

Achenbach, T. M. (1997). *Manual for the Young Adult Self-Report and Young Adult Behavior Checklist*. Burlington: University of Vermont Department of Psychiatry.

Cederblad, M., B. Höök, M. Irhammar, and A. M. Mercke (1999). "Mental health in international adoptees as teenagers and young adults: An epidemiological study." *Journal of Child Psychological Psychiatry* 40, 1239–48.

Cicchetti, D., and F. A. Rogosch (2001). "The impact of child maltreatment and psychopathology on neuroendocrine functioning." *Developmental Psychopathology* 13, 677–720.

Golombok, S., R. Cook, A. Bish, and C. Murray (1995). "Families created by the new reproductive technologies: Quality of parenting and social and emotional development of the children." *Child Development* 66, 285–98.

Heim, C., J. Newport, R. Bonsall, A. H. Miller, and C. B. Nemeroff (2001). "Altered pituitary-adrenal axis responses to provocative challenge tests in adult survivors of childhood abuse." *American Journal of Psychiatry* 158, 575–81.

Hjern, A., F. Lindblad, and B. Vinnerljung (2002). "Suicide, psychiatric illness, and social maladjustment in intercountry adoptees in Sweden: A cohort study." *Lancet* 360, 443–48.

Hofstra, M. B., J. Van der Ende, and F. C. Verhulst (2000). "Continuity and change of psychopathology from childhood into adulthood: A fourteen-year follow-up study." *Journal of the American Academy of Child Adolescent Psychiatry* 39, 850–58.

Huizink, A., E. J. H. Mulder, and J. K. Buitelaar (2004). "Prenatal Stress and Risk for Psychopathology: Specific Effects or Induction of General Susceptibility?" *Psychological Bulletin* 130, 115–42.

Juffer, F., and M. H. Van IJzendoorn (2005). "Behavior problems and mental health referrals of international adoptees. A meta-analysis." *Journal of the American Medical Association* 293, 2501–15.

Lindblad, F., A. Hjern, and B. Vinnerljung (2003). "Intercountry adopted children as young adults—a Swedish cohort study." *American Journal of Orthopsychiatry* 73, 190–202.

Meany, M. J. (2001) "Maternal care, gene expression, and the transmission of individual differences in stress reactivity across generations." *Annual Review of Neuroscience* 24, 1161–92.

NRC-Handelsblad (2007). *India eist gestolen adoptiekind terug*, 22 mei 2007. Amsterdam: NRC-Handelsblad.

O'Connor, T. G., R. S. Marvin, M. Rutter, J. T. Olrick, P. A. Britner, and the English and Romanian Adoptees Study Team (2003). "Child-parent attachment following early institutional deprivation." *Developmental Psychopathology* 15, 19–38.

Rutter, M., L. Andersen-Wood, C. Beckett, D. Bredenkamp, J. Castle, J. Dunn, and the English and Romanian Adoptees Study Team. (1998) "Developmental catch-up, and deficit, following adoption after severe global privation." *Journal of Child Psychological Psychiatry* 39, 465–76.

Rutter, M., E. Colvert, J. Kreppner, C. Beckett, J. Castle, C. Groothues, A. Hawkins, T. G. O'Connor, S. E. Stevens, and E. J. Sonuga-Barke (2007). "Early adolescent outcomes for institutionally deprived and non-deprived adoptees, I: disinhibited attachment." *Journal of Child Psychological Psychiatry* 48, 17–30.

Selman, P. (2000). "The demographic history of intercountry adoption." In P. Selman, ed., *Intercountry adoption, Development and trends and perspectives*. London: British Agencies for Adoption and Fostering. 15–39.

———. (2005). *Trends in intercountry adoption 1998–2003P: A demographic analysis. Paper presented at the First Global Conference on Adoption Research*. Denmark: Copenhagen.

Tieman W., J. Van der Ende, and F. C. Verhulst (2005). "Psychiatric disorders in young adult intercountry adoptees: an epidemiological study." *American Journal of Psychiatry* 162, 592–98.

———. (2006). "Social functioning of young adult intercountry adoptees compared to nonadoptees." *Society of Psychiatry and Psychiatric Epidemiology* 41, 68–74.

Tizard, B. (1977). *Adoption: A Second Chance*. New York: The Free Press.

Van der Vegt, E. J. M., W. Tieman, J. Van der Ende, R. F. Ferdinand, F. C. Verhulst, and H. Tiemeier (submitted a) "Impact of early childhood adversities on adult psychiatric disorders: A study of international adoptees."

Van der Vegt, E. J. M., J. Van der Ende, C. Kirschbaum, F. C. Verhulst, and H. Tiemeier (submitted b) "Early childhood adversities affect diurnal cortisol patterns in adults: A study of international adoptees."

Van der Vegt, E. J. M., J. Van der Ende, A. C. Huizink, F. C. Verhulst, and H. Tiemeier (submitted c) "Pregnancy modifies the effect of early childhood adversities on cortisol levels."

Van Egmond, G. (2001). *Verbinding verbroken*. Baarn: Ambo.

———. (1987). *Bodemloos bestaan: problemen met adoptiekinderen*. Baarn: Ambo.

Van IJzendoorn, M. H., and F. Juffer (2006). "The Emanuel Miller Memorial Lecture 2006: Adoption as intervention. Meta-analytic evidence for massive catch-up and plasticity in physical, socio-emotional, and cognitive development." *Journal of Child Psychology and Psychiatry* 47, 1228–45.

Verhulst, F. C., M. Althaus, and H. J. Versluis-den Bieman (1990a). "Problem behavior in international adoptees, I: An epidemiological study." *Journal of the American Academy of Child Adolescent Psychiatry* 29, 94–103.

———. (1990b). "Problem behavior in international adoptees, II: Age at placement." *Journal of the American Academy of Child Adolescent Psychiatry* 29, 104–11.

———. (1992). "Damaging backgrounds—later adjustment of international adoptees." *Journal of the American Academy of Child and Adolescent Psychiatry* 31, 518–24.

Verhulst, F. C., and H. J. Versluis-den Bieman (1995). "Developmental course of problem behaviors in adolescent adoptees." *Journal of the American Academy of Child Adolescent Psychiatry* 34, 151–59.

Versluis-den Bieman, H. J., and F. C. Verhulst (1995). "Self-reported and parent reported problems in adolescent international adoptees." *Journal of Child Psychological Psychiatry* 36, 1411–28.

Weaver, I. C., N. Cervoni, F. A. Champagne, A. C. D'Alessio, S. Sharma, J. R. Seckl, S. Dymov, M. Szyf, and M. J. Meaney (2004). "Epigenetic programming by maternal behavior." *Nature Neuroscience* 7, 847–54.

World Health Organization (1993). *Composite International Diagnostic Interview (CIDI), core version 1.1*. Geneva, WHO.

To write this review, we searched the main electronic databases, psychiatric journals, and reference lists of all studies identified as potentially relevant, with special emphasis on knowledge based on empirical evidence as it applies to the "African-Caribbean" group. This means that work specifically about the African community in Britain has been excluded.

HISTORICAL BACKGROUND AND CONTEXT

Large-scale migration from the Caribbean to the British Isles began after World War II, when the government encouraged immigration as a means of addressing labor shortages. It peaked in the early 1960s and started to reduce in the mid-1970s. By 2001, African-Caribbeans were making up 1 percent of the general population in England (Office for National Statistics, 2001); currently more than half the African-Caribbean population is UK-born and is therefore well established. Although the background of people migrating to the UK from the Caribbean region is heterogeneous—as they have come from different islands with varied cultures, languages, and colonial histories—there are strong community links between them.

SOCIAL ADVERSITY

Like many immigrant populations, the African-Caribbean community in the UK has faced economic hardship, adversity, and discrimination. This has been apparent in patterns of employment and housing (Daniel, 1968; Commission for Racial Equality, 1990) with comparatively higher rates of manual occupations, especially in males, and unemployment, more social rental housing (Office of the Deputy Prime Minister, 2003) in overcrowded flats, perception of discrimination, and experience of racial harassment (Nazroo, 1997), all of which can be related to mental health adjustment. On the other hand recent data suggests that young Black females have been able to achieve significant advances and higher incomes in the employment market compared with White females (Whitmarsh and Harris, 1996; Karlsen and Nazroo, 2002). African-Caribbeans have also achieved high levels of social mixing and prominence in popular and urban youth culture.

IDENTITY AND FAMILY ORGANIZATION

The Fourth National Survey of Ethnic Minorities (Nazroo, 1997) in the United Kingdom showed that assimilation level (i.e., self-identification as British only) presented a high degree of intragroup variation among the

African-Caribbean community. Thus a number of the younger Caribbeans (some of them "mixed parentage": White English–Black Caribbean) appear to be reviving the assimilative hopes of the earliest migrants. Nevertheless, there is also evidence of alienation from or a rejection of Britishness among the young, as more than a quarter did not regard themselves as British. In-depth interviews revealed that skin color ("Black") is prominent in self-descriptions. Only 18 percent of 16- to 35-year-olds said that religion was *very important* to how they led their lives (5 percent of Whites had a similar opinion) (Modood, 2005).

African-Caribbean family organization within the UK shows both similarities and differences with that of White British families. An early study (Rutter et al., 1975) compared the home circumstances and family patterns of African-Caribbean families with 10-year-old children living in an inner London borough, with that of non-immigrant White families. It found that African-Caribbeans had significantly larger families; otherwise the quality of marital and parent-child relationships and patterns of discipline was similar with that of White English families (Rutter et al., 1975). African-Caribbean children were considered more "self reliant" (i.e., a high proportion cleaned their own shoes, tidied their own things, made their own beds, traveled by bus alone, and used the cooker without supervision), but their parents exercised more control on how they spent their free time.

The high level of assimilation and mixing of the African-Caribbean with the White British community occurs in peer groups between neighbors and in educational and employment contexts (Baumann, 1995). It is reflected in the high rate of intermarriage and mixed unions that disproportionately characterize the African-Caribbean group (Berthoud, 2000): surveys have shown that among the British-born with a partner, half of African-Caribbean men and one-third of African-Caribbean women have a White partner.

However the African-Caribbean population has significant characteristics in family structure that may affect the risk for child psychopathology. Thus 40 percent of Caribbean men and women do not have a partner (compared to the national average of 20 percent) and about half of the children of Caribbean origin are living with only one parent (compared to a sixth of children nationally) (Modood, 2005). Moreover fewer Caribbeans—in comparison with the White group—have ever lived with a partner or are in a formal marriage, and the proportion of those separated or divorced is twice as high as it is for Whites across all age groups under sixty years of age.

For some time evidence has accumulated that African-Caribbean children are over-represented within the care system (Bebbington and Miles, 1989; Barn, 1990; Barn, 1993; Ford et al., 2007). More Black than White children are admitted into care for "absent parenting," and fewer are admitted for neglect/abuse; they are also more likely to remain in regular parental contact. Nevertheless children and adolescents who experience family breakdown and are in the care of the local authority generally have a high rate of psychiatric disorder and poor social adjustment (McCann et al., 1996): increased use of the care system therefore represents an added risk factor for the children's mental health.

BEHAVIOR AND ADJUSTMENT IN SCHOOL

For three decades there has been concern about the progress of African-Caribbean children within British schools, reflecting behavior and attendance problems and school exclusions rather than scholastic attainment (the latter having been extensively reviewed by Maughan, 2005).

Regarding primary schools, attendance has been found to be better among African-Caribbean pupils than in other groups (Mortimer et al., 1988), with indications that they have higher rates of staying in school than Whites, and are more motivated to obtain educational qualifications (Smith and Tomlinson, 1989). On the other hand, there is also some evidence that Caribbean males have the most confrontational relationships with teachers, they are the group teachers feel most threatened by, and one that experiences high rates of disciplinary action and exclusion from school (Modood, 2003). High rates of permanent school exclusion of African-Caribbean children have been a cause for concern though this has improved considerably over time (Parsons et al., 2004).

Bullying is another possible risk factor for problems in psychiatric adjustment. In a large survey of bullying in British schools more than half reported having been bullied and the rate was highest in ethnic minority children; this would have included Caribbean children. In fact one quarter of ethnic minority children said they were severely bullied (as opposed to 13 percent of White pupils) (Katz, Buchanan, and Bream, 2001).

CONDUCT DISORDER

Past research—including studies of the community (Nicol, 1971; Earls and Richman, 1980) and school (Cochrane, 1979), across a broad age range (3- to 14-years)—indicated that rates of disturbance in African-Caribbean children as a whole were similar to those in indigenous children. However a number of specific differences have emerged with more conduct disorder in African-Caribbean (Rutter et al., 1974; Cochrane, 1979) and more school-based conduct disorder (e.g., based on teacher, not parental reports) among African-Caribbean children (Rutter et al., 1974). Reading delay and learning difficulties are commonly linked to conduct disorder. Reading delay is more prevalent among African-Caribbean children (Maughan, 2005) and this may lead to behavior disturbance at school that does not generalize to the home environment. Alternatively, African-Caribbean parents may have different expectations from White English parents and be more tolerant of their children's behavior which would be perceived as a symptom by other parents.

A more recent large epidemiological survey in Great Britain (Meltzer et al., 2000) has reported higher rates of conduct disorder in Black than in White 5- to 15-year-olds (8.6 percent and 5.4 percent respectively), but the difference was largely accounted for by higher rates in adolescent Black boys, and the results need to be taken with caution since the Black children's sample was comparatively small (140 boys and 132 girls) and there were wide confidence intervals. If the suggestion of increased conduct disorder is correct, this may have developed against the background of a history of more social and economic adversity faced by this population, urban dwellings, family organization, and possibly attendance to poorly organized schools (Quinton, 1988; Mortimer et al., 1988; Quinton, 1994; Loeber and Hay, 1994; Goodman and Richards, 1995; Rutter, Giller, and Hagell, 1998). This may partly be as a result of area effects, as these young people tend to live in inner cities and they are also more likely to be excluded from school (Department for Education and Employment, 1998).

CRIME AND DELINQUENCY

A review of the evidence suggests that the crime rate among African-Caribbeans and Black Africans is substantially higher than among the White majority (and among the other ethnic minorities). However, the interpretation of this finding is not clear-cut (Smith, 2005). We will proceed to present some of these findings and suggest likely explanations for the considerable difference in offending patterns between the African-Caribbeans and others.

Until the 1970s, crime rates in African-Caribbeans were thought to be similar to or below the rates for their White peers, but since then there is evidence of strikingly increased rates of arrest and imprisonment in the second and subsequent generations. This rise coincides with a secular rise in offending between 1950 and 1980 that affected all population groups. However, offending rose more among African-Caribbeans than with other groups (none of the South Asian immigrant groups, for example, showed a similar change) (Smith, 2005). Mobile telephone robbery and violent offences are more likely to be carried out by Black people (Home Office, 2001a; Graham and Bowling, 1995). At the same time, victim surveys of young people over sixteen years of age reveal that Black people are also more likely to have been victims of personal and household crimes (Whitmarsh and Harris, 1996), of assaults and acquisitive crime, such as burglaries and car thefts, as well as robberies or thefts from the person, and that they experience more fear of crime (Fitzgerald and Hale, 1996; Home Office, 2000).

Attention has been given to the fact the increased arrests of Black citizens could be a reflection of selective response and bias on the part of the police, and concern that the criminal justice system may discriminate against those from Black communities at each stage from arrest to imprisonment. However, a number of leading reviewers have argued that racial discrimination alone does not account for the higher levels of African-Caribbeans in the criminal justice system (Rutter, Giller, and Hagell, 1998; Smith, 1994; Smith, 1997; Smith, 2005). Among the reasons are the findings that other immigrant ethnic groups are also subject to discriminatory treatment by many institutions but have low levels of involvement with the criminal justice system.

In conclusion, there do appear to be substantial differences in rates of crime among ethnic groups. The causes of the higher rates of offending are not fully understood and are likely to be multifactorial. Both employment and cohesive marriage have been associated with desistance from offending: African-Caribbean males have less stable relationships than their White or Asian counterparts, and experience higher unemployment than White men. There may also be less desistance because it is more difficult for them to move outside inner city areas where there is less offending (Osborn, 1980). Individual factors may interact with the range of family and social processes described above.

It is also striking that in many other countries certain ethnic minority youths have higher rates of offending than majority peers (Rutter, Giller, and Hagell, 1998). Investigation of the causes of the onset and persistence of offending in these communities is important. Smith offers a range of explanations for the elevated crime rates among African-Caribbeans in the second and subsequent generations in the UK that may provide a starting point for further research, and may be applicable in part across other countries and ethnic groups. He makes the case for (1) the long-term consequences of slavery have profoundly influenced relations between men, women, and children among the descendants of slaves over many generations as discussed previously in family organization, (2) the adoption of an outgoing, integrative style among African-Caribbean migrants led them to encounter more discrimination and prejudice than other ethnic groups, and to compare themselves unfavorably with reference groups in Britain rather than in their country of origin, (3) a sequence of interactions between young Black people and the police has led to spiraling hostility and the stigmatization of Black people as criminals; their behavior is often interpreted as antisocial where similar behavior among Whites or other ethnic groups would not be. There is the possibility that these ascriptions could permanently shape Black identities affecting their behavior in the long term, and (4) the growth of oppositional and confrontational styles as sources of identity may have drawn young people into dangerous situations and criminal behavior. Most convincing models of pathways to antisocial behavior and offending involve multiple risk factors. They might operate to increase risk against the background of more ethnically specific adversity that has been previously described.

SUBSTANCE MISUSE

Substance misuse among British adolescents has been on the increase in recent decades (Silbereisen, Robins, and Rutter, 1995). In addition, the rates of consumption of cigarettes, alcohol, and illicit drugs have risen rapidly in the early teenage years (Sutherland and Shepherd, 2001). Some British studies have shown high rates of drug experimentation in 15- and 16-year-olds (Miller and Plant, 1996) with the risk of smoking and illicit drug use particularly high in adolescents who report high levels of drunkenness (Sutherland and Willner, 1998). Since 1996, there have been many large studies based on self-reported illegal drug use in African-Caribbean children and other ethnic minorities. The key findings are presented in table 5.1.

Self-report studies are of course subject to limitations such as omissions from the sample, lack of responses, and doubts regarding their veracity but it is unclear if these problems influence the findings. In the majority of these studies, African-Caribbean adolescents (as well as those of other ethnic minority groups) have lower rates of illicit drug use than their White counterparts; only in the two most recent studies were the results different. One of these studies suggested that there may be an ethnic-specific pattern of alcohol and tobacco use in adolescents: Black children who drink and smoke or have tried alcohol or tobacco had an average earlier onset age of smoking and drinking, while Asian children had the lowest rates for initiation and regular use and the highest mean age of starting to experiment with tobacco and alcohol (Best et al., 2001). Religious and peer influences might possibly affect ethnic groups differently in terms of their involvement in substance use. Another study implied a possible association between higher levels of substance misuse with lower familial and religious influence and higher level of peer influence (Karlsen, Rogers, and McCarthy, 1998).

AFFECTIVE AND ANXIETY DISORDERS

There is little research regarding affective and anxiety disorders in ethnic minority children and adolescents and these disorders are mostly considered

Table 5.1. Self-reported drug use studies and ethnic minority differences

Study/year	Sample/Design	General Findings	Ethnic Differences
Ramsay and Percy, (1996)	10,000 16–59 years England & Wales	Ecstasy use is lower than generally estimated and magic mushrooms is higher.	Lower rates for ethnic minorities compared with White youths.
Ramsay and Spiller, (1997)	13,488 16–59 years England & Wales	Highest prevalence in prosperous professionals in metropolitan areas, especially in 16–29 age group. Cannabis highest use and heroin/crack very low.	Whites have considerably higher prevalence levels than Afro-Caribbeans, who in turn have higher levels than Indians or Pakistanis / Bangladeshis.
Karlsen, Rogers, and McCarthy, (1998)	132 12–13 years Two inner London boroughs	Higher levels of drug use in young people with lower levels of familial and religious influence or higher levels of peer influence.	Bangladeshi adolescents have lower levels of drug use, while Whites have higher rates. Black Africans and Black Caribbeans have intermediate levels.
Flood-Page et al., (2000)	4,848 12–30 years England & Wales	Most illicit drug use is relatively controlled "recreational" use of cannabis and ecstasy.	Whites have considerably higher prevalence levels than Afro-Caribbeans.
Sharp et al., (2001)	13,300 16–59 years England & Wales	No significant increases in drug use among 16–24 year olds from 1998 survey.	Drug use is less prevalent in ethnic groups compared with White youths. Only significant increase for young Indians.

Study	Sample	Findings	Conclusions
Best et al., (2001)	1,777 11–14 years 8 schools in southwest London	Importance of sociocultural factors in relation to race and gender in predicting onset and escalation of drug use. Age of onset does not appear to be a significant determinant of transition rate from initiation to regular use.	White adolescents are more likely to have ever smoked tobacco and drunk alcohol than Blacks or Asians. Whites are more likely to do so on regular basis. Blacks who drink or smoke had an earlier age of onset of smoking and drinking.
Rodham et al., (2005)	6,020 15–16 years old 41 schools in England	The results confirm gender differences in substance use (males reported drinking and drug taking more often and females smoking) and demonstrate that there are different patterns of drug use among ethnic groups.	Black male adolescents are more likely than Whites to have used cannabis, opiates, and other drugs. Asian and Black males and females are less likely to report drinking during a typical week compared to Whites.
Jayakody et al., (2006)	2,789 11–14 years 28 schools in East London	Ethnic differences in drug use were found and statistically significant differences for Black adolescents.	Cannabis use in the previous month was significantly higher among Black Caribbeans, compared with White British, with similar findings in lifetime cannabis use.

under the broader diagnostic categories of emotional disorder or psychological distress.

Rates of emotional disorders in Great Britain are broadly comparable in
Black and in White children and young people, with a trend for fewer problems in primary school Black boys and adolescent Black girls (Meltzer et al.,
2000). A large questionnaire survey carried out in East London assessed
psychological distress in adolescents from ethnic minority groups. All ethnic groups experienced high levels of familial social disadvantage compared
with the national average, but the results showed that rates of psychological
distress were similar to rates in UK national samples in boys and girls.
Moreover depressive symptoms and psychological distress had little consistent association with social disadvantage. This could be explained by the
lack of variability within their cohort regarding socioeconomic level, all lying in the bottom quintile of the government's index for deprivation (Stansfeld et al., 2004).

A large study of attendees to a child psychiatric clinic found that the diagnosis of emotional disorder was significantly more rare in second-generation African-Caribbean children than in the predominantly White comparison group (17.8 percent versus 27.1 percent). It also revealed that both
groups of children with emotional disorders had very similar emotional
symptoms. The most striking exception to this was the relative rarity of refusal or reluctance to attend school among African-Caribbean children
compared to the comparison group (12 percent versus 43 percent respectively, p<0.001). Although emotional disorders were less frequent in
African-Caribbean primary school age girls than in the comparison group
(23 percent versus 42 percent), this difference was virtually obliterated in
the teenage years (with rates of 51 percent versus 55 percent). In contrast,
in boys the difference between groups widened with age. The authors suggested that the low proportion of emotional disorder in younger African-
Caribbean girls could be related to group differences in self-esteem (Goodman and Richards, 1995).

EATING DISORDERS

In recent years, the links between culture and eating disorders has attracted
much attention (Dolan, 1991; Vandereycken and Hoek, 1992; Nasser,
1997). Earlier views that these disorders occur exclusively in young White
women from affluent Western societies have been challenged by their identification in many sociocultural groups, including Black American (Robinson and Andersen, 1985) and Black British women (Holden and Robinson,
1988; Lacey and Dolan, 1988; Dolan, Lacey, and Evans, 1990). Nevertheless, there is a consistent finding that culture is an important determinant

of attitudes to body shape, fatness, and dieting (Furnham and Alibhai, 1983; Wardle and Marsland, 1990; Furnham and Baguma, 1994). Cross-cultural studies have indicated that young women from culturally English backgrounds dislike body fat and plumper figures, and diet more as compared to age-matched peers from African-Caribbean and African backgrounds. No epidemiological studies have been carried out to investigate eating disorders among adolescent African-Caribbeans in the United Kingdom. The existing literature consists of case reports and some community studies investigating eating attitudes (Reiss, 1996) and bulimia nervosa among adult African-Caribbean British (Lacey and Dolan, 1988).

The small number of reports of anorexia nervosa in African-Caribbean adolescents suggests it is very rare (Holden and Robinson, 1988). It is striking that most reports of anorexia nervosa among ethnic minority adolescents in the UK concern South Asian youngsters (Markantonakis, 1990; Bendal, Hamilton, and Holden, 1991; Bryant-Waugh and Lask, 1991). Bulimia nervosa also appears to be very rare among adolescent African-Caribbean adolescent females. This may be because the disorder typically starts in late adolescence or early adulthood, and perhaps because it occurs less in this community (Lacey and Dolan, 1988).

It is important to consider why African-Caribbean female adolescents may be protected against developing eating disorders compared with their peers. Two factors appear relevant. Firstly, attitude to body shape and dieting is relevant because dislike of fatness and associated dieting are important in leading to the onset of eating disorders (Patton et al., 1990; Patton et al., 1999). There is consistent evidence that African-Caribbean female adolescents are more positive toward their body shape than their peers and that these attitudes may be culturally mediated. A study of adolescents aged eleven to eighteen in London secondary schools has shown that the African-Caribbean girls have less dissatisfaction with their body shape and less dieting compared with White and South Asian peers (Wardle and Marsland, 1990). This was in spite of higher body mass index (their weight was greater in relation to their height) in this group. These questionnaire studies are entirely consistent with anthropological accounts that indicate that a fuller body shape has positive associations with fecundity and maturity (MacCormack and Draper, 1987).

Proponents of the sociocultural model of eating disorders have suggested that ethnic differences in body dissatisfaction may be diminishing as the thin ideal of beauty becomes more widely disseminated among minority women. A meta-analysis conducted in 2006 confirmed more favorable body image evaluations among Black than White females, with the greatest differences in the age period of the early twenties. Although results confirmed that ethnic differences have diminished, this trend was only limited to weight-focused measures while on more global body image measures,

in a small sample of African-Caribbean adolescents aged sixteen to nineteen (Harrison, 1997). The Aetiology and Ethnicity in Schizophrenia and Other Psychoses (AESOP) study, a population-based study of 568 patients aged fifteen and older who presented to secondary services with first-episode psychosis found that African-Caribbeans had significantly higher incidence of schizophrenia and mania, with modest increase in depressive psychosis (Fearon et al., 2006).

African-Caribbeans have more psychotic symptoms on psychosis screening questionnaires when compared to Whites (King et al., 2005). A community sample study raised the possibility of cultural differences in the experience and the reporting of non-psychotic hallucinations, since Caribbean people reported higher rates of hallucinations without being associated with increased rates of psychosis (Johns et al., 2002).

Comparison of outcome in African-Caribbeans, other immigrants (Asians), and UK Whites has led to inconsistent conclusions. Some studies suggest a poorer outcome for African-Caribbean patients than White or Asian patients (Birchwood et al., 1992; Eagles, 1993; McGovern et al., 1994; Bhugra et al., 1997) while another describes less self-harm, more rated "recovered," and less time spent in hospital in African-Caribbeans (McKenzie et al., 1995).

There has been much debate about aetiological factors that may contribute to the reported increase in the rates of schizophrenia in African-Caribbeans in the United Kingdom (Fearon et al., 2006). Genetic factors are probably not relevant since rates of schizophrenia in countries of origin— Jamaica, Trinidad, and Barbados—are not increased (Hickling and Rodgers-Johnson, 1995; Bhugra et al., 1996). Furthermore while rates in parents are comparable, those in siblings of second generation African-Caribbeans are higher than in siblings of White probands (Sugarman and Crawford, 1994; Hutchinson et al., 1996). These findings suggest environmental factors acting specifically on the second generation.

Possibilities include low birth weight and birth complications (Eagles, 1991), viral infections (Fahy et al., 1993), cannabis consumption, socio-economic adversity, and racism. However, none of these has adequate supporting evidence (King et al., 1994; Bartlett and Fiander, 1995; McKenzie et al., 1995; Hutchinson et al., 1997). More recent studies have emphasized the importance of social environment and cognitive factors (Sharpley et al., 2001). One study has showed that the incidence of psychoses in a non-White ethnic minority group is greater when the group represents a smaller proportion of the local population (Boydell et al., 2001) suggesting the influence of wider social supports. Another study indicates the possible contribution of unemployment: African-Caribbeans with first-onset schizophrenia living in London had much higher levels of unemployment than their patient counterparts in Trinidad (Bhugra et al., 2000). Moreover the rates of psychotic illness are higher in inner city areas as well as in more deprived areas where the African-Caribbean population tends to be over-represented. Poor housing conditions have also been suggested as a potential contributory risk factor (Mallett et al., 2004).

Nevertheless, focusing on adversity in adult life (e.g., poverty, unemployment, and the like) as an explanation may be inappropriate because the population groups most subject to adversity (White people in the lowest socioeconomic groups and Black immigrants in the United Kingdom) appear not to have comparably large increases of psychoses (Cooper, 2005) and the possible role of racism in the development of psychosis remains unclear (Bhugra and Ayonrinde, 2001).

Do the findings in adult patients apply to children and adolescents? There is some support for the conclusion that they do. A study of London child and adolescent clinic attendees found that psychotic disorders were over-represented in second generation African-Caribbeans (Goodman and Richards, 1995). If this finding reflects genuine community differences in rates, this would be in line with adult studies.

A recent survey of London adolescents admitted to psychiatric in-patient units found an over-representation of Black adolescents in the psychotic group, but concluded that this over-representation was mainly due to the high numbers of adolescents of African origin: these made up 20 percent (11/55) of all adolescents with psychosis (Tolmac and Hodes, 2004). The authors also found diagnostic differences among different ethnic groups: only one of the eleven African adolescents had a diagnosis of schizophrenia in contrast with six of the eight adolescents in the other Black groups (Black Caribbean and Black British). Nevertheless, the small size of the African-Caribbean group meant that no definitive conclusion about this group could be drawn.

DEVELOPMENTAL DISORDERS

There is emerging evidence that autism is increased among African-Caribean children—especially girls—attending child and adolescent mental health services and that similarly severe mental retardation is comparatively increased among Caribbean attendees (Wing, 1979; Goodman and Richards, 1995). It seems unlikely that socioeconomic adversity contributes to an increase of autism in this population since social class and immigrant status are not specially associated with autism (Fombonne, 1999).

There is little research on mental retardation in African-Caribbeans in the United Kingdom. One study found that children from ethnic minorities with severe mental retardation had more severe disabilities (including sensory impairments, neurological functioning, and social behavior) (Akinsola and Fryers, 1986) but the sample size did not allow the examination of possible contributory etiological factors such as communicable diseases or perinatal damage.

LIMITATIONS OF RESEARCH

This review has been generally based on studies with small sample sizes and an absence of a truly social and cultural perspective. The same is likely to apply to research into other immigrant and ethnic groups in other countries. The term "culturally informed" refers to research that investigates the relevance of the specific aspects of a particular culture and family and social organization that may be relevant for the shaping and onset of psychiatric disorder and poor social adjustment. Equally important would be investigation of factors that are protective of specific disorders and problems, as a way of understanding resilience within communities. Such a perspective would also need to investigate issues such as racial discrimination in its various manifestations, and how this may contribute to poorer mental health (Chakraborty and McKenzie, 2002).

A further issue is the relevance of cultural notions of health and illness, and how these influence the appraisal of difficulties. The presence of culturally specific ideas about illness, including mental health, has been suggested (Littlewood, 2001) and may persist across second- or third-generation immigrants, as well as among the newly arrived, and those whose parents may have traditional ideas and beliefs which are relevant to family and community response. There has also been a lack of social, anthropological, and qualitative investigation of the Caribbean and of other populations that might complement the psychiatric research using survey methods.

Of relevance is also the extent to which racial and cultural bias and stereotyping may contribute toward research findings and their interpretation. This can become a particularly sensitive issue regarding the investigation of conduct disorder, antisocial behavior, and offending among young African-Caribbean British males as there could be discriminatory policing, convictions, and sentencing in the courts (Smith, 1994). The practical relevance for the research is that checks need to be carried out to clarify whether these biases are operating within a specific field of inquiry.

The fourth methodological issue that will become increasingly important for all research with ethnic minorities, and indeed all people living in cosmopolitan cities, concerns the methods for describing ethnicity and the extent to which there is homogeneity amongst the group of people being investigated. The African-Caribbean region is itself heterogeneous (Smith, 1988; Hutchinson and McKenzie, 1995), and the community in the UK reflects this. In addition there is diversity caused by different degrees of assimilation and effects associated with occupational status. Children of mixed African-Caribbean/White parentage vary in the extent to which they regard themselves as Black although many do (Tizard and Phoenix, 1993). This is reflected in significant numbers of youngsters, including those who access mental health services, not "fitting" into the standard ethnic categories used for monitoring and service planning (Hodes, Creamer, and Walley, 1998). The mismatch between how youngsters of mixed parentage view themselves and how others see them may also be of relevance. More sophisticated means are required for describing ethnic group membership and identity (Entwistle and Astone, 1994; Hutchinson and McKenzie, 1995).

FUTURE INVESTIGATIONS

Despite the limitations in the available literature, current findings do suggest a number of directions in which future research should be directed. There should be adequate epidemiological studies to investigate the prevalence of the main psychiatric disorders, learning disabilities, and psychosocial problems such as offending and substance misuse, levels of associated impairment and mental health service utilization and a study of possible contributory etiological factors. Special attention may be given to the epidemiology of psychotic disorders in young people. New studies require a longitudinal perspective; for example, to clarify factors associated with entry into or avoidance of delinquency, and it is important to investigate in much more detail the cultural attitudes and practices that may be associated with specific risk and protective factors. The use of anthropological and qualitative techniques may be especially appropriate.

REFERENCES

Akinsola, H. A. and T. Fryers. "A comparison of disability in severely mentally handicapped children of different ethnic origins." *Psychological Medicine* no. 16 (1986), 127–33.

Balarajan, R. "Ethnicity and variations in the nation's health." *Health Trends* no. 27 (1995), 114–19.

Barn, R. "Black children in local authority care: Admission patterns." *New Community* no. 16 (1990), 239–63.

Barn, R. *Black Children in the Public Care System* (London: BT Batsford Ltd., 1993).

Bartlett, A. and M. Fiander. "Commentary on incidence of psychotic illness in London: Comparison of ethnic groups by Michael King, et al." *British Medical Journal* no. 310 (1995), 332.

Baumann, G. "Managing a polyethnic milieu: kinship and interaction in a London suburb." *Journal of the Royal Anthropological Institute* (N.S.), no. 1 (1995), 725–41.

Bebbington, A. and J. Miles. "The background of children who enter local authority care." *British Journal of Social Work* no. 19 (1989), 349–68.

Bebbington, P. E., J. Hurry, and C. Tennant. "Psychiatric disorders in selected immigrant groups in Camberwell." *Social Psychiatry* no.16 (1981), 43–51.

Bendal, P., M. Hamilton, and N. Holden. "Eating disorders in Asian girls." *British Journal of Psychiatry* no. 159 (1991), 441.

Berthoud, R. *Family Formation in Multicultural Britain: Three Patterns of Diversity* (University of Essex: Institute for Social and Economic Research, 2000).

Best, D., S. Rawaf, J. Rowley, et al. "Ethnic and gender differences in drinking and smoking among London adolescents." *Ethnicity and Health* no. 6(1) (2001), 51–57.

Bhugra, D. and O. Ayonrinde. "Racism, racial life events and mental ill health." *Advances in Psychiatric Treatment* no. 7 (2001), 343–49.

Bhugra, D. and R. Cochrane. *Psychiatry in Multicultural Britain* (London: Gaskell, 2001).

Bhugra, D., M. Hilwig, B. Hossein, et al. "First-contact incidence rates of schizophrenia in Trinidad and one-year follow-up." *British Journal of Psychiatry* no.169 (1996), 587–92.

Bhugra, D., M. Hilwig, R. Mallett, et al. "Factors in the onset of schizophrenia: A comparison between London and Trinidad samples." *Acta Psychiatrica Scandinavica* no. 101(2) (2000), 135–41.

Bhugra, D., J. Leff, R. Mallett, et al. "Incidence and outcome of schizophrenia in Whites, African-Caribbeans and Asians in London." *Psychological Medicine* no. 27 (1997), 791–98.

Bhugra, D., N. Thompson, J. Singh, and E. Fellow-Smith. "Inception rates of deliberate self-harm among adolescents in West London." *International Journal of Social Psychiatry* no. 49(4) (2003), 247–50.

Birchwood, M., R. Cochrane, F. Macmillan, et al. "The influence of ethnicity and family structure on relapse in first-episode schizophrenia. A comparison of Asian, Afro-Caribbean, and White patients." *British Journal of Psychiatry* no.161 (1992), 783–90.

Blatchford, P., "Pupils' self-assessments of academic attainment at 7, 11, and 16 years: Effects of sex and ethnic group." *British Journal of Educational Psychology* no. 67 (1997), 169–84.

Boydell, J., J. van Os, K. McKenzie, et al. "Incidence of schizophrenia in ethnic minorities in London: Ecological study into interactions with environment." *British Medical Journal* no. 323 (2001), 1336–38.

Bryant-Waugh, R. and B. Lask. "Anorexia nervosa in a group of Asian children living in Britain." *British Journal of Psychiatry* no. 158 (1991), 229–33.

Carpenter, L. and I. F. Brockington. "A Study of mental illness in Asians, West Indians and Africans living in Manchester." *British Journal of Psychiatry* no.137 (1980), 201–5.

Chakraborty, A. and K. McKenzie. "Does racial discrimination cause mental illness?" *British Journal of Psychiatry* no. 180 (2002), 475–77.

Cochrane, R., "Mental illness in immigrants to England and Wales: An analysis of mental hospital admissions." *Social Psychiatry* no. 12 (1977), 25–35.

Cochrane, R., "Psychological and behavioral disturbance in West Indians, Indians and Pakistanis in Britain." *British Journal of Psychiatry* no. 134 (1979), 201–10.

Cochrane, R. and S. S. Bal, "Mental hospital admission rates of immigrants to England: A comparison of 1971 and 1981." *Social Psychiatry and Psychiatric Epidemiology* no. 24 (1989), 2–11.

Commission for Racial Equality, *Annual Report* (London: CRE, 1990).

Cooper, B., "Immigration and schizophrenia: The social causation hypothesis revisited." *British Journal of Psychiatry* no. 186 (2005), 361–63.

Daniel, W. W., *Racial Discrimination in England* (Harmondsworth: Penguin, 1968).

Dean, G., D. Walsh, H. Downing, et al. "First admissions of native-born and immigrants to psychiatric hospitals in South-East England 1976." *British Journal of Psychiatry* no. 139 (1981), 506–12.

Department for Education and Employment (DFEE), *Permanent Exclusions from Schools in England 1996/1997 and Exclusion Appeals Lodged by Parents in England (451/98)* (Darlington: DFEE News, 1998).

Department of Health, *Mental Health Policy Implementation Guide* (London: Department of Health, 2000).

Dolan, B., "Cross-cultural aspects of anorexia nervosa and bulimia: A review," *International Journal of Eating Disorders* no. 10 (1991), 67–78.

Dolan, B., J. H. Lacey, and C. Evans. "Eating behavior and attitudes to weight and shape in British women from three ethnic groups." *British Journal of Psychiatry* no. 157 (1990), 523–28.

Eagles, J. M. "The relationship between schizophrenia and immigration. Are there alternatives to psychosocial hypotheses?" *British Journal of Psychiatry* no. 159 (1991), 783–89.

Eagles, J. M. "Commentary on ethnicity and relapse in schizophrenia by Birchwood, et al." *British Journal of Psychiatry* no. 162 (1993), 846.

Earls, F. and N. Richman. "The prevalence of behavior problems in three-year-old children of West Indian–born parents." *Journal of Child Psychology and Psychiatry* no. 21 (1980), 99–106.

Entwistle, D. R. and N. M. Astone. "Some practical guidelines for measuring youth's race/ethnicity and socio-economic status." *Child Development* no. 65 (1994), 1521–40.

Fahy, T. A., P. B. Jones, P. C. Shaw, et al. "Schizophrenia in Afro-Carribeans in the U.K. following parental exposure to the 1957 A2 Influenza pandemic." *Schizophrenia Research* (1993), 132.

Fearon, P., J. B. Kirkbride, et al. (AESOP Study Group) "Incidence of schizophrenia and other psychoses in ethnic minority groups: results from the MRC AESOP Study." *Psychological Medicine* no. 36(11) (2006), 1541–50.

Fitzgerald, M. and C. Hale. *Ethnic Minorities, Victimisation and Racial Harassment, Research Findings No. 39* (Home Office Research and Statistics Directorate, 1996).

Flood-Page, C., S. Campbell, V. Harrington, and J. Miller. *Youth crime: Findings from the 1998/1999 Youth Lifestyle Survey* (London: Home Office, Home Office Research Study no. 209, 2000).

Fombonne, E., "The epidemiology of autism: a review." *Psychological Medicine* no. 29(4) (1999), 769–86.

Ford, T., P. Vostanis, H. Meltzer, and R. Goodman. "Psychiatric disorder among British children looked after by local authorities: Comparison with children living in private households." *British Journal of Psychiatry* no. 190 (2007), 319–25.

Furnham, A. and N. Alibhai. "Cross cultural differences in the perception of female body shapes." *Psychological Medicine* no. 13 (1983), 829–37.

Furnham, A. and P. Baguma. "Cross-cultural differences in the evaluation of male and female body shapes." *International Journal of Eating Disorders* no. 15 (1994), 81–89.

Goddard, N., F. Subotsky, and E. Fombonne. "Ethnicity and Adolescent Deliberate Self Harm." *Journal of Adolescence* no. 19 (1996), 513–21.

Goodman, R. and H. Richards. "Child and adolescent psychiatric presentations of second-generation Afro-Caribbeans in Britain." *British Journal of Psychiatry* no. 167 (1995), 362–69.

Graham, J. and B. Bowling. *Young People and Crime* (London: Home Office, Home Office Research Study no. 145, 1995).

Harrison, G., C. Glazebrook, J. Brewin, et al. "Increased incidence of psychotic disorders in migrants from the Caribbean to the United Kingdom." *Psychological Medicine* no. 27 (1997), 799–806.

Harrison G., D. Owens, A. Holton, et al. "A prospective study of severe mental disorder in Afro-Caribbean patients." *Psychological Medicine* no. 18 (1988), 643–57.

Harvey, I., M. Williams, P. McGuffin, et al. "The functional psychoses in Afro-Carribeans." *British Journal of Psychiatry* no. 157 (1990), 515–22.

Hickling, F. W. and P. Rodgers-Johnson. "The incidence of first contact schizophrenia in Jamaica." *British Journal of Psychiatry* no.167 (1995), 193–96.

Hill, A. J., C. Weaver, and J. E. Blundell. "Dieting concerns of 10-year-old girls and their mothers." *British Journal of Clinical Psychology* no. 29 (1990), 346–48.

Hodes, M., J. Creamer, and J. Walley. "The cultural meanings of ethnic categories." *Psychiatric Bulletin* no. 22 (1998), 20–24.

Hodes, M., C. Jones, and H. Davis. "Cross-cultural differences in maternal evaluation of children's body shapes." *International Journal of Eating Disorders* no. 19 (1996), 257–63.

Holden, N. and P. H. Robinson. "Anorexia nervosa and bulimia nervosa in British Blacks." *British Journal of Psychiatry* no. 152 (1988), 544–49.

Home Office, *Mobile Phone Theft. Home Office Research Study no. 235* (London: Home Office, 2001a).

Home Office, *The 2000 British Crime Survey. Home Office Statistical Bulletin 18/00* (London: Home Office, 2000).

Hutchinson, G. and K. McKenzie. "What is an Afro-Caribbean? Implications for psychiatric research." *Psychiatric Bulletin* no. 19 (1995), 700–702.

Hutchinson, G., N. Takei, D. Bhugra, et al. "Increased rate of psychosis among African-Caribbeans in Britain is not due to an excess of pregnancy and birth complications." *British Journal of Psychiatry* no. 171 (1997), 145–47.

Hutchinson, G., N. Takei, T. A. Fahy, et al. "Morbid risk of schizophrenia in first degree relatives of White and African-Caribbean patients with psychosis." *British Journal of Psychiatry* no. 169 (1996), 776–80.

Jarvis, E., "Schizophrenia in British Immigrants: recent findings, issues and implications." *Transcultural Psychiatry* no. 35 (1998), 39–74.

Jayakody, A. A., R. M. Viner, et al. "Illicit and traditional drug use among ethnic minority adolescents in East London." *Public Health* no. 120 (4) (2006), 329–338.

Johns, L. C., J. Y. Nazroo, P. Bebbington, and E. Kuipers. "Ocurrence of hallucinatory experiences in a community sample and ethnic variations." *British Journal of Psychiatry* no. 180 (2002), 174–78.

Karlsen, S. and J. Y. Nazroo. "Relation between racial discrimination, social class, and health among ethnic minority groups." *American Journal of Public Health* no. 92 (2002), 624–31.

Karlsen, S., A. Rogers, and M. McCarthy. "Social environment and substance misuse: A study of ethnic variations among inner London adolescents." *Ethnicity and Health* no. 3(4) (1998), 265–73.

Katz, A., A. Buchanan, and V. Bream. *Bullying in Britain: Testimonies from Teenagers* (London: Young Voice, 2001).

King, M., E. Coker, and G. Leavey. "Authors reply to commentary on incidence of psychotic illness in London: comparison of ethnic groups." *British Medical Journal* no. 310 (1995), 333.

King, M., E. Coker, G. Leavey, et al. "Incidence of psychotic illness in London: Comparison of ethnic groups." *British Medical Journal* no. 309 (1994), 1115–19.

King, M., J. Y. Nazroo, S. Weich, et al. "Psychotic symptoms in the general population of England—a comparison of ethnic groups (the Empiric study)." *Social Psychiatry and Psychiatric Epidemiology* no. 40 (5) (2005), 375–81.

Lacey, J. H. and B. M. Dolan. "Bulimia in British Blacks and Asians. A catchment area study." *British Journal of Psychiatry* no. 152 (1988), 73–79.

Littlewood, R., "Psychopathology and personal agency: Modernity, culture change and eating disorders in South Asian societies." *British Journal of Medical Psychology* no. 68 (1995), 45–63.

Littlewood, R., "Caribbean immigration to Britain: Mental health of the migrants and their British-born families," in A. T. Yilmaz, M. G. Weiss, and A. Riecher-Rossler, eds., *Cultural Psychiatry: Euro-International Perspectives* (Basel: Karger, 2001), 81–102.

Littlewood, R. and M. Lipsedge. "Acute psychotic reactions in Caribbean-born patients." *Psychological Medicine* no. 11 (1981a), 303–18.

Littlewood, R. and M. Lipsedge. "Some social and phenomenological characteristics of psychotic immigrant." *Psychological Medicine* no. 11 (1981b), 289–302.

Loeber, R. and D. F. Hay. "Developmental Approaches to Aggression and Conduct Problems," in M. Rutter and D. F. Hay, eds., *Development Through Life: A Handbook for Clinicians* (Oxford: Blackwell Scientific Publications, 1994), 488–516.

MacCormack, C. P. and A. Draper. "Social and cognitive aspects of female sexuality in Jamaica," in P. Caplan, ed., *The Cultural Construction of Sexuality* (New York: Routledge, 1987), 143–65.

Mallett, R., J. Leff, D. Bhugra., et al. "Ethnicity, goal striving and schizophrenia: A case-control study of three ethnic groups in United Kingdom." *International Journal of Social Psychiatry* no. 50(4) (2004), 331–44.

Markantonakis, A. "Anorexia nervosa in people of Asian extraction." *British Journal of Psychiatry* no. 157 (1990), 783.

Maughan, B. "Educational Attainments. Ethnic differences in the United Kingdom," in M. Rutter and M. Tienda, eds., *Ethnicity and Causal Mechanisms* (Cambridge: Cambridge University Press, 2005), 80–106.

McCann, J. B., A. James, S. Wilson, et al. "Prevalence of psychiatric disorders in young people in the care system." *British Medical Journal* no. 313 (1996), 1529–30.

McClure, G. M. G., "Suicide in children and adolescents in England and Wales 1970–1998." *British Journal of Psychiatry* no. 178 (2001), 469–74.

McGovern, D., P. Hemmings, R. Cope, et al., "Long-term follow-up of young Afro-Caribbean Britons and White Britons with a first admission diagnosis of schizophrenia." *Social Psychiatry and Psychiatric Epidemiology* no. 29 (1994), 8–19.

McKenzie, K., J. van Os, T. Fahy, et al. "Psychosis with good prognosis in Afro-Caribbean people now living in the United Kingdom." *British Medical Journal* no. 311 (1995), 1325–28.

Meltzer, H., R. Gatward, R. Goodman, et al. *Mental Health of Children and Adolescents in Great Britain. Office for National Statistics* (London: The Stationary Office, 2000).

Merril, J. and J. Owens. "Ethnic differences in self poisoning: A comparison of West-Indian and White groups." *British Journal of Psychiatry* no. 150 (1987), 765–68.

Miller, P. M. and M. Plant. "Drinking, smoking, and illicit drug use among 15 and 16 year olds in the United Kingdom." *British Medical Journal* no. 313 (1996), 394–97.

Modood, T., "Ethnic differences in educational performance," in D. Mason, ed., *Explaining Ethnic Differences: Changing Patterns of Disadvantage in Britain* (Bristol: Policy Press, 2003), 53–68.

Modood, T., "Ethnicity and intergenerational identities and adaptations in Britain: The socio-political context," in M. Rutter and M. Tienda, eds., *Ethnicity and Causal Mechanisms* (Cambridge: Cambridge University Press, 2005), 281–300.

Mortimer, P., P. Sammons, L. Stoll, et al. *School Matters: The Junior Years* (London: Paul Chapman Publishing, 1988).

Mukai, T., M. Crago, and C. M. Shisslak. "Eating attitudes and weight preoccupation among female high school students in Japan." *Journal of Child Psychology and Psychiatry* no. 35 (1994), 677–88.

Nasser, M. *Culture and Weight Consciousness* (New York: Routledge, 1997).

Nazroo, J. Y. *Ethnicity and Mental Health: Fourth National Survey of Ethic Minorities* (London: Policy Studies Institute, 1997).

Neeleman, J., V. Mark, and S. Wessley. "Suicide by age, ethnicity group, coroners' verdicts and country of birth." *British Journal of Psychiatry* no. 171 (2001), 463–67.

Nicol, A. R. "Psychiatric disorder in the children of Caribbean immigrants." *Journal of Child Psychology and Psychiatry* no. 12 (1971), 273–81.

Office for National Statistics. *Census 2001* (2001).

Office of the Deputy Prime Minister. *English Housing Condition Survey,* no. 4 (2003).

Office of the Deputy Prime Minister. *Survey of English Housing Provisional Results: 2002–2003,* no. 18 (2003).

Osborn, S. G. "Moving home, leaving London and delinquent trends." *British Journal of Criminology* no. 20 (1980), 54–61.

Parsons, C., R. Godfrey, G. Annan, et al. *Minority Ethnic Exclusions and the Race Relations (Amendment) Act 2000* (London: DfES Publications, 2004).

Patton, G. C., E. Johnson-Sabine, K. Wood, et al. "Abnormal eating attitudes in London schoolgirls—a prospective epidemiological study: outcome at twelve-month follow-up." *Psychological Medicine* no. 20 (1990), 383–94.

Patton, G. C., R. Selzer, C. Coffey, et al. "Onset of adolescent eating disorders: Population based cohort study over 3 years." *British Medical Journal* no. 318 (1999), 765–68.

Quinton, D. "Urbanism and child mental health." *Journal of Child Psychology and Psychiatry* no. 29 (1988), 11–20.

Quinton, D. "Cultural and Community Influences" in M. Rutter and D. Hay, eds., *Development Through Life: A Handbook For Clinicians* (Oxford: Blackwell Scientific Publications, 1994), 112–34.

Ramsay, M. and A. Percy. *Drugs Misuse Declared: Results of the 1994 British Crime Survey* (London: Home Office, Home Office Research Study, 1996), no. 33.

Ramsay, M. and A. Spiller. *Drugs Misuse Declared in 1996: Latest Results from the British Crime Survey* (London: Home Office, Home Office Research Study, 1997), no. 172.

Reiss, D. "Abnormal eating attitudes and behaviors in two ethnic groups from a female British urban population." *Psychological Medicine* no. 26 (1996), 289–99.

Roberts, A., T. F. Cash, A. Feingold, and B. T. Johnson. "Are black-white differences in females' body dissatisfaction decreasing? A meta-analytic review." *Journal of consultant clinical psychology* no. 74 (6) (2006), 1121–31.

Robinson, P. H. and A. Andersen. "Anorexia nervosa in American blacks." *Journal of Psychiatric Research* no. 19 (1985), 183–88.

Rodham, K., K. Hawton, E. Evans, and R. Weatherall. "Ethnic and gender differences in drinking, smoking and drug taking among adolescents in England: A self report school-based survey of 15 and 16 year olds." *Journal of Adolescence* no. 28 (2005), 63–73.

Rutter, M., H. Giller, and A. Hagell. *Antisocial Behavior by Young People* (Cambridge: Cambridge University Press, 1998).

Rutter, M., W. Yule, M. Berger, et al. "Children of West Indian immigrants, I. Rates of behavioral deviance and of psychiatric disorder." *Journal of Child Psychology and Psychiatry* no. 15 (1974), 241–62.

Rutter, M., B. Yule, J. Morton, et al. "Children of West Indian immigrants. III. Home circumstances and family patterns." *Journal of Child Psychology & Psychiatry* no. 16 (1975): 105–23.

Shaffer, D. and J. Piacenti. "Suicide & attempted suicide," in M. Rutter, E. Taylor, and L. Hersov, eds., *Child & Adolescent Psychiatry, Modern Approaches* (Oxford: Blackwell Scientific Publications, 1994), 407–24.

Sharp, C., P. Baker, Goulden, et al. *Drugs Misuse Declared in 2000: Results from the British Crime Survey* (London: Home Office, Home Office Research Study, 2001), no. 224.

Sharpley, M., G. Hutchinson, K. McKenzie, et al. "Understanding the excess of psychosis among the African-Caribbean population in England." *British Journal of Psychiatry* no. 78 (suppl.40) (2001), 60–68.

Silbereisen, R. K., L. Robins, and M. Rutter. "Secular trends in substance use: Concepts and data on the impact of social change on alcohol and drug abuse," in M. Rutter and D. J. Smith, eds., *Psychosocial Disorders in Young People—Time Trends and Their Causes* (Chichester: John Wiley & Sons Ltd, 1995).

Smith, R. T. *Kinship and Class in the West Indies* (Cambridge: Cambridge University Press, 1988).

Smith, D. J. "Race, crime and criminal justice," in M. Maguire, R. Morgan, and R. Reiner, eds., *The Oxford Handbook of Criminology* (Oxford: Clarendon Press, 1994), 1041–18.

Smith, D. J. "Ethnic origins, crime and criminal justice in England and Wales," in M. Tonry, ed., *Ethnicity, Crime and Immigration: Comparative and Cross-National Perspectives* (Chicago: University of Chicago Press, 1997), 1101–82.

Smith, D. J. "Explaining ethnic variations in crime and antisocial behavior in the UK," in M. Rutter and M. Tienda, eds., *Ethnicity and Causal* Mechanisms (Cambridge: Cambridge University Press, 2005), 174–203.

Smith, D. J. and S. Tomlinson. *The School Effect: A Study of Multi-racial Comprehensives* (London: Policy Studies Institute, 1989).

Soni Raleigh, V., "Suicide levels and trends among immigrants in England and Wales." *Health Trends* no. 24 (1992), 91–94.

Soni Raleigh, V. "Suicide patterns and trends in people of Indian subcontinent and Caribbean origin in England and Wales." *Ethnicity and Health* no. 1 (1996), 55–63.

Stansfeld, S. A., M. M. Haines, J. A. Head, et al. "Ethnicity, social deprivation and psychological distress in adolescents." *British Journal of Psychiatry* no. 185 (2004), 233–38.

Striegel-Moore, R. H. "Etiology of binge eating: A developmental perspective" in C. G. Fairburn and G. T. Wilson, eds., *Binge Eating. Nature, Assessment, and Treatment* (New York and London: Guilford Press, 1993), 144–72.

Sugarman, P. A. "Outcome of schizophrenia in the Afro-Caribbean community." *Social Psychiatry and Psychiatric Epidemiology* no. 27 (1992), 102–5.

Sugarman, P. A. and D. Crawford. "Schizophrenia in the Afro-Caribbean community." *British Journal of Psychiatry* no. 164 (1994), 474–80.

Sutherland, I. and J. P. Shepherd. "The prevalence of alcohol, cigarette and illicit drug use in a stratified sample of English adolescents." *Addiction* no. 96 (2001), 637–40.

Sutherland, I. and P. Willner. "Patterns of alcohol, cigarette and illicit drug use in English adolescents." *Addiction* no. 93 (1998), 1199–208.

Thomas, C. L., A. C. James, and M. O. Bachmann. "Eating attitudes in English secondary school students: Influence of ethnicity, gender, mood and social class." *International journal of eating disorders* no. 31(1) (2002), 92–96.

Tizard, B. and A. Phoenix. *Black, White or Mixed Race? Race and Racism in the Lives of Young People of Mixed Parentage* (London: Routledge, 1993).

Tolmac, J. and M. Hodes. "Ethnic variation among adolescent psychiatric in-patients with psychotic disorders." *British Journal of Psychiatry* no. 184 (2004), 428–31.

Van Os, J., D. J. Castle, N. Takei, et al. "Psychotic illness in ethnic minorities: Clarification from the 1991 census." *Psychological Medicine* no. 26 (1996), 203–8.

Vandereycken, W. and H. W. Hoek. "Are eating disorders culture-bound syndromes?" in K. A. Halmi, ed., *Psychobiology and Treatment of Anorexia Nervosa and Bulimia Nervosa* (Washington, DC: American Psychiatric Press, 1992), 19–36.

Wardle, J. and L. Marsland. "Adolescent concerns about weight and eating; A social-developmental perspective." *Journal of Psychosomatic Research* no. 34 (1990), 377–91.

Whitmarsh, A. and T. Harris. *Social Focus on Ethnic Minorities* (London, HMSO: J. Church & C. Summerfield, 1996).

Wing, L. "Mentally retarded children in Camberwell (London)," in H. Hafner, ed., *Estimating Needs for Mental Health Care* (Berlin: Springer Verlag, 1979).

II

CULTURAL ASPECTS OF SPECIFIC
MENTAL HEALTH DISORDERS
IN CHILDREN

HISTORY

Hysteria, which stems from the Greek word for uterus—"hystera" or "hysterikos"—has been known since the ancient Greece or even earlier. Approximately 4,000 years ago "bizarre physical and mental symptoms produced by the movement of the uterus" were recorded in the Egyptian medical papyrus "Kahun." Hippocrates (460 B.C.) described how "the female reproductive parts caused dizziness, motor paralysis and sensory disturbance" and Galen (129 A.D.) argued about "hysteria as an illness caused by lack of sexual activity" where marriage or pregnancy was the first choice of treatment.

In 1682, Thomas Sydenham portrayed both the physical and the psychological symptoms of hysteria and underlined that these symptoms could mimic all of the physical illnesses, but Paul Briquet was the first physician who studied systematically on hysteria. In 1859, he described a clinical picture with the help of a somatic symptoms list, which later was referred to as Briquet's Syndrome. His views were to a great extent influenced by the French neuropathologist Jean-Martin Charcot, who believed that hysteria was the result of a weak neurological system, which was hereditary. He hypnotized his patients in order to study their symptoms and found that he could implant suggestions that dramatically improved the clinical condition under hypnosis. Dr. Charcot's students Pierre Janet and Sigmund Freud were also impressed by him and went on to use hypnosis. Janet's most important contribution to the area was the introduction of the concept "dissociation." Although John Ferriar originated the term "hysterical conversion," Sigmund Freud was to revive the term a century later in referring to the "conversion of intrapsychic distress into physical symptoms." He came to the conclusion that these symptoms were strongly associated with, and symbolized the patients' traumatic memories, which were usually of sexual nature. Josef Breuer, Freud's mentor and coauthor of his first psychoanalytical work "Studies on Hysteria," speculated that "the abnormal excitability of the nervous system" was responsible for producing pathological ideas, which were converted into somatic symptoms.

Over the course of the early twentieth century, there has been a decline in the recorded incidence of hysteria, perhaps partly due to the fact that many previously described symptoms and syndromes were reassigned to organic disorders with the improvement of diagnostic techniques. It has been argued that even patients Freud thought were hysterical may actually have suffered from organic illnesses, such as "Anna O." (Orr-Andrewes, 1987). The decline was sharper in Western countries probably due to both the sexual liberalization and the significant increase in public awareness about the psychology behind hysteria, which is stigmatized and no longer got the desired attention from society.

NOSOLOGY

In the first edition of the Diagnostic and Statistical Manual of Mental Disorders (1952), hysteria was divided into two categories; namely "dissociative reaction" that represented the mental symptoms like amnesias, fugue states, or multiple personalities, and "conversion reaction," to refer to somatic symptoms. In the DSM-II (1968), where symptoms were recognized as reflections of underlying conflicts or maladaptive reactions to life problems, these terms were transformed into "hysterical neurosis, dissociation type" and "hysterical neurosis, conversion type." DSM-III (1980), introduced "somatization disorder" as a new diagnostic category. The psychodynamic view was abandoned, and a categorization based on clinical phenomenology rather than etiological assumptions was preferred in the DSM-III, resulting in the elimination of "hysterical neurosis" and its replacement by "dissociation disorders" and "conversion disorders." DSM-IV (1994) used a conceptually different approach and more detailed descriptions for the types of symptoms or deficits in conversion disorder.

The International Statistical Classification of Diseases and Related Health Problems (ICD) preferred to separate somatoform and dissociative disorders. The major difference was that conversion disorder fell under the category of dissociative disorders in the ICD classification system, whereas the DSM categorized it as a somatoform disorder. ICD-9 (1978) defined conversion disorder as "a disorder whose predominant feature is a loss or alteration in physical functioning that suggests a physical disorder but that is actually a direct expression of a psychological conflict or need." In the ICD-10 (1994), the term "conversion" took a parenthetical place in the dissociative [conversion] disorders.

There is an ongoing discussion on the classification of many psychiatric disorders, but somatoform disorders are among the most controversial diagnostic category. It is difficult to claim that the current definitions or classification systems have developed a better understanding on the terms of "conversion" and "dissociation," which were used for the first time in the nineteenth century, and the term "hysteria" coming from the time of Hippocrates.

The DSM-IV-TR defines dissociation as "the splitting off of clusters of mental contents from conscious awareness, a mechanism central to hysterical conversion and dissociative disorders; the separation of an idea from its emotional significance," while International Classification of Diseases (ICD-10) offers a more inclusive scheme and defines dissociation as "a partial or complete loss of the normal integration between memories of the past, awareness of identity and immediate sensations, and control of body movements." Yet, it seemed problematic to affirm the classification of CD without any memory deficits or loss of consciousness under dissociative disorders. In addition, it may be more acceptable not to classify all conversion seizures under convulsive disorders, but to classify syncopes (temporary loss of consciousness) as dissociative disorders.

The confusion in the definition of somatoform disorders asserts itself in publications with a remarkable amount of synonyms for CD or psychogenic seizures (for example, nonepileptic psychogenic seizure, nonepileptic attack disorder, nonepileptic events, nonepileptic conversion seizure, pseudoseizure, pseudoepileptic seizure, pseudoepilepsy, pseudoepileptic attacks, convulsive pseudoseizure, hysterical seizures, hysterical epilepsy, hysterical attacks, hysteroepilepsy, epileptiform hysteria, psychogenic attacks, functional seizures, psycho seizures, conversion seizure).

An additional problem concerning child psychiatry is that the diagnostic classification of somatoform disorders in children and adolescents are identical to adults. In other words, adult diagnostic criteria are applied to diagnose somatoform disorders in children.

EPIDEMIOLOGY

There are a small number of studies on the prevalence and incidence of childhood conversion disorder with contradictory results. The fact that conversion symptoms generally are present in a primary care setting and often resolves without psychiatric evaluation causes an additional difficulty in determining true incidence. Literature from the Western countries appears to indicate that a diagnosis of CD is relatively rare in children and adolescents: DSM-IV-TR reports the prevalence rate of 0.01–0.3 percent for conversion disorder in the general population, while the prevalence of CD among hospitalized children and adolescents were reported as 0.5 percent (Goodyer, 1981) and the incidence between 2.3 and 4.2/100,000 (Kozlowska et al., 2007). In contrast to Western samples the epidemiological or clinical data from developing countries such as India and Turkey suggest higher incidence rates. CD is reported to be the most prevalent psychiatric problem for children and adolescents in India (Chandra et al., 1993). Srinath et al. found that 14,8 percent of the psychiatric outpatients and 30.8 percent of psychiatric hospitalizations were diagnosed as CD (Srinath et al., 1993). Relatively low but still remarkable prevalence rates ranging from 2.3 percent to 8.9 percent were reported in studies coming from Turkey (Avci and Aslan, 1995; Baysal et al., 1995; Kerimo lu and Yalin, 1992). Although the prevalence of CD in children and adolescents is believed to be low in Western countries, medically unexplained pain symptoms especially headache and recurrent abdominal pain, and other somatic complaints like dizziness, nausea, and fatigue are relatively frequent. CD is more common in adolescents when compared with children, and rarely seen in preschoolers (Akdemir and Unal,

2006). In most of the studies the prevalence rates increase with age, and girls outnumber boys by three to one. It is also reported that CD is more prevalent among children and adolescent coming from rural area or living in poor socioeconomic status families (Ercan et al., 2003).

ETIOLOGY

Various theories have been suggested on the etiology of hysteria, which has changed in historical development. At present, both neurobiological and psychosocial variables are considered as significant factors for the etiology of CD. It is obvious that all of the psychiatric disorders should be evaluated within the frame of biopsychosocial perspective. However, psychosocial and cultural factors have a more important influence in the etiology of CD as compared with most of the other psychiatric disorders.

Neurobiological Factors

Although conversion disorder refers to functional or unexplained neurological deficits that are "not caused by organic lesions in the nervous system," several studies in adults tried to identify the neurophysiological basis for conversion symptoms using functional brain imaging techniques.

In most of these studies, striatothalamocortical circuits controlling sensorimotor function and voluntary motor behavior were examined (Spence et al., 2000; Vuilleumier et al., 2001; Yazici et al., 2004; Yazici and Kostakoglu, 1998). Using SPECT, Vuilleumier et al. were able to demonstrate a consistent decrease of regional cerebral blood flow in the thalamus and basal ganglia contralateral to the deficit in patients with unilateral hysterical sensorimotor loss, which resolved after recovery (Vuilleumier et al., 2001). Volumetric studies supported this finding by showing that patients with CD had significantly smaller mean volumes of the caudate nucleus, lentiform nucleus and the right thalamus (Atmaca et al., 2006). On the other hand, several neuroimaging results have shown increased activation in limbic regions, such as cingulate or orbitofrontal cortex during conversion symptoms (Vuilleumier, 2005).

According to the somatosensory amplification view, individuals may pay more attention to normal physiological sensations and the somatic components of affect, thus amplify or misinterpret these sensations (Barsky et al., 1988). From a neurobiological point of view, conversion symptoms are explained as primitive reflexive mechanisms of protection and alertness, reflecting either errors in how information about body state is processed and represented, or the motor component of an automatic emotional response. Within this evolutionary framework, Kozlowska argued that "mind

In some cultures or languages there may be a lack of words to express one's emotions or may be the expression of emotions through body language is completely normal. The connection between love and heart is well known in all cultures. In Turkish, "dizzying" or "head spinning" are the idioms used for pleasure, while "breath taking" is preferred for admiration, "feeling nauseous" for hatred, "heart pumping" for excitement, "headache" for a person causing trouble, "stomachache" for an annoying person, "to have nine births in a row" or "to hold breath" for a troubled waiting, "to take an easy breath" for the good ending of a troubled waiting, "explosion of the gall bladder" for fear, "wet one's pants" both for fear and laughter, and "drooling" for desire. That is, the culture not only provides specific and appropriate terms for the perception of the illness and the functioning of the body, but also lets the individual interpret the changes in him/herself through these terms (Arsan et al., 1985).

The symptoms of conversion may be regarded as a communicative tool for the emotions and thoughts, which are banned to be expressed because of cultural factors. Gender roles, religious beliefs, and sociocultural influences reinforce these prohibitions. The fact that the conversion symptoms and especially psychogenic seizures are more frequent in the girls whose sexuality and aggression expressions are suppressed or who are afraid to report sexual abuse supports this view. Verbal expression is more censored in the societies where the traditional lifestyle is more dominant. Therefore, these individuals experience difficulties in coping with the negative life events due to both psychosocial censure and difficulties in separation-individuation process. Gender differences in the prevalence of CD can be explained with higher socioeconomical and sociocultural pressure on girls. An important indicator of this sociocultural impact on gender is the increasing ratio of somatic symptoms in girls compared to boys during adolescence, while there are no significant differences during the childhood. This increase underlines the difference between "being born as a woman" and "becoming a woman."

Family factors

Findings suggest that in the families of children with CD, conflicts or communication difficulties usually exist and the psychiatric disorder rates are significantly higher than those of the control groups (Ercan et al., 2003; Pehlivanturk and Unal, 2002). Thus, the psychiatric evaluation of every family member is recommended.

It is also indicated that children with CD are conscientious, obedient, accommodating, and perfectionist children whose families are shown to have worries about illnesses and high expectations from their children. Similarly, the families of children and adolescents with CD are found to be overprotective with high rates of separation anxiety disorder (Bhatia and Sapra, 2005).

Marital problems are especially reported among the parents of these patients and the studies emphasize the important role of family functioning in the etiology of CD in children (Campo et al., 1999). According to family systems theory, conversion symptoms may protect and maintain the family functioning and may even prevent conflicts in the family system. For instance, these symptoms may keep the family together, prevent it from separation, or end ongoing conflicts.

Family Role Allocation, Role Identifications, and Child-Rearing Models

Ozturk asserted that there are strikingly special relationships between the parents and the child with CD. She suggested that "the parents may give the child a special place, a special role or a special responsibility which causes early and excessive sexual role identification and consequently builds a personality which yields to the development of hysterical symptoms" (Ozturk, 1976).

The privileged or special place of the child in the family may arise from special conditions like resemblance to grandparents or other relatives who had a special meaning for the father or mother. Furthermore, the special role in the family usually has its source in unresolved oedipal conflicts. On the other hand, the special responsibility is characterized by parents' intense delegation of their own chores and duties to the child in his/her early ages. Girls who behave like a mother to their siblings in their childhood constitute the majority of conversion disorder cases.

These special roles or responsibilities identified during childhood may become a burden for the child. When the children or adolescents who were given a special role or responsibility encounter a traumatic event that they cannot cope with or when they become incapable of fulfilling the responsibilities of the expected role, conversion symptoms may occur.

Child-rearing styles vary greatly among societies with regard to nutrition, protection, toilet training, and sexuality throughout the child's development. The continuity of care style along with the social attitudes seems to be more effective on personality than a specific rearing style. Family dynamics, personality theories, and some aspects of developmental psychology, which are mostly claimed to be universally valid paradigms, could actually be cultural-specific theoretical concepts (Sayar, 2003). For example, processes such as autonomy, separation, and individuation might only be relevant to Western cultures. Accordingly, autonomous individuals and well-defined boundaries are beneficial for a healthy interaction in the family, whereas blurred interpersonal boundaries or enmeshed families are perceived as pathological compositions. On the other hand, in some non-Western societies, personality is relational and contextually determined, instead of an emphasis on interpersonal boundaries or separation and individuation processes. Autonomy and relatedness are viewed as basic human needs, and though apparently conflicting, are proposed to be compatible. Similarly, the concept of self is variously understood in different cultural contexts. Individualistic cultures encourage a sense of bounded, separate, independent, and autonomous self, whereas collectivistic cultures foster a fluid, relational, interdependent, and porous self. It is concluded that these notions had roots in the traditions of cultures and are deeply embedded in child-rearing practices. Thus, differences in child-rearing practices can be seen as a reflection of these traditions.

In Eastern cultures, parents teach their children to adjust to their environment while in Western cultures parents encourage their children to show their talents. Being aware of the negative aspects of their own behavior is one of the major goals of child-rearing practices in an interdependent culture. For this reason, the most negative feeling in Japan for example, is disturbing other people. Despite different child-rearing practice implementations, a similar socialization of interdependence is also reported in Indian and Turkish societies.

Life Events

In the diagnosis of CD, psychological stress factors are required to be associated with the initiation or exacerbation of the symptoms. The psychosocial stress factors such as violence, depression, or bereavement in the family increase the risk for CD. In a Turkish study with children and adolescents with CD, it is indicated that relationship problems, medical or psychiatric illness in the family, and academic problems play an important role as precipitating factors (Pehlivanturk and Unal, 2000).

In many studies, children and adolescents who have been diagnosed as CD had a higher rate of sexual and physical abuse history compared to the normal control groups. History of sexual abuse was found especially in the patients who have psychogenic seizures or dissociative disorders (Alper et al., 1993; Erdinc et al., 2004). In the adult CD patients, early childhood traumas were observed frequently.

The social challenges such as low educational level, poverty, having multiple children, inaccessibility of opportunities elicited by consuming society, fast urbanization, and immigration may cause psychological trauma on children and adolescents. Furthermore, violence and oppressive attitudes toward women and early marriage are also among the important challenging life events. In Turkey, the difficulty of the examination system for high school and university education also serves as an additional stress source for the adolescents.

Iatrogenic—Attitudes of Physicians

Since physicians experience difficulties in handling conversion symptoms and in referring these patients to mental health services, they play an important role in the maintenance of these symptoms.

Both in Western and developing countries, physicians have difficulties in recognizing the psychiatric disorders in primary health services (Kramer and Garralda, 1998). Despite the fact that CD is a prevalent psychiatric disorder in Turkey, it either is misdiagnosed or treated with improper methods in the emergency services. Moreover, the repetitive and advance investigations for any organic etiology may increase the anxiety and thus cause the duration of the illness to be prolonged. It should be noted that the physicians are also members of the same society as the patient and the reasons that shape the patients' thoughts about the illness are valid for the physicians.

In a study by Goodyer and Mitchel, 29 percent of children and adolescents used prescribed medication before they were referred to a psychiatry service. In children and adolescents who had psychogenic seizures the medication rate was found to be higher (56 percent) when compared with the other groups (Goodyer and Mitchell, 1989). In a study from Turkey, the misdiagnosis rate, which was higher among the children under twelve and children from rural areas, was reported to be 37 percent. Similarly, unnecessary medication was used in 31 percent of these children (Pehlivanturk and Unal, 2000).

Some physicians may experience anger with the thought that these patients are escaping from their responsibilities, acting deliberately, or at least deviating the symptoms. Since telling the patient that "the symptoms are imaginary," or blaming the patient for "pretending" worsens the symptoms and causes the situation to become persistent, it is not a recommendable attitude. Inappropriate attitudes of physicians (for example, painful injections, lemon juice application to the eyes) are beyond the ethical boundaries. In a Turkish study with primary health physicians, the ignorance of the physicians about the subject matter is more influential on the treatment of CD than the physicians' emotional state. This finding suggests that training on CD may increase the physicians' approach quality to the patients (Bediz et al., 2004). Physician training should also include the conceptual framework for approaching patients from a different culture (Rosenberg et al., 2007).

Cultural Factors

Culture is the sum of tangible and intangible elements that people produce throughout their social and historical development and transfer from generation to generation. Cultural elements are learned within a society

cieties, the psychiatric disorders are not distinguished from physical ill-nesses and in effect they are not stigmatized.

The notion, which accepts Western cultures above other cultures, affirms that other cultures would come to the same level of Western cultures with social development. Yet, in recent years, a new notion that accepts all cultures at an equal level has started to dominate cultural psychiatry. This notion requires the consideration for the differences of the illnesses across the cultures rather than the similarities and requires the investigation of how each culture experiences somatization. The somatic expression of stress may even be a practical choice in cultures where psychological health services are not accessible or in cultures where psychiatric disorders are stigmatized. In such societies the somatization of distress may help the patient to get social support that s/he needs and consequently without any damage or malfunctioning, it may help to maintain the balance. Thus, somatization serves as a communication tool that prompts social support rather than simply being an illness.

When somatization is considered as "an escape from psychological stigmatization," the continuous change in its appearance may be better understood. In other words, in different cultures, somatization may manifest itself in different versions. In Western cultures it can be recognized that somatization actually disguises itself behind several popular illnesses such as neurasthenia, chronic fatigue syndrome, immune deficiency syndrome, environmental illness, fibromyalgia, or reactive hypoglycemia.

In studies on cross-cultural comparison of the depressive symptomatology, Turkish patients are found to have significantly higher somatic symptoms compared to German and English patients. These findings indicate that there are some similarities in the symptoms of depression between cultures, but also differences in their predominant mode of expression (Diefenbacher and Heim, 1994; Ulusahin et al., 1994).

Although somatic symptom rates are found to be higher in non-Western cultures, there are also studies that display no cross-cultural differences in the rates of somatoform disorders (Gureje et al., 1997; Piccinelli and Simon, 1997). According to these results, conversion symptom is questioned to be whether a disorder on its own or an accompanying symptom to psychiatric disorders. The conversion symptoms in the clinical picture may mask the underlying psychiatric disorder. When we consider conversion as a communication style, it is quite a possibility that patients who have been diagnosed with CD may actually have undiagnosed depression or anxiety disorders.

In the etiology of conversion symptoms, there are multiple and complex biopsychosocial factors. Thus, it is necessary to study CD with a multidimensional perspective. That somatization is more prevalent in the developing countries should not cause any prejudice to suggest that somatization is a specific disorder in the undeveloped societies and any depreciatory attitude.

Our knowledge on the psychological and biological etiologies of depression, anxiety disorders, and schizophrenia has increased remarkably within the last fifty years. Although there has been an important leap with Freud's psychoanalytical explanation on somatoform disorders, in the following years they have been left out of the attention of the researchers, as if the underlying reasons were completely understood or an effective treatment was developed. Even though in the recent years it has started to be seen less frequently, it is still prevalent in the developing countries and thus more research is needed on the factors that affect CD etiology.

With a better understanding of present cultural conditions, the comprehension of the special meanings of emotions, behaviors, and attitudes will be achieved. In the international classification systems, there is a need that cultural factors get more emphasis in the definition of somatoform disorders. These systems should also include the items specific to non-Western cultures and in the research designs, cultural factors should be taken into consideration.

CLINICAL FEATURES

CD is an illness where emotional problems and conflicts find expression in voluntarily controlled or sense-perception organs. Most of the CD symptoms influence sensory motor functioning and mimic neurological illnesses. Psychogenic seizures, coordination or balance problems, paralysis or weakness, aphasia, gait disturbance, dysphagia, blindness, tunnel vision, deafness, blurred vision, glove anesthesia, and paresthesias are the most common presenting features, whereas rare symptoms such as coughing, sneezing, hiccupping, belching, vomiting, hallucinations, and stridor are also reported among children and adolescents with CD.

In Turkey and India the most frequent conversion symptom is psychogenic seizures while in Western countries motor symptoms are more common (Kozlowska et al., 2007; Pehlivanturk and Unal, 2000; Srinath et al., 1993). Although CD rates are lower in Western countries, unexplained pain complaints are frequent in children and adolescents.

Polysymptomatic presentations are indicated to be more frequent than monosymptomatic presentations and several somatic pain or gastrointestinal symptoms usually accompany the clinical picture (Grattan-Smith et al., 1988). Polysymptomatic CD in childhood and adolescence may constitute a different entity from monosymptomatic conversion disorder and may be an early manifestation or incomplete form of somatization disorder. Accordingly, family histories of psychiatric disorders are more frequent in children and adolescents with polysymptomatic CD, and the prognoses are reported to be poorer (Murase et al., 2000).

In many cases CD may be comorbid with, or secondary to a medical condition. Usually, a mild illness or a trauma may be the precursor of CD. The lack of worry related to the illness (la belle indifference) may be observed in CD but since this finding varies in children, it should not be considered as a typical characteristic of conversion.

Prolonged conversion symptoms such as paralysis may cause muscle atrophy, demineralization, and contractures. Another risk is the iatrogenic interventions such as various diagnostic investigations, medical treatments, or surgical procedures.

CD usually exhibits an acute onset of symptoms. However, there are also cases with slow progressive worsening of symptoms. Psychological conflicts or other stress factors are temporally linked to the onset or exacerbation of the symptoms. Symptoms may develop after a physical illness or an accident. It is reported that there are several conflicts, communication difficulties, and high rates of psychiatric disorders in these families. The average time interval between the onset of the symptoms and referral to a psychiatric clinic is reported to be around one year in a Turkish study (Pehlivanturk and Unal, 2000). The uncertainty about how far the medical investigations for identifying a physical cause should go is an additional reason for the increase of this time interval.

Personality Characteristics

Conversion symptoms may be observed in all personality types, but children with histrionic personality characteristics are thought to be more prone to develop CD. These children usually have a low frustration threshold, and also show narcissistic, immature, and dependent features.

The children with CD in Turkey are reported to be excessively cooperative, perfectionist, introverted, insecure, and mostly have difficulties in the expression of emotions. Contrary to this profile, though rare, CD may be seen in children and adolescents with conduct problems (Ozturk, 1976).

Comorbid Disorders

It is stated that CD generally accompanies other psychiatric disorders in children and adolescents, and in studies where these patients are compared to healthy control groups, psychiatric disorders, especially anxiety and depression, symptoms are common. Especially in children with prepubertal depression, somatic symptoms are found to be more frequent compared to adolescents or adults. During the prepubertal period, a child is rarely brought to the physician only with depressive symptoms. For many researchers, conversion symptoms are components of other psychiatric disorders such as adjustment disorder, separation anxiety, depression, psychosis, or organic brain syndrome. Pehlivanturk and Unal (2000) reported that 15.7 percent of the children and adolescents with CD had comorbid major depression and 37.2 percent had comorbid anxiety disorders. They also indicated that the prevalence of depressive disorders increased with age. Similarly, Ercan et al. found 10 percent of adolescents with CD had adjustment disorder, 25 percent had major depression, and 19 percent had dysthymia (1998). Although the rate of children and adolescents who applied primarily with a psychiatric problem to pediatric clinics is reported to be 2 percent, this figure is corrected up to 38 percent after these patients were psychiatrically assessed. These data indicate that children who actually have psychiatric problems may be referred to pediatric clinics with somatic complaints (Kramer and Garralda, 1998).

Diagnostic Difficulties

Psychogenic seizures may mimic any kind of epileptic seizure. The differential diagnosis between epileptic seizures and psychogenic seizures can be difficult despite detailed physical and neurological examinations and investigations. A great proportion of the patients have an artistic tendency to mimic real epileptic seizures. The coincidence of epilepsy and psychogenic seizures is an additional diagnostic problem (Karacan et al., 1996). After the implementation of videoelectroencephalography (Video-EEG), 10 to 30 percent of the patients who previously diagnosed with psychogenic seizures are shown to have real epileptic seizures. Similarly, some of the patients were exposed to unnecessary medication with antiepileptic drugs, although they had psychogenic seizures.

The most important factors that increase the difficulties in diagnosis are the lack of specific findings, the coexistence of epileptic and psychogenic seizures, possibility of an underlying physical illness such as frontal lobe seizures or reflex epilepsies, and the uncertainty encountered about for how far the investigations for physical causes should go. Since EEG abnormalities are not rare among healthy population (10 percent), routine EEG does not always help for the differential diagnosis. Similarly, due to individual differences in baseline levels, serum prolactin levels do not either be of help during the routine practice. However, Video-EEG is observed to have a very important role in differentiating pseudo seizures from epilepsy.

TREATMENT

Since the appearance of the illness is almost always physical, children and adolescents with conversion disorder are usually presented to the pediatrician or the primary health care provider at first. The evaluation of possible physical disorder and reassurance that the symptoms do not indicate a serious underlying disease can solely be therapeutic in some cases. However, a more thorough approach and referral for psychiatric treatment are required in many cases.

The literature on the treatment of CD in children or adolescents mostly consists of case reports using several approaches, including play therapy, educational therapy, art therapy, psychodynamic therapy, cognitive-behavioral therapy, biofeedback, physiotherapy, affect regulation techniques, guided imagery techniques, hypnotherapy, Eye-Movement Desensitization-Reprocessing, family therapy, pharmacotherapy, and hospitalization (Diseth and Christie, 2005). The most successful treatment approach seems to be the most eclectic (see text box 6.1); however, controlled clinical trials of these interventions are lacking.

The goals of these treatment modalities can be summarized as to give information about the nature of the disorder and to facilitate the parents' engagement in treatment, encourage insight gaining about factors initiating or aggravating the symptoms, to intervene as appropriate for any associated family dysfunction, parental psychopathology or other source of family stress that may impede recovery, decrease the need for secondary gains, build self-esteem, teach nonsomatic ways to express distress, and to remove the somatic symptoms without creating new symptoms.

Inpatient/residential treatment is indicated if outpatient treatment is ineffective or if there is a treatment resistant comorbid psychopathology. Sometimes hospitalization is very useful only because it removes children from their pathological home environments.

OUTCOME

The findings of follow-up studies in children and adolescents with conversion disorder suggest clinical improvement rates varying from 56 to 100 percent. This indicates generally a better outcome compared to the clinical improvement rates in adults (Wyllie et al., 1991). Many cases recover within three months, and when diagnosed early, some conversion symptoms can even remit spontaneously or with minimal intervention after a few days or weeks (Turgay, 1990). Long-term follow-up showed also favorable outcome rates; Pehlivanturk and Unal reevaluated forty children and adolescents four years later and found that 85 percent had completely recovered from their conversion symptoms (Pehlivanturk and Unal, 2002).

Despite the investigation of numerous variables as the predictors of prognosis in CD, some results are conflicting. For example, Goodyer and Mitchell showed that recovery rates for psychogenic seizures (62.5 percent) were significantly lower than other conversion symptoms (90 percent) (1989), while others reported high recovery rates for psychogenic seizures ranging from 78 percent to 100 percent (Pehlivanturk and Unal, 2002). Similarly, several studies demonstrated the association of comorbid anxiety disorders, depression, or preceding conduct disorders with poor outcome (Chandra et al., 1993), whereas Wyllie et al. (1999) found no significant effect. However, there is almost a consensus that polysymptomatic presentation, chronicity of the symptoms, poor capacity to gain insight, severe internal conflicts, history of sexual abuse, and serious family dysfunction are poor prognostic factors; while younger age, early diagnosis, good premorbid adjustment, close liaison between pediatricians and child psychiatrists, the presence of an easily identifiable stressor, cooperation of the child and the family are generally associated with favorable outcome (Pehlivanturk and Unal, 2002).

CONCLUSION

Despite its high prevalence in non-Western countries, our knowledge about CD in children and adolescents appeared to be limited. It is also difficult to claim that the current definitions or classification systems have developed a better understanding on CD. The international classification systems should include the items specific to non-Western cultures, and cultural factors should be taken into consideration in the research designs. Despite living in the era of globalization, it is essential to protect different cultures and to realize their impact on psychiatric illnesses. Contemporary cultural psychiatry recognizes that psychiatric disorders should be assessed in a culture-specific perspective, instead of simply comparing the differences between cultures.

Although CD is universal, it should be remembered that the conversion symptom formation is shaped by culture, and in some cultures it may be only a representation of anxiety or depressive disorders. In all cultural groups, it is known that the physical symptoms are the most common personal expressions of social problems and emotional distress. Yet, in some cultures or languages the expression of emotions through body language can be accepted as completely normal. In these cultures, medically unexplained symptoms usually do not cause help-seeking behaviors or cannot be accounted for a psychiatric disorder. It should be kept in mind that conversion symptoms can be seen as a culturally approved coping mechanism rather than an illness.

It is observed that negative thoughts and attitudes toward patients with CD are not prevailing and psychiatric disorders presented with physical symptoms are not stigmatized in Turkish society. However, it is surprising that the physicians tend to stigmatize CD more than the laypeople in Turkey. The clinicians should be aware that conversion symptoms are shaped by social and cultural factors and inform their patients about the nature of these symptoms.

Even though CD has started to be seen less frequently in recent years, it is still prevalent in developing countries, thus more research is needed on the etiology, comorbid disorders, and treatment alternatives for this disorder. Cultural-specific factors such as circumcision, child-rearing styles, and family role allocations should also be investigated.

Box 6.1.   Case Study of CD.

A 10-year-old boy, O., is a fourth grader and is the first child of an extended traditional farmer family of a low-middle income level, consisting of grandfather, grandmother, uncle, aunt, cousins, and a seven-year-old brother.

He was referred to a child psychiatry clinic because of a tremor in his right hand and arm lasting all day for one month. Two months before his tremor began, he also had a history of headache, palpitation, and abdominal pain. After being evaluated by physicians at his hometown, he was referred to a doctor in child neurology. His physical and neurological examinations and laboratory investigations were found to be within normal limits. It was observed that, when he was distracted somehow, his tremor ceased.

O. had been described as an introverted child, but also congenial and successful who behaved more mature than his age. Due to his accomplishments at school, he was praised by his teachers and was admired by his peers. He was expected to contribute to his father's work after school. He had a special place within the family among other children and was in an exemplary position. His grandparents had treated him prestigiously as he was the first grandchild.

The primary school he was going to was a small village school where there was a single classroom and a single teacher. The students in all grades studied together in this single class. In the beginning of his fourth year in this school, after his teacher extended these expectations by demanding help for younger children with their homework at school, his tremor began and his neat handwriting deteriorated. He was reluctant to go to school and his teacher, in an effort to try to support him, had stated that he might not come to school if he wished to. All his family members, especially his mother, were so anxious and concerned about his situation that she had started feeding him.

Although he looked younger than his age, he wore a black suit and talked in a manner above his age. He was highly anxious and depressive, and was preoccupied with his tremor and school absenteeism. The patient was diagnosed with conversion and anxiety disorders. An effective treatment was accomplished by both analyzing the relationship patterns in the family, handling their child-rearing styles, reconstructing his special place, role, and responsibilities, which may lead to early sexual role identification and antidepressant medication. His tremor disappeared in four months and he could go back to school.

REFERENCES

D. Akdemir and F. Unal. "Early onset conversion disorder: A case report." *Turkish Journal of Psychiatry* 17(2006): 65–71.

K. Alper, O. Devinsky, K. Perrine, B. Vazquez, and D. Luciano. "Nonepileptic seizures and childhood sexual and physical abuse." *Neurology* 43(1993): 1950–53.

C. Arsan, B. Erdo an, and O. Aslan. "Somatization and its importance in medical practice" (in Turkish; English summary) *Dirim* 60(1985): 323–32.

M. Atmaca, A. Aydin, E. Tezcan, A. K. Poyraz, and B. Kara. "Volumetric investigation of brain regions in patients with conversion disorder." *Progress in Neuropsychopharmacology and Biological Psychiatry* 30(2006): 708–13.

A. Avc› and H. Aslan. "Obsessive Compulsive Disorder and Conversion Disorder in Children: A Comparative Clinical Study." *Turkish Journal of Psychiatry* 6(1995): 49–53.

A. J. Barsky, J. D. Goodson, R. S. Lane, and P. D. Cleary. "The amplification of somatic symptoms." *Psychosomatic Medicine* 50(1988): 510–19.

Z. B. Baysal, F. Öktem, F. Ünal, and B. Pehlivantürk. "The change in the adolescent psychiatric population in ten years" (paper presented at the Fourth International Congress of ISAP, Athens, Greece, 1995).

U. Bediz, C. Aydemir, A. D. Basterzi, C. Kısa, S Cebeci, and E Göka. "Factors influencing physicians approach to conversion disorder." *Clinical Psychiatry* 7(2004): 73–79.

M. S. Bhatia and S. Sapra. "Pseudoseizures in children: A profile of 50 cases." *Clinical Pediatrics* 44, no. 7(September 2005): 617–21.

J. V. Campo, L. Jansen-McWilliams, and K. J. Kelleher. "Somatization in pediatric primary care: Association with psychopathology, functional impairment and use of services." *Journal of the American Academy of Child and Adolescent Psychiatry* 38(1999): 1093–1101.

R. Chandra, S. Srinivasan, R. Chandrasekaran, and S. Mahadevan. "The prevalence of mental disorders in school-age children attending a general pediatric department in southern India." *Acta Psychiatrica Scandinavica* 87(1993): 192–96.

A. Diefenbacher and G. Heim. "Somatic symptoms in Turkish and German depressed patients." *Psychosomatic Medicine* 56(1994): 551–56.

T. H. Diseth and H. J. Christie. "Trauma-related dissociative (conversion) disorders in children and adolescents—an overview of assessment tools and treatment principles." *Nordic Journal of Psychiatry* 59(2005): 278–92.

S. E. Dündar, F. Aldanmaz, A. Oguz. "Attitudes of laypeople towards conversion disorder, obsessive compulsive disorder, anxiety disorder and impotence" (in Turkish; English summary). *Kriz Dergisi* 3(1995): 250–57.

C. Eggers. "Conversion symptoms in childhood and adolescence." *Praxis der Kinderpsychologie und Kinderpsychiatrie* 47, no. 3(1998): 144–56.

E. S. Ercan, A. Varan, and B. Veznedaro lu. "Associated features of conversion disorder in Turkish adolescents." *Pediatrics International* 45(2003): 150–55.

E. S. Ercan, A. Varan, B. Veznedaro lu, F. Akdeniz, and C. Ayd›n. "Associated Features of Conversion Disoder in Adolescents." *Turkish Journal of Psychiatry* 9(1998): 165–72.

B. Erdinc, C. B. Sengul, N. Dilbaz, and S. Bozkurt. "A case of incest with dissociative amnesia and post traumatic stress disorder." *Turkish Journal of Psychiatry* 15, no. 2(2004): 161–65.

I. M. Goodyer. "Hysterical conversion reactions in childhood." *Journal of Child Psychology and Psychiatry, and Allied Disciplines* 22(1981): 179–88.

I. M. Goodyer and C. Mitchell. "Somatic emotional disorders in childhood and adolescence." *Journal of Psychosomatic Research* 33(1989): 681–88.

P. Grattan-Smith, M. Fairley, and A. P. Procopis. "Clinical features of conversion disorder." *Archives of Disease in Childhood* 63(1988): 408–14.

O. Gureje, G. E. Simon, T. B. Ustun, and D. P. Goldberg. "Somatization in cross-cultural perspective: A World Health Organization study in primary care." *American Journal of Psychiatry* 154(1997): 989–95.

E. Karacan, S. Senol, and S. Sener. "Psychogenic seizures secondary to epilepsy: Two case studies" (in Turkish; English summary). *Cocuk ve Genclik Ruh Sagligi Dergisi* 3(1996): 144–49.

E. Kerimo lu and A. Yabn. "Obsessive-compulsive disorder and hysteria (conversion reaction) in children." *Journal of Ankara Medical School* 14(1992): 11–18.

K. Kozlowska, K. P. Nunn, D. Rose, A. Morris, A. Ouvrier, and J. Varghese. "Conversion disorder in Australian pediatric practice." *Journal of the American Academy of Child and Adolescent Psychiatry* 46(2007): 68–75.

T. Kramer and M. E. Garralda. "Psychiatric disorders in adolescents in primary care." *British Journal of Psychiatry* 173(1998): 508–13.

M. Kuloglu, M. Atmaca, E. Tezcan, O. Gecici, and S. Bulut. "Sociodemographic and clinical characteristics of patients with conversion disorder in Eastern Turkey." *Social Psychiatry and Psychiatric Epidemiology* 38(2003): 88–93.

S. Murase, T. Sugiyama, T. Ishii, R. Wakako, and T. Ohta. "Polysymptomatic conversion disorder in childhood and adolescence in Japan. Early manifestation or incomplete form of somatization disorder?" *Psychotherapy and Psychosomatics* 69(2000): 132–36.

A. Orr-Andrewes. "The case of Anna O: A neuropsychiatric perspective." *Journal of Psychoanalytic Association* 35(1987): 387–19.

M. Ozturk. "The special role of children with hysterical symptoms in their family" (in Turkish; English summary). *Çocuk Sagligi ve Hastaliklari Dergisi* 19(1976): 93–107.

B. Pehlivanturk and F. Unal. "Conversion disorder in children and adolescents: Clinical features and comorbidity with depressive and anxiety disorders." *Turkish Journal of Pediatrics* 42(2000): 132–37.

P. Pehlivanturk and F. Unal. "Conversion disorder in children and adolescents: A 4-year follow-up study." *Journal of Psychosomatic Research* 52(2002): 187–91.

M. Piccinelli and G. Simon. "Gender and cross-cultural differences in somatic symptoms associated with emotional distress. An international study in primary care." *Psychological Medicine* 27, no. 2(March 1997): 433–44.

E. Rosenberg, L. J. Kirmayer, S. Xenocostas, M. D. Dao, and C. Loignon. "GPs' strategies in intercultural clinical encounters." *Family Practice* 24, no 2(April 2007): 145–51.

K. Sayar. "Self and personality from a cultural viewpoint." (in Turkish; English summary). *Yeni Symposium* 41(2003): 78-85.

S. A. Spence, H. L. Crimlisk, H. Cope, M. A. Ron, and P. M. Grasby. "Discrete neurophysiological correlates in prefrontal cortex during hysterical and feigned disorder of movement." *Lancet* 355, no. 9211(April 2000): 1243–44.

S. Srinath, S. Bharat, S. Girimaji, and S. Seshadri. "Characteristics of a child inpatient population with hysteria in India." *Journal of the American Academy of Child and Adolescent Psychiatry* 32(1993): 822–25.

A. Turgay. "Treatment outcome for children and adolescents with conversion disorder." *Canadian Journal of Psychiatry* 35(1990): 585–88.

A. Ulusahin, M. Basoglu, and E. S. Paykel. "A cross-cultural comparative study of depressivesymptoms in British and Turkish clinical samples." *Social Psychiatry and Psychiatric Epidemiology* 29(1994): 31–39.

F. R. Volkmar, J. Poll, and M. Lewis. "Conversion reactions in childhood and adolescents." *Journal of the American Academy of Child and Adolescent Psychiatry* 23(1984): 424–30.

P. Vuilleumier. "Hysterical conversion and brain function." *Progress in Brain Research* 150 (2005): 309–29.

P. Vuilleumier, C. Chicherio, F. Assal, S. Schwartz, D. Slosman, and T. Landis. "Functional neuroanatomical correlates of hysterical sensorimotor loss." *Brain* 124(2001): 1077–90.

J. R. Weisz, S. Suwanlert, W. Chaiyasit, B. Weiss, and E. W. Jackson. "Adult attitudes toward over- and undercontrolled child problems: Urban and rural parents and teachers from Thailand and United States." *Journal of Child Psychology and Psychiatry, and Allied Disciplines* 32(1991): 645–54.

E. Wyllie, D. Friedman, H. Luders, H. Morris, D. Rothner, and J. Turnbull. "Outcome of psychogenic seizures in children and adolescents compared with adults." *Neurology* 41(1991): 742–44.

E. Wyllie, J. P. Glazer, S. Benbadis, P. Kotagal, and B. Wolgamuth. "Psychiatric features of children and adolescents with pseudoseizures." *Archives of Pediatrics and Adolescent Medicine* 153(1999): 244–48.

K. M. Yazici, M. Demirci, B. Demir, and A. Ertu rul. "Abnormal somatosensory evoked potentials in two patients with conversion disorder." *Psychiatry and Clinical Neurosciences* 58(2004): 222–25.

K. M. Yazici and L. Kostakoglu. "Cerebral blood flow changes in patients with conversion disorder." *Psychiatry Research* 83(1998): 163–68.

BIBLIOGRAPHY

American Psychiatric Association. *Diagnosis and Statistical Manual of Mental disorders. 4th ed. Text Revision.* Washington, DC: American Psychiatric Association, 2000.

Baskak, B., and A. Çevik. "Cultural aspects of somatization" (in Turkish; English summary). *Türkiye'de Psikiyatri* 9(2007): 50–57.

Campo, J. V., and S. L. Fritsch. "Somatization in children and adolescents." *Journal of American Academy of Child and Adolescent Psychiatry* 33(1994): 1223–35.

Cimilli, C. "Social evolution of somatization" (in Turkish; English summary). *Türkiye Klinikleri* 1(1999): 34–43.

Fabrega, H. "The concept of somatization as a cultural and historical product of Western medicine." *Psychosomatic Medicine* 52(1990): 653–72.

Ford, C. V. "Somatization and fashionable diagnoses: illness as a way of life." *Scandinavian Journal of Work, Environment and Health* 23(1997): 7–16.

Fritz, G. K., S. Fritsch, and O. Hagino. "Somatoform disorders in children and adolescents: a review of the past 10 years." *Journal of American Academy of Child and Adolescent Psychiatry* 36(1997): 1329–38.

Garralda, E. "Somatization and somatoform disorders." *Psychiatry* 4, no. 8(2005): 97–100.

——. "A selective review of child psychiatric syndromes with a somatic presentation." *British Journal of Psychiatry* 161(1992): 759–73.

Göka, E. "Body as language and symptom flora" (in Turkish; English summary). *Türkiye Klinikleri* 1(1999): 18–26.

Goodyer, I. M., and D. C. Taylor. "Hysteria." *Archives of Disease in Childhood* 60(1985): 680–81.

Güleç, C. "A transculturel perspective to the disease and health concepts in the anatolian culture," (in Turkish; English summary). *Klinik Psikiyatri* 3(2000): 34–39.

Halligan, P. W., and A. S. David. "Conversion hysteria: Towards a cognitive neuropsychological account." *Cognitive Neuropsychiatry* 4(1999): 161–63.

Illis, L. S. "Hysteria." *Spinal Cord* 40(2002): 311–12.

Kagitcibasi, C. "Autonomy and relatedness in cultural context-implications for self and family." *Journal of Crosscultural Psychology* 36(2005): 403–22.

——. "The autonomous-relational self: a new synthesis." *European Psychologist* 1(1996): 180–86.

Kirmayer, L. J., and A. Young. "Culture and somatization: Clinical, epidemiological, and ethnographic perspectives." *Psychosomatic Medicine* 60(1998): 420–30.

Kirmayer, L. J., and K. J. Looper. "Abnormal illness behaviour: Physiological, psychological and social dimensions of coping with distress." *Current Opinion in Psychiatry* 19(2006): 54–60.

Kozlowska, K. "Healing the disembodied mind: contemporary models of conversion disorder." *Harvard Review of Psychiatry* 13, no. 1(2005): 1–13.

Looper, K. J., and L. J. Kirmayer. "Perceived stigma in functional somatic syndromes and comparable medical conditions." *Journal of Psychosomatic Research* 57(2004): 373–78.

Mayou, R., L. J. Kirmayer, G. Simon, K. Kroenke, and M. Sharpe. "Somatoform disorders: time for a new approach in DSM-V." *American Journal of Psychiatry* 162(2005): 847–55.

Micale, M. S. "On the 'Disappearance' of Hysteria: A Study in the Clinical Deconstruction of a Diagnosis." *Isis* 84(1993): 496–526.

Ozturk, O. M. *Ruh Sağliği ve Bozukluklari* (Mental Health and Disorders; in Turkish). Ankara: Medikomat, 2001.

Sayar, K. "Self and personality from a cultural viewpoint" (in Turkish; English summary). *Yeni Symposium* 41(2003): 78–85.

7

Cultural and Clinical Aspects of Depressive Disorders in Tunisian Children and Adolescents

Asma Bouden and Iméne Gasmi

INTRODUCTION

Depression in children has only relatively recently received clinical recognition. It was, in fact, only around the 1960s–1970s that clinicians learned to detect behind a screen of other symptoms the depressive affect and mood. Thus was born the concept of "masked depression," a term which speaks to its disconcerting nature and, at the same time, its difficulty to diagnose. Many symptoms can hide depression from the view of even the well-trained clinician, for example, somatic complaints, disturbance of sleep, eating disorders, elimination disorders, psychosomatic disorders, and behavioral disorders. These symptoms may present themselves to make up for a failure that is more pronounced the younger the patient, namely the inability to express and verbalize emotions. Consequently, from lack of insight, the child reveals his mental suffering by making his body telling it for him. This characteristic is not specific to childhood and immaturity, it is also observed in certain cultures. In fact, the physical expression of affect in the form of complaints or somatic conversion is very frequent in the southern countries and in particular the Maghreb (Douki et al., 1989). Thus in these regions it is more common to diagnose "depressive equivalents" than the typical syndrome.

All authors agree regarding the irrevocable existence of a common core of depression, which may be said to be universal. At the same time, it is also recognized that the mark of culture does not fail to color the expression of symptoms. Few controlled studies have examined the variation in the semiological register from one culture to another. Several studies, however, have shown the difficulty in applying the diagnostic scales from one cultural context to another, and the necessity of adapting certain items to the group being studied (Knight et al., 1994). Classification tools have attempted to respond to these difficulties, but have not always been able to solve them. Some rare psychological disorders cannot be placed in any diagnostic category. In child psychiatry, the problem is even more complex given that certain symptoms, which are particularly frequent in depressed children, such as somatic complaints and social withdrawal, are not among the diagnostic criteria for major depressive disorder in international classifications (Bailly, 1996).

The lack of data on the symptomatic variations of depression according to culture affects the reliability of the assessment of the child's psychological suffering within its cultural surroundings. Cultural belonging influences the presentation, the expression of affect, and the quality of personal interaction as much as other elements to be taken into account in the diagnosis of depressive syndrome. Thus, symptomatic analysis of psychological functioning cannot be projected without care from one cultural context to another. Cultures produce particular organizations of syndromes which have their own semiology and which must be analysed cautiously so that they may be reattached to a nosological category.

This set of problems has led us to the study of the semiology of depression in Tunisian children, using a structured diagnostic questionnaire that was completed by a standard clinical examination. The results were then compared to those found in the literature.

A STUDY OF DEPRESSIVE FEATURES
AMONG TUNISIAN CHILDREN

We aimed to study depression in Tunisian children and to search for possible cultural specificities. This was a descriptive, retrospective, cross-sectional study covering a period of twenty-six months, between January 2005 and February 2007.

The study included boys and girls aged six to seventeen years in mainstream education attending the outpatient clinic of the department of Child Psychiatry at the Razi Hospital in Tunis, suffering from an episode of major depression, dysthymic disorders, or adjustment disorder with depressive mood, according to DSM-IV-R criteria (APA, 2003). Children with ongoing organic pathology or with medium, severe, or profound mental retardation were excluded. The evaluation tools included a standardized semistructured interview: the Schedule for Affective Disorders and Schizophrenia for School-Age Children, lifetime version (Kiddie-SADS-PL) (Kaufman et al., 1997).

Seventy-five patients were included in the study: one-third was pre-adolescent children and two-thirds were adolescents; the average age was 12.5 years. The group was fairly evenly distributed according to gender. About half came from an urban area and a quarter each from rural or semirural areas. Two-thirds came from low-income households and only 4 percent were from families with a high level of income. A total of 72 percent of the group had one or two parents who were unemployed or worked only as day workers (62.7 percent). As for parental educational level, about two-thirds came from families with little or no formal education and about a quarter from moderately educated families (parents with secondary school level education). In 8 percent parents had had a university education.

CLINICAL CHARACTERISTICS

The diagnostic distribution is given in figure 7.1. About two-thirds had a DSM-IV-R episode of major depression, 14 percent dysthymia or adjustment disorder with depressive mood, the rest having a nonspecific depression (figure 7.1). There was no significant difference in the diagnostic distribution according to the main age brackets (children and adolescents) or gender.

Psychiatric comorbidy was common (figure 7.2) and present in nearly half the sample, mostly separation anxiety disorder (in 40 percent), but also posttraumatic stress disorder, generalized anxiety, elimination, and conduct

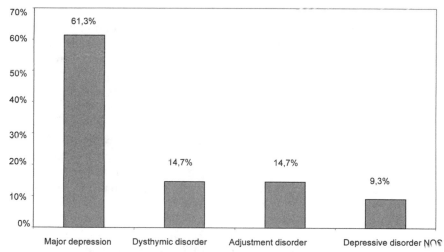

Figure 7.1.   Types of depressive disorders in the population

COMORBID DISORDERS Frequency	
Separation anxiety disorders	40.5%
Posttraumatic stress disorders	19.0%
Generalized anxiety	16.2%
Elimination disorders	18.9%

Figure 7.2.   Comorbid Disorders

disorders. Younger children had more comorbid disorders (63 percent) than adolescents (35 percent), a statistically significant difference (p=0.02). While elimination and separation anxiety disorders were identified at a higher rate in children, conduct and generalized anxiety disorders were statistically more frequent in adolescents (p=0.03). However there were no differences in comorbidity according to gender.

THE SEMIOLOGICAL CHARACTERISTICS OF THE DEPRESSIVE EPISODE

Symptoms According to K-SADS Criteria

The most frequent symptoms (see figure 7.3) were depressive mood, and in descending order: irritability, sadness, anhedonia, sensitivity to rejection and suicidal thoughts, feelings of worthlessness, pessimism, and feelings of guilt. In terms of psychomotor symptoms concentration difficulties were most frequent followed by asthenia and lack of reactivity; psychomotor retardation and agitation were reported equally commonly. In addition anxiety was found in a third of cases, and insomnia and anorexia were also common. Elimination disorders were recognized in 18 percent and were classed as comorbid disorders.

Other Symptoms Found on Clinical Examination

Somatic complaints were reported by 41 percent. These amounted essentially to headache (70 percent), abdominal pain (19 percent), arthralgia (6 percent), and palpitations (3 percent). Somatic complaints were more frequent (50 percent) among patients with comorbid anxiety (36 percent in those without associated anxiety disorders) but this difference was not statistically significant.

Other associated symptoms were somatic and psychological conversion, though these did not necessarily fulfil the DSM-IV-R criteria for conversion and dissociative disorders. They were encountered in 41 percent of cases

Symptoms	Total	Age			Gender		
		6–11 Years	12–17 Years	P	Masculine	Feminine	P
Irritability	69.3%	77.8%	64.4%	0.17	68.4%	70.3%	0.53
Depressive mood	64.0%	59.3%	66.7%	0.34	65.8%	62.2%	0.46
Anhedonia	40.0%	37.0%	41.7%	0.44	34.2%	45.9%	0.21
Sensitivity to rejection	32%	29.6%	33.3%	0.47	28.9%	35.1%	0.37
Thoughts of suicide	32%	14.8%	41.7%	0.01	28.9%	35.1%	0.37
Feelings of worthlessness	30.7%	25.9%	33.3%	0.34	31.6%	29.7%	0.53
Feelings of hopelessness	26.7%	25.9%	27.1%	0.56	28.9%	24.3%	0.42
Feelings of guilt	17.3%	7.4%	22.9%	0.07	13.2%	21.6%	0.25
Decrease in ability to concentrate	64.0%	66.7%	62.5%	0.45	71.7%	56.8%	0.14
Exhaustion	41.3%	40.7%	41.7%	0.56	34.2%	48.6%	0.15
Psychomotor retardation	21.3%	25.9%	18.8%	0.32	13.2%	29.7%	0.07
Agitation	20.0%	22.2%	18.8%	0.46	28.9%	10.8%	0.04
Anxiety	37.3%	48.1%	31.3%	0.11	39.5%	35.1%	0.44
Insomnia	40.0%	37%	41.7%	0.44	36.8%	43.2%	0.37
Loss of appetite	36.0%	3.7%	20.8%	0.04	5.3%	24.3%	0.02
Somatic complaints	41.3%	48.1%	37.5%	0.25	39.5%	43.2%	0.46
Conversion symptoms	41.3%	40.7%	41.7%	0.56	34.2%	48.6%	0.15

Figure 7.3. Symptom rates according to gender and age groups

(somatic conversions in 33 percent and psychological conversions in 8 percent). The former (somatic conversions) included mainly loss of consciousness (nonspecified dissociative disorder in 38 percent), isolated dyspnoea (conversion disorder) without anxiety (19 percent), and paresthesia (conversion disorder) (6 percent). The psychological conversions which do not correspond to any diagnostic classification criteria were made up of loss themes (death, separation) and visual or imaginative experiences (visions of scenes) with no associated consciousness disorder or anxiety. All these symptoms were concurrent with the depressive episodes. Conversions were more frequent (52 percent) among patients with comorbid anxiety (30 percent among those without anxiety disorders). This difference was statistically significant (p=0.05).

Associations

- *With age*: Only suicidal thoughts, feelings of guilt, and weight loss were statistically more frequent in adolescents (see figure 7.3).
- *With gender*: Weight loss, psychomotor retardation, as well as symptoms of somatic conversion were statistically more frequent in girls, while agitation was more frequent in boys (see figure 7.3).
- *With education level of the parents*: The frequency of conversion was higher among patients with parents with a low level of education (illiterate and primary school level). However, this difference was not statistically significant. Losses of consciousness were significantly more frequent among children from families with poor education (p=0.027).
- *With socioeconomic level*: Somatic complaints and conversions were statistically more frequent in low-income families (p=0.02). Symptoms in the psychomotor domain like asthenia and agitation were statistically more frequent in patients from destitute families (p=0.09 and p=0.06 respectively). There was no significant difference in other symptoms of depression.
- *With geographic origin*: Patients living in rural areas showed more symptoms of conversion (57 percent) compared to those in urban areas (34 percent). This difference was statistically significant (p=0.003). As for somatic complaints, they were more frequent in rural (57 percent) than in urban areas (36 percent), but this difference was not statistically significant. There was no association between type of complaint and geographic origin of the patient.

Comments

In our Tunisian sample of young people attending a psychiatric unit, two in three were adolescents; the over-representation of this age bracket is recognized in the literature with prevalence in the general population of 3 to 5 percent (compared to approximately 1 percent in younger children) for major depressive disorder and dysthymia (Birmaher et al., 1999; Cohen et al., 1993; Ford et al., 2003).

Sociodemographic Associations

Our population includes as many boys as girls. A sex ratio near to one is especially found in most epidemiological studies in children, even though from the beginning of adolescence the sex ratio favors girls by two to one. This ratio is similar to that observed in the adult population for major depressive disorder (Angold, 1988; Birmaher et al., 1999). This female predominance is not found in our sample, which is surprising. Indeed, in our sociocultural context, and as is the case for other conservative cultures, puberty can be experienced in a negative manner in girls and linked with a tempestuous relationship to parents (because of lack of freedom over outings and over choice of clothing, and of the greater value of and protection of virginity). This intergenerational conflict is even more acute nowadays because young Tunisians are immersed in and influenced by Western culture via the media and new technologies.

Close to half of the sample lived in an urban area (Greater Tunis), while the other half was equally divided between rural and semirural areas. This distribution is in fact representative of the pattern of recruitment of the child psychiatry department in Tunis (Mezghani, 2005).

The parents' socioeconomic level and education—made up of a large majority of poor families with little or no formal education at all—is comparable to those of all patients consulting our service at large (Mezghani, 2005). In order to better study these variables and notably their role as risk factors for the occurrence of depressive disorders, it is necessary to compare a large sample to a control group (patients suffering from another pathology). Indeed, difficult social conditions have been incriminated in the literature as a predictive factor in the recurrence and early onset of depressive disorders (Lewinsohn et al., 1994; Rao et al., 1995).

Diagnostic Groups

More than half our sample was made up of patients suffering from an episode of major depression (61 percent), while only 14 percent had dysthymic disorders. It is currently recognized in the literature that major depressive disorders and dysthymic disorders have the same prevalence (Birmaher et al., 1999; Garrison et al., 1992; Garrison et al., 1997; Plaino-Lorente and Domèneche, 1993): approximately 1 percent in children and 3 to 5 percent in adolescents in the general population. The difference in the frequency found in our sample between these two types of depressive disorders can be explained by the fact that in Tunisia it is the acute and disruptive pathologies that lead parents to overcome the resistance that is imposed by the still very strong stigmatization of mental pathology. This stigmatization is emphasized by the fact that our department is located in a psychiatric hospital that was formerly an asylum. Moreover, dysthymia is a pathology that remains underdiagnosed, possibly due to its chronic and sometimes subclinical character (Birmaher et al., 1999), which makes parents less likely to seek psychiatric care.

Comorbidity

Close to half the sample presented a comorbid disorder, particularly the younger patients. This fact is found in most studies (Kessler and Walters, 1998; Angold and Costello, 1993): It is thought that comorbidity may be even more frequent than in adults (Rohde et al., 1991). This elevated rate of comorbidity raises the question of its legitimacy: Is it really comorbidity or rather the result of current classification systems fragmenting more classic syndromes? Anxiety, for example, one of the major symptoms of depressive disorder (as described in the classical nosography) becomes, with the current classification tools, an independent psychiatric disorder needing an independent and complementary therapeutic process. Clinical experience teaches us that it is not always necessary to follow such nosographic categories except when the anxiety disorders predate the depression; in fact, it is only in these clinical situations that the therapeutic and preventative implications are legitimized. Indeed, certain anxiety disorders like separation anxiety disorder, panic, and phobic disorders are identified risk factors for depressive disorders in young subjects. In our sample, anxiety was concurrent to and associated with depression in a third of cases. This rate is close to those from the literature identifying anxiety disorders as the most frequent comorbidity of depressive disorders, and present in between 40 percent and 70 percent (Angold and Costello, 1993; Kendall et al., 1992; Kovacs et al., 1994). Anxiety themes change according to developmental stages. Thus in our sample, separation anxiety disorder was the most frequent comorbid disorder in children and generalized anxiety disorder in adolescents. Elimination disorders in our sample were more frequent in children, conduct disorders in adolescents. These results corroborate those found in the literature (Riggs et al., 1995). Comorbidity with posttraumatic stress disorders, observed in 19 percent of cases, in fact may express a depressive episode secondary to the traumatic event.

Main Symptoms

Considering depressive semiology and in reference to K-SADS items and DSM-IV-R diagnostic criteria, diagnostic tools adequately identify the core depressive symptoms of our sample. Irritability and sadness were the predominant means of expressing depressive mood, whereas verbalization of the real-life experience through feelings of guilt, pessimism, and feelings of worthlessness were reported less frequently. Only feelings of guilt and suicidal thoughts were statistically more frequent in adolescents. It is indeed currently recognized that the behavioral and somatic manifestations that are frequent in children evolve into a more elaborated semiological expression by adolescence (Mitchell et al., 1988; Ryan et al., 1987). Thus, pessimism, feelings of guilt, suicidal thoughts, and anhedonia increase from childhood to adolescence (Sorensen et al., 2005; Weiss and Garber, 2003).

In the psychomotor domain, concentration difficulties followed by asthenia were most frequent, found with the same frequency in children and in adolescents. These two symptoms along with disturbance of sleep should be the most independent from developmental factors (Ryan et al., 1987). Insomnia tops the list of vegetative manifestations exhibited by our patients, followed by anorexia and weight loss. This last symptom is statistically more frequent in adolescents (Mouren-Siméoni, 1998; Sorensen et al., 2005). This is explained by the fact that it is difficult to characterize a weight loss in the youngest patients, which in any case is replaced in the DSM-IV-R by an absence of the expected weight gain for children.

Somatic Symptoms

Close to 42 percent of subjects in our sample reported a somatic complaint. This amounted to headaches in the majority of cases, followed by abdominal pain. Somatic complaints were strongly associated with depressive mood and did not increase in a significant manner in the subgroup with comorbid anxiety. An elevated frequency of somatic complaints during depression is found in Western literature (Masi et al., 2000; McCauley et al., 1991; Sorensen et al., 2005). These somatic complaints are more frequent in depressed children, compared to those suffering from anxiety disorders, and would be even more frequent in the most severe depressive cases (Egger and Costello., 1999; McCauley et al., 1991). In the literature, headache would be the most frequent complaint, followed by abdominal pain (Masi et al., 2000).

For certain authors like J. Angst (1973), somatic complaints would be an invariable and universal symptom of depression whereas for others the frequency and acuteness of this symptomatic category remains influenced by cultural factors. Already in 1962, Prince in Nigeria affirmed that depression was one of the most common syndromes in Africa, if "we include in depression somatic complaints." For this author, somatic symptoms dominate the features of depression and are often emphasized by the patient, preventing a deeper exploration of disorders thereby masking a depressive

Angold A., and E. J. Costello. "Depressive comorbidity in children and adolescents: Empirical, theoretical, and methodological issues." *American Journal of Psychiatry* 150, no. 12 (1993): 1779–91.

Angst, J. "La dépression masquée du point de vue transculturel," in P. Kielholz, ed., *La dépression masquée* (Paris: Masson, 1973).

APA (American Psychiatric Association). *Diagnostic and Statistical Manual of Mental Disorders.* Fourth Edition revised (DSMIV-R). (Washington, DC: American Psychiatric Association, 2003).

Bailly, D. "Le diagnostic de dépression chez l'enfant et l'adolescent: un problème résolu?" *Dépression* no. 2 (1996): 13–16.

Birmaher, B., N. D. Ryan, D. E. Williamson et al., "Childhood and adolescent depression: a review of the past 10 years." *Part I. Journal American Acad. Child Adolescent Psychiatry* 35, no. 11 (1999): 1575–82.

Cohen, P., J. Cohen, S. Kasen, C. N. Velez, C. Hartmark, J. Johnson, M. Rojas, J. Brook, and E. L. Streuning. "An epidemiological study of disorders in late childhood and adolescence: Age and gender specific prevalence." *Journal of Child Psychol. Psychiatry* 34, no. 6 (1993): 851–67.

Douki, S., D. Moussaoui, and F. Kacha. *Manuel du Praticien Maghrébin* (Paris: Masson, 1989).

Egger, H. L., and E. J. Costello. "Somatic complaints and psychopathology in children and adolescents: Stomach aches, musculoskeletal pains, and headaches." *Journal of American Acad. Child Adolescent Psychiatry* 38, no.7 (1999): 852–60.

Ezin Houngbe, J., *Les états dépressifs chez le noir Africain*, November 11, 2005, at transfer 32.bj.refer.org/jezin/cours.html.

Ford, T., R. Goodman, and H. Meltzer, "The British child and adolescent mental health survey 1999: The prevalence of DSM-IV disorders." *Journal of American Acad. Child Adolescent Psych.* 42, no. 10 (2003): 1203–211.

Garrison, C. Z., C. L. Addy, K. L. Jackson et al. "Major depressive disorder and dysthymia in young adolescents." *American Journal of Epidemiology* 135, no. 7 (1992): 792–802.

Garrison, C. Z., J. L. Waller, S. P. Cuffe et al. "Incidence of major depressive disorder and dysthymia in young adolescents." *Journal of American Acad. Child Adolescent Psychiatry* 36, no 4 (1997): 458–65.

Kaufman, J., B. Birmaher, D. Brent et al., "Schedule for affective disorders and schizophrenia for school-age children, present and lifetime version (K-SADS-PL): Initial reliability and validity data." *Journal of American Acad. Child Adolescent Psychiatry* 36 (1997): 980–88.

Kendall, P. C., E. Kortlander, T. E. Chansky, and E. U. Brady. "Comorbidity of anxiety and depression in youth: Treatment implications." *Journal of Consult. Clin. Psychology* 60, (1992): 869–80.

Kessler, R. C., and E. E. Walters, "Epidemiology of DSM-III-R major depression and minor depression among adolescents and young adults in the National Comorbidity Survey." *Depress. Anxiety* 7, no. 1 (1998): 3–14.

Knight, G. P., L. M. Virdin, and M. Roosa, "Socialization and family correlates of mental health outcomes among Hispanic and Anglo-American children: consideration of cross-ethnic scalar equivalence." *Child Development* 65, no. 1 (1994): 212–24.

Kovacs, M., S. Akiskal, C. Gastonis, and P. L. Parrone. "Childhood-onset dysthymic disorder." *Arch. Gen. Psychiatry* 51 (1994): 365–74.

Lewinsohn, P. M., G. N. Clarke, J. R. Seeley, and P. Rohde. "Major depression in community adolescents: Age at onset, episode duration and time to recurrence." *Journal of American Acad. Child Adolescent Psychiatry* 33, no 6 (1994): 809–18.

Masi, G., L. Favilla, S. Millepiedi, and M. Mucci. "Somatic symptoms in children and adolescents referred for emotional and behavioral disorders." *Psychiatry* 63, no.2 (2000): 140–49.

McCauley, E., G. A. Carlson, and R. Calderon. "The role of somatic complaints in the diagnosis of depression in children and adolescents." *Journal of American Acad. Child Adolescent Psychiatry* 30, no. 4 (1991): 631–35.

Mezghani, L. "Profil clinique et socio-démographique des consultants du service de Pédopsychiatrie de l'Hôpital Razi de Tunis." *Thèse de Doctorat en Médecine*, Soutenue publiquement à la Faculté de Médecine de Sfax (Juillet 2005).

Mitchell, J., E. McCaulley, M. Burke, and S. L. Moss, "Phenomenology of depression in children and adolescents." *Journal of American Acad. Child Adolescent Psychiatry* 27 (1988): 12–20.

Mouren-Siméoni, M. C. "Dépression de l'enfant: aspects cliniques, évolutifs et thérapeutiques." *Médecine thérapeutique/Pédiatrie* 1, no.1 (1998): 65–70.

Pehlivanturk, B., and F. Unal. "Conversion disorder in children and adolescents: clinical features and comorbidity with depressive and anxiety disorders." *Turk. Journal of Pediatry* 42, no. 2 (2000): 132–37.

———. "Conversion disorder in children and adolescents: A 4-year follow-up study." *Journal of Psychosom. Research* 52, no. 4 (2002): 187–91.

Plaino-Lorente, A., and E. Domèneche. "Prevalence of childhood depression: results of the first study in Spain." *Journal of Child Psychology* 34, no. 6 (1993): 1007–17.

Prince, R. "Functional symptoms associated with study in Nigerian students." *West Afr. Med. Journal* 11 (1962): 198–206.

Rao, U., N. D. Ryan, B. Birmaher et al. "Unipolar depression in adolescents: Clinical outcome in adulthood." *Journal of American Acad. Child Adolescent Psychiatry* 34, no. 5 (1995): 21–27.

Riggs, P. D., S. Baker, S. K. Mikulich, S. E. Young, and T. J. Crowley. "Depression in substance-dependent delinquents." *Journal of American Acad. Child Adolescent Psychiatry* 34 (1995): 764–71.

Rohde, P., P. M. Lewinsohn, J. R. Seeley. "Comorbidity of unipolar depression: II. Comorbidity with other mental disorders in adolescents and adults." *Journal Abnormal Psychology* 100 (1991): 214–22.

Ryan, N. D., J. Puig-Antich, P. Ambrosini et al. "The clinical picture of major depression in children and adolescents." *Journal of American Acad. Child Adolescent Psychiatry* 44 (1987): 854–61.

Sorensen, M. J., J. Becker Nissen, O. Mors, and P. Hove Thomsen. "Age and gender differences in depressive symptomatology and comorbidity: An incident sample of psychiatrically admitted children." *Journal of Affect. Disord.* 84, no.1 (2005): 85–91.

Weiss B., and J. Garber. "Developmental differences in the phenomenology of depression." *Dev. Psychopathology* 15, no.2 (2003): 403–30.

8

Suicide in Children and Adolescents

A Japanese Perspective

Yoshiro Ono

INTRODUCTION

Suicide is one of the major public health issues for children and adolescents as well as adults. Although there are substantial differences in the reported suicide rates across the various regions in the world, suicide is a universal concern. The World Health Organization (WHO) has launched a world-wide initiative for the prevention of suicide (SUPRE) in response to the current worrisome high rates. The WHO has estimated that approximately one million people died from suicide in the year 2000, representing a "global" mortality rate of 16 per 100,000. As suicide is now among the three leading causes of death in people aged fifteen to forty-four, prevention is an issue that must be addressed by the international community as a whole (World Health Organization, 2007).

Suicide is a form of violence directed to the self. There are levels of suicidal behavior ranging from thinking about intentional self-injury or death (suicidal ideation) through actual intentional self-injury (suicidal attempt) to death (suicide) (Pfeffer, 2002). Since suicide attempts are at least ten to twenty times more frequent than completed suicides and suicidal ideation much more common than suicide attempts (Sudak, 2005), the prevention of suicide must address a broad range of mental health issues. Those mental health issues are strongly influenced by sociocultural factors (Bertolote

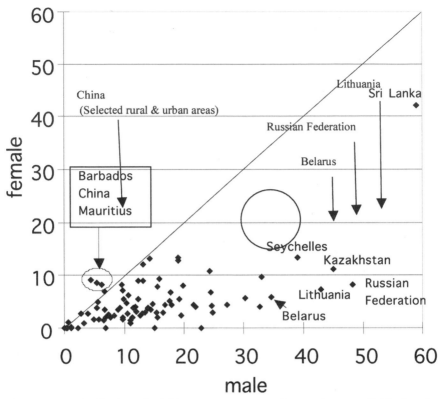

Figure 8.2.   Distribution of suicide rates per 100,000 by sex (latest available data for each country and area) in adolescents aged 15–24 years

2007). Suicide rates in both males and females are lower than overall rates, especially among males. Countries with high overall suicide rates had high rates in the fifteen to twenty-four age group, but Sri Lanka and the Seychelles had high suicide rates as well (figure 8.2).

The pattern of gender difference in suicide rates for young people was somewhat different from those of overall rates. Although all countries except China had higher rates in males in the overall population, Barbados, Mauritius, and China had higher female than male rates for the fifteen to twenty-four population. More counties had male to female ratios close to one in the figure 8.2, suggesting a tendency for the gender difference in suicide rate among young people to be smaller than those in the general population. The relatively high suicide rates in young females may be partially explained by the fact that suicide attempts are two to three times more frequent in female adolescents compared to male adolescents (Lewinsohn et al., 2001), and that past suicide attempts are the strongest predictor of future suicidal attempts and completion (Shaffer et al., 1996; Brent et al., 1999). Moreover, suicide in childhood and early adolescence occurs almost as often in females as in males, suggesting that the male predominance is related to gender difference developing after puberty.

Even though the rate of suicide among young people is relatively low, its impact on public health is great. The relatively low mortality of young people from physical disease elevates the rank order of suicide as a cause of death. Suicide is a leading cause of death, along with transport accidents, other accidents, and assaults in the fifteen to twenty-four age group in many countries (Wasserman et al., 2005). Furthermore, suicide rates among people under forty-four years of age have increased from 1950 to 1998, and it is currently the group at highest risk in one-third of all counties in the developed or developing world (World Health Organization, 2007). Although suicide rates escalated from the mid-1960s until the mid-1980s and then declined in the United States and many other countries, they are still high or increasing in some countries, particularly non-European countries (Wasserman et al., 2005).

The Clinical Characteristics of Suicide in Young People

Suicide under the age of ten is very rare, but it increases rapidly in mid-adolescence. In most countries, suicide rates for children aged ten to fourteen are below 1.0 per 100,000 (World Health Organization, 2007). However, suicidal ideation is not rare among young children who are likely to have impulsive thoughts of hurting themselves. The impulsiveness of young children can provoke dangerous behavior such as hanging or jumping from heights, even though drugs and firearms are likely to be out of their reach (Pfeffer, 2002).

Suicide by hanging is the most common method in general, but firearms are predominant in several countries such as the United States (Shaffer et al., 2002). In contrast, there is almost no suicide by firearm in Japan where guns are strictly controlled and almost impossible to access by ordinary citizens (Ojima et al., 2004). In 2005, there were only seventy-six gunshot cases and twenty-two gunshot deaths in Japan (National Police Academy, 2006). Although drug overdose is a common method of attempting suicide, it does not usually result in death because many psychotropic medicines or over-the-counter analgesics are usually not lethal (Brent et al., 1999; Shaffer et al., 2002). Pesticide ingestion is an exception, because it is difficult to treat, especially in rural areas where emergency medical care systems are lacking or difficult to access (Shaffer et al., 2002).

Methods of suicide may also be influenced by the media. Researchers have described the suicide cluster, an excessive number of suicides occurring in close temporal and geographic proximity, presumed to be related to imitation (Brent et al., 1989; Gould et al., 1990a, 1990b, 1994). In these cases, suicides might be triggered by publicity about actual or fictional suicides via novels, films, or television, the so-called Werther effect (Gould et al, 1986; Schmidtke et al., 1988). Suicide clusters have been recognized in many countries including Japan (Ishii, 1991; Stack, 1996). Recently, the Internet has influenced suicidal behavior in young people in many developed countries. Suicide Web sites exchange information concerning suicide and provide instruction on how to commit it. In Japan, for example, carbon monoxide poisoning (from burning charcoal in a confined area) was popularized on these Web sites; a group of youths who met on the Internet were recently involved in a suicide pact by this method (*Japan Times*, 2004; Rajagopal, 2004). Similar suicide pacts have occurred in Hong Kong and Taiwan (Liu et al., 2007).

Risk Factors

Research on suicidal behavior in children and adolescents has found a number of risk factors involving individual psychopathology, the family, and stress.

Individual Psychopathology

The most influential risk factor is psychosis. Psychological autopsy studies of adolescents who had completed suicides indicate that more than 90 percent of adolescent suicide victims have had a psychiatric disorder (Brent et al., 1999; Marttunen et al., 1991; Shaffer et al., 1996). The most common disorders are depression, substance and alcohol abuse, and disruptive behavior disorder. In community samples, suicidal risk was most associated with current depression and anxiety (specifically, generalized anxiety disorder) and depression together with disruptive disorder (Foley et al., 2006). A study of a nationally representative sample in the United States revealed that delinquency is associated with an increased risk of suicidal ideation, suicidal attempt, and treatment for attempt one year later, and to ideation and attempt seven years later (Thompson et al., 2007). Prior suicidal attempt is a strong risk factor for suicide in both children and adolescents (Shaffer et al., 1996; Brent et al., 1999). Hopelessness (Shaffer et al, 1996), aggression (Gould et al, 1998), and sexual orientation (Russell et al., 2001) have been identified as risk factors.

Family Factors

A family history of suicidal behaviors increases the risk of suicidal behavior (Brent et al., 1996; Shaffer et al., 1996; Lieb et al., 2005), particularly depression and substance abuse (Hollis, 1996; King et al., 2001). Parental psychopathology directly affects children through an adverse life environ-ment, and suicidal behavior may have a hereditary component. Some twin studies indicate an increased risk of suicide (Roy et al., 1991) and suicide attempts (Roy et al., 1995) for monozygotic twin pairs. The serotonin func-tion abnormalities (e.g., reduction of serotonin activity or serotonin dys-regulation in the CNS) observed in individuals with suicidality, impulsive-ness, or aggressiveness may have a genetic background (Gould et al., 2003).

Stress

Stressful life events are important precipitants for suicidal behavior, re-gardless of age. Such life events include the loss of important persons, rup-tured romantic relationships, and a fight among friends; family discord, family violence, and a family history of suicide; and school-related prob-lems such as academic failure, disciplinary crises, and bullying (Gould et al., 2003). It should be noted that being bullied by others, bullying others, and a combination of the two are significant risks for suicidal behaviors in adolescents (Kaltiala-Heino et al., 1999; Kim et al., 2005; Klomek et al., 2007). Suicidal behavior is associated with the experience during childhood of child abuse and neglect, especially physical abuse and sexual abuse (Sil-verman et al., 1996).

TRENDS OF SUICIDE IN JAPAN

Japan has a high suicide rate (Yamamura et al., 2006). In 2005, there were 30,553 deaths by suicide and the suicide rate was 24.2 per 100,000, the highest since the 1950s (Ministry of Health, Labour and Welfare, 2007). Al-though the suicide rates of most Western countries (except Hungary and the Russian Federation) have been stable for the last half-century, the rates in Japan and South Korea have shown a rapid growth in the latest decade (fig-ure 8.3). The recent increase in Japan and South Korea has been explained by economic hardship in the last decade (Araki et al., 1987; McCurry, 2006), but economic reverses have not always affected the suicide rates in Japan (Yamamura et al., 2006). The suicide rate in South Korea has been growing faster than in Japan until, in 2005, it surpassed that of Japan (*Korea Times*, 2004; 2005).

The age distribution of suicide rates in Japan is unique. Suicide rates usu-ally gradually increase after adolescence until the oldest population shows the highest suicide rates for both sexes. Males and females in Japan demon-strated almost the same trend of suicide rates until middle age, but the rate in males of forty-five to sixty-four years of age is 25 percent to 56 percent higher than the global rate and that of females over fifty-five years is almost 100 percent higher (figure 8.4). More than half (57.1 percent) of Japanese

ten to fourteen years, the second rank in the age group fifteen to nineteen years, and the leading cause from twenty through forty-four years. For females, suicide was the fourth most common cause of death in the age group ten to fourteen years, and the leading cause from fifteen to thirty-four years (Ministry of Health, Labour and Welfare, 2007).

Cases of youth suicide have often appeared in newspapers and television news, drawing public attention, and making it a nationwide issue. Recent suicides committed by children and adolescents who were exposed to bullying by classmates were reported extensively. School systems were blamed for overlooking bullying and failing to prevent victimization. Media publicity may be problematic because it can induce suicide clusters, but no media guidelines for suicide reporting have been proposed and implemented in Japan.

In Japan, suicide in children and adolescents was studied mostly in the 1980s, reflecting the surge of suicide in adolescents in the 1960s and early 1970s. Since then, suicide has not been a subject of research until recently. Studies in the 1980s and recent years have highlighted particular aspects of suicide in Japanese children and adolescents in regard to psychopathology and psychosocial stressors.

Psychosocial Factors Related to Suicidal Behaviors in Japan

In contrast to the studies from Western countries which emphasize psychopathology such as depression, substance abuse/dependency, and disruptive behavior as risk factors for suicide, most of studies on suicide in young people in Japan deal with the social, familial, and school environment.

Ohara et al. (1963) investigated suicide cases, in children aged ten to fourteen years, as reported in national newspapers from 1952 to 1961. They found the chief precipitants to be family or school problems, especially disciplinary issues. They also surveyed thirty-eight cases of suicide and suicidal attempts in children that were reported by child-serving agencies such as family courts, psychiatric clinics, and child welfare centers, and found that twenty-one children had conduct problems such as stealing or running away from home. The high percentage of conduct problems should be carefully interpreted because most of the cases were reported by public child welfare centers that had the responsibility for delinquent children younger than fifteen years.

In the 1980s, Kitamura and his colleagues (1981) investigated suicidal behaviors in a large sample of adolescents who attended a university child and adolescent psychiatry clinic. They found that academic/school difficulty (38.3 percent) was the most frequent antecedent to a suicide attempt, followed by family problems (34.6 percent). They concluded that suicide attempts precipitated by school problems (typically, failure to attend school) were a characteristic of Japanese adolescents. The predominance of school-related problems in Japanese adolescents was also demonstrated in a comparative study of suicidal behavior in Japanese and German adolescents (Kitamura, 1983). However, because school problems, especially school refusal, were the most common reason in Japan for children and adolescents to attend a psychiatrist in the 1980s and the 1990s (see, for example, Nakane, 1996), the school-related conflict might be overrepresented.

Recently, two independent studies found that family and interpersonal conflict were more prevalent among suicide attempters than school conflict. Murase et al. (2004) investigated eight adolescents consecutively admitted over three years to an intensive care ward due to life-threatening suicidal attempts. Most (75 percent) were females who had attempted suicide by overdose (87.5 percent). Although four adolescents had a history of school refusal, family problems (especially mother-child conflict) were the most common psychosocial stressors.

Mikami et al. (2006a) investigated the psychiatric features of adolescent suicidal attempts in a consecutive series of thirty-four patients treated at the emergency department of a university medical center. Thirty females (88 percent) and twenty-seven adolescents (79.4 percent) had attempted suicide by overdose. Parent-child conflict was the leading psychosocial factor (50 percent), while academic problems were found in only 17.6 percent, suggesting school-related problems might not be the predominant antecedent to adolescent suicidal attempts in Japan. A similar pattern was reported in relation to deliberate self-harm (DSH). Takei et al. (2006) investigated seventy-two adolescents with DSH. They found that conflict with parents (39.0 percent) and problems with same-sex friends (25.4 percent) were common antecedent to self-injurious behavior, whereas school problems were less common (11.7 percent).

Because there have been no psychological autopsy studies of young victims of suicide, knowledge is incomplete. However, some figures are available from the police and education systems. In the statistics of the National Police Agency, causes of suicide are identified from suicide notes. Although only 28 percent of victims under the age of twenty left notes, in 2005, health problems (28.2 percent) and school problems (20.6 percent) were more frequent than family problems (10.0 percent) (National Police Agency, 2006). The Ministry of Education, Culture, Sports, Science and Technology reports the causes of suicide in public school children annually. In 2005, 103 students died from suicide. Family problems (10.7 percent), school problems (9.7 percent), and mental disorders (9.7 percent) were main causes. However, causes were not identified in 58.3 percent of cases (Ministry of Education, Culture, Sports, Science and Technology, 2006). Further research is necessary.

Even though the major stresses related to suicidal behavior are familial and interpersonal, contemporary children and adolescents still suffer heavy burdens in the highly competitive education system. School/education-related stress should be carefully addressed. In Taiwan, the most common antecedent for suicide attempts among adolescents was school stress (Chiou et al., 2006). Academic stress in the Taiwanese education system is very high, as it is in Japan.

Psychopathology Related to Suicidal Behavior in Japan

It has been established in many parts of the globe that psychopathology such as mood disorders, substance use disorders, and disruptive behavior disorders are strong risk factors for suicidal behavior in children and adolescents (Gould et al., 2003). That is also true for Japanese children and adolescents, though there are only a few researches addressing the psychopathology of suicide in young people. Among eight adolescents in hospitals after a life-threatening suicide attempt, six were diagnosed as having depressive disorder. None had substance use disorder and only one had conduct disorder (Murase et al. 2004). Among thirty-four consecutive cases of adolescent suicidal attempt, the majority (79.4 percent) had a psychiatric diagnosis, the most common of which was mood disorder (26.5 percent) and adjustment disorder (23.5 percent); whereas disruptive behavior disorder (5.9 percent) and substance use disorder (2.9 percent) were rather uncommon (Mikami et al. 2006a). Although there are no epidemiological data concerning the prevalence of substance use disorder among adolescents in Japan, both substance abuse and conduct disorder are uncommon diagnoses in clinical settings of child and adolescent psychiatry.

Pervasive developmental disorder has been found in association with suicidal behavior. Among thirty-four adolescent suicide attempters reported by Mikami et al (2006a), four adolescents (11.8 percent) had pervasive developmental disorder (PDD): three had Asperger's disorder, and one had PDD not otherwise specified. Despite the report of suicidal behavior in an adolescent with Asperger's disorder (Mikami et al., 2006b), it is controversial whether PDD is a true risk factor for suicide. Comorbid psychopathology including mood and anxiety disorder might contribute to suicidal behavior in adolescents with PDD, who should be regarded as at risk, and carefully followed.

Ken, a 13-year-old boy with Asperger's disorder, exhibited ritualistic behavior in the morning: going for a walk with his dog, watching particular TV programs recorded on videotape, and going to school by school bus. He often had a tantrum if he could not complete these rituals in time for the school bus. Once, he had a tantrum in which he bit his own hand and said, "I am very unhappy and want to die." He had become interested in suicide and often visited suicide Web sites. One day, after he returned home, he had a tantrum when he had interrupted prerecorded programs by accidentally pressing the remote-control button. He was found hanging in his room and taken to an emergency room. Fortunately, he regained consciousness on the way to the hospital. Next day, he disclosed that he had imitated a hanging he saw on a television cartoon. The distress associated with frustrated rituals and a preoccupation with suicide, both symptoms of Asperger's disorder, appeared to be the antecedent of the suicide attempt.

CHALLENGES AND FUTURE DIRECTION

Efforts to prevent suicide should involve not only public health and mental health facilities but also politics, education, social services, and policy development. Strategies for preventing suicide include promoting public awareness, identifying those at high risk, and providing appropriate and timely care (U.S. Public Health Services, 1999). Of particular importance is identifying the psychopathology known to foreshadow suicidal behaviors. In this aspect, mental health has a primary responsibility to prevent suicide in children and adolescents. In Japan, the paucity of child and adolescent mental health care resources must be rectified.

Although depression is a risk factor (Murase et al, 2004; Mikami et al, 2006a), its importance has not been adequately recognized by parents, teachers, or mental health professionals. Instead, reflecting anecdotal media reports, the public tends to regard bullying as the most important cause of suicide in this age group. Even though bullying is common in schools in every country, and a proven risk factor for suicidal behavior (Smith et al., 1999), the importance of mood disorders should not be underestimated.

In reality, however, mood disorders in children and adolescents have been underestimated or almost ignored in Japanese psychiatry. In the United States, it was believed that depressive disorder was uncommon among the young and preadolescent children were thought to be incapable of experiencing depression (Harrington, 2002). There was almost no description of mood disorders in the textbook of child psychiatry such as *Child Psychiatry*, by Leo Kanner (1935). Currently, depressive disorder is one of the most commonly diagnosed psychiatric disorders in children and adolescents in the United States (U.S. Department of Health and Human Services, 1999). In Japan, in contrast, depressive disorders are seldom diagnosed in this age group and are not recognized as a major issue of child and adolescent mental health.

Recently, several researchers have conducted surveys of depressive symptoms in school-age children and adolescents. Although the prevalence of depressive disorders was relatively low, Sugawara and his colleagues (1999) reported that the prevalence of DSM-III-R depressive disorder in eight-year-old boys, by structured interview, was 3.5 percent, or comparable to that reported in the United States and New Zealand. Other researchers, using a questionnaire, revealed that 7.8 percent to 13.3 percent of elementary school pupils and 21.9 to 22.8 percent of junior high school pupils had depressive symptoms (Murata et al., 1992; Denda et al., 2006; Sato et al., 2006). Moreover, in a study comparing major depression in the United States and Japan, there was a great difference of the overall prevalence for twelve- to fifteen-year-old adolescents, but after sociodemographic variables such as gender, age, guardian status, parental education, and family financial status were adjusted, the apparent association between adolescent major depression and ethnicity disappeared (Doi et al., 2001). Thus, depressive disorders in Japanese adolescents are as common as in American adolescents.

Nevertheless, the number of children and adolescents diagnosed as having mood disorder is disproportionately low, in most Japanese clinics. According to the classification of the ICD-10 (World Health Organization, 1992), "Neurotic, stress-related, and somatoform disorders (F4)," "Disorders of psychological development (F8)," and "Behavioural and emotional disorders with onset usually occurring in childhood and adolescence (F9)" are usually the most common categories. "Mood disorders (F3)" comprise only a few percent of total patients (Ono, 2006). Many children and adolescents have the chief complaint of school refusal, and most of them were classified in the F4 category. It is assumed that many with depressive disorder are diagnosed as having anxiety or adjustment disorders because they avoid stressful situations like schools.

The disparity between the likely prevalence of depressive disorder and clinical outpatient statistics reflects a number of issues associated with current mental health service systems, particularly lack of resources and accessibility, insufficient public awareness of mood disorders in children and adolescents, reluctance by youth and families to attend psychiatrists, and the stigma of mental illness. To eliminate all these barriers to early identification and treatment, child and adolescent mental health services should be familiar and easy to access. An awareness of depression as a major mental health issue in children and adolescents should be promulgated for the public, educationists, mental health professionals, and primary health providers.

Japan has one of the highest suicide rates in the world. The prevention of suicide should be a national priority. Although the majority of the victims of suicide are middle-aged or older persons, mental health problems, particularly depression, are common at all ages. In 2006, the Japanese government enacted the Basic Law on Measures to Prevent Suicide, and a Cabinet Office panel went on to compile a proposal to help prevent suicide. The law defined establishing mental health service systems in communities, workplaces, and schools as an obligation of the central and local governments. To facilitate information and data collecting, research, policy making, and developing services, the Suicide Prevention Center was established in the National Institute of Mental Health, the National Center of Neurology and Psychiatry, in Tokyo in October 2006. The development and implementation of the evidence-based mental health service systems to prevent suicide in people of all ages are expected to be propelled by the national policy.

CONCLUSION

Suicide is a major public health problem for all ages, worldwide. Research into suicide in children and adolescents has revealed a set of risk factors: individual psychopathology, familial factors, and stress. Socioeconomic, cultural, and ethnic factors are also involved. In spite of relatively high suicide rates in North Asian countries (Japan, South Korea, and China), insufficient information is available.

In Japan, recent researches have revealed that the comorbidity of suicide with substance abuse and conduct problems is less frequent than in other countries. In contrast, children and adolescents with pervasive developmental disorder might be at risk. Depressive disorders are an important and common risk factor for Japanese children and adolescents as in most other countries. However, since depressive disorders have been under-recognized in children and adolescents, the detection of high-risk individuals is hampered. Along with suicide prevention programs, more effective mental health care systems for children and adolescents are required.

ACKNOWLEDGEMENT

The author acknowledges Professor Barry Nurcombe, Emeritus Professor of Child and Adolescent Psychiatry, The University of Queensland, and Professor of Child and Adolescent Psychiatry and Paediatrics, the University of Western Australia, for his generous assistance in preparation of the manuscript.

REFERENCES

Araki, S. and K. Murata. (1987). Suicide in Japan: socioeconomic effects on its secular and seasonal trends. *Suicide Life Threat Behavior* 17, 64–71.
Bertolote, J. M. and A. Fleischmann. (2002). A global perspective in the epidemiology of suicide. *Suicidologi* 7, 6–8.

Brent, D. A., M. M. Kerr, C. Goldstein, J. Bozigar, M. E. Wartella, and M. J. Allan. (1989). An outbreak of suicide and suicidal behavior in high school. *Journal of American Acad. Child Adolescent Psychiatry* 28, 918–24.

Brent, D. A., M. Baugher, J. Bridge, T. Chen, and L. Chiappetta. (1999). Age- and sex-related risk factors for adolescent suicide. *Journal of American Acad. Child Adolescent Psychiatry* 38, 1497–1505.

Brent, D. A., J. Bridge, B. A. Johnson, and J. Connolly. (1996). Suicidal behavior runs in families: A controlled family study of adolescent suicide victims. *Arch. Gen. Psychiatry* 53, 1145–52.

Chiou, P., Y. Chen, and Y. Lee. (2006). Characteristics of adolescent suicide attempters admitted to an acute psychiatric ward in Taiwan. *Journal of Chinese Med. Association* 69, 428–35.

Denda, K., Y. Kako, N. Kitagawa, and T. Koyama. (2006). Assessment of depressive symptoms in Japanese school children and adolescents using the Birleson Depression Self-rating Scale. *International Journal of Psychiatry Med.* 36, 231–41.

Doi, Y., R. E. Roberts, K. Takeuchi, and S. Suzuki. (2001). Multiehinic comparison of adolescent major depression based on DSM-IV criteria in a U.S.-Japan study. *Journal of American Acad. Child Adolescent Psychiatry* 40, 1308–15.

Foley, D. L., D. B. Goldston, E. J. Costello, and A. Angold. (2006). Proximal psychiatric risk factors for suicidality in youth: The Great Smoky Mountains Study. *Arch. Gen. Psychiatry* 63, 1017–24.

Gould, M. S., T. Greenberg, D. M. Velting, and D. Shaffer. (2003). Youth suicide risk and preventions: A review of the past 10 years. *Journal of American Acad. Child Adolescent Psychiatry* 42, 386–405.

Gould, M. S., R. King, S. Greenwald, P. Fisher, M. Schwab-Stone, R. Kramer, A. J. Flisher, S. Goodman, G. Canino, and D. Shaffer. (1998). Psychopathology associated with suicidal ideation and attempts among children and adolescents. *Journal of American Child Adolescent Psychiatry* 37, 915–23.

Gould, M. S., K. Petrie, M. Kleinman, and S. Wallenstein. (1994). Clustering of attempted suicide: New Zealand national data. *International Journal of Epidemiology* 23, 1185–89.

Gould, M. S., and D. Shaffer. (1986). The impact of suicide in television movies. Evidence of imitation. *New England Journal of Medicine* 315, 690–94.

Gould, M. S., S. Wallenstein, and M. Kleinman. (1990a). Time-space clustering of teenage suicide. *American Journal of Epidemiology* 131, 71–78.

Gould, M. S., S. Wallenstein, M. Kleinman, P. O'Coarroll, and J. Mercy. (1990b). Suicide clusters: An examination of age-specific effects. *American Journal of Public Health* 80, 211–12.

Harrington, R. (2002). Affective disorders. In M. Rutter and E. Taylor (eds.) *Child and adolescent psychiatry,* fourth edition. Malden, MA: Blackwell Science, pp. 463–85.

Hollis C. (1996). Depression, family environment, and adolescent suicidal behavior. *Journal American Acad. Child Adolescent Psychiatry* 35, 622–30.

Ishii, K. (1991). Measuring mutual causation: Effects of suicide news on suicide in Japan. *Social Science Research* 20, 188–95.

Japan Times. (2004). Seven people die in group suicide pact. October 13, 2004.

Kaltiala-Heino, R., M. Rimpela, M. Marttunen, A. Rimpela, and P. Rantanen. (1999). Bullying, depression, and suicidal ideation in Finish adolescents: School survey. *BMJ* 319, 348–51.

Kanner, L. (1935). *Child Psychiatry*. Springfield, IL: Charles C. Thomas.

Kim, Y. S., Y. Koh, and B. Leventhal. (2005). School bullying and suicidal risk in Korean middle school students. *Pediatrics* 115, 357–63.

King, R. A., M. Schwab-Stone, A. J. Flisher, S. Greenwald, R. A. Kramer, S. H. Goodman, B. B. Lahey, D. Shaffer, and M. Gould. (2001). Psychosocial risk behavior correlates of youth suicide attempts and suicidal ideation. *Journal of American Acad. Child Adolescent Psychiatry* 40, 837–46.

Kitamura, A. (1983). Comparative study of attempted suicide among young persons in Germany and Japan. *Seishin Shinkeigaku Zasshi* 85, 54–68 (in Japanese).

Kitamura, A., K. Wada, Y. Kitamura, Y. Inoue, and A. Yamamoto. (1981). Longitudinal studies of attempted suicide among young people. *Seishin Shinkeigaku Zasshi* 83, 372–85 (in Japanese).

Klomek, A. B., F. Marrocco, M. Kleinman, I. S. Schonfeld, and M. S. Gould. (2007). Bullying, depression, and suicidality in adolescents. *Journal of American Acad. Child Adolescent Psychiatry* 46, 40–49.

Korea Times. (2004). Suicide rate grows faster in OECD. June 4, 2005.

Lewinsohn, P. M., P. Rohde, J. R. Seeley, and C. L. Baldwin. (2001). Gender differences in suicide attempts from adolescence to young adulthood. *Journal of American Acad. Adolescent Psychiatry* 40, 427–34.

Lieb, R., T. Bronish, M. Hofler, A. Schreier, and H. U. Wittchen. (2005). Maternal suicidality and risk of suicidality in offspring: findings from a community study. *American Journal of Psychiatry* 162, 1665–71.

Liu, K. Y., E. Caine, K. Chan, A. Chao, Y. Conwell, C. Law, D. Lee, P. Li, and P. Yip. (2007). Charcoal burning suicides in Hong Kong and urban Taiwan: An illustration of the impact of a novel suicide method on overall regional rates. *Journal of Epidemiol. Community Health* 61, 248–53.

Marttunen, M. J., H. M. Aro, M. M. Henriksson, and J. K. Lonnqvist. (1991). Mental disorders in adolescent suicide: DSM-III-R Axis I and II diagnosis in suicides among 13- to 19-year-olds in Finland. *Arch. Gen. Psychiatry* 48, 834–39.

McCurry, J. (2006). Japan promises to curb number of suicides. *Lancet* 367, 383.

Mikami, K., S. Inomata, N. Hayakawa, A. Ohyama, H. Andoh, H. Ohzono, A. Ichimura, and H. Matsumoto. (2006a). Clinical features of serious suicide attempts among adolescents in Japan. *Book of abstract, 17th World Congress of the International Association for Child and Adolescent Psychiatry and Allied Professionals*, p. 158.

Mikami, K., K. Ohya, K. Akasaka, and H. Matsumoto. (2006b). Attempted suicide of youth with Asperger's disorder. *Seishin Shinkeigaku Zasshi* 108, 587–96 (in Japanese).

Ministry of Education, Culture, Sports, Science and Technology. (2006). *Statistics of Issues Related to School Guidance in 2005*. Ministry of Education, Culture, Sports, Science and Technology (in Japanese).

Ministry of Health, Labour and Welfare. (2007). *Vital Statistics of Japan, 2005*. Tokyo: Health & Welfare Statistic Association (in Japanese).

Murase, S., S. Honjo, H. Kaneko, S. Arai, K. Nomura, O. Hashimoto, and T. Ohta. (2004). Clinical characteristics of serious Japanese adolescent suicide-attempters admitted to an intensive care ward. *Jan. Journal of Child Adolescent Psychiatry* 45 Supplement, 25–34.

Murata, T., T. Tsutsumi, Y. Sarada, Y. Nakaniwa, Y. Shinpo, and R. Kobayashi. (1992). Childhood depressice condition in Japan. In "Collected Papers of the 12th Congress of the IACAPAP," *Challenge of Child and Adolescent Psychiatry Toward 21st Century*. Tokyo: Seiwa Shoten Publishers, pp. 532–44 (in Japanese).

Nakane, A. (1996). Nonattendance at school (school phobia): Clinical aspects and psychopathology, in M. Shimizu (ed.), *Recent Progress in Child and Adolescent Psychiatry*, pp. 64–71. Tokyo: Springer-Verlag.

National Police Academy. (2006). Crimes in Japan in 2005. http://www.npa.go.jp/english/seisaku5/20061211.pdf

National Police Agency. (2006). *Statistics of suicide in 2005*. National Police Agency (in Japanese).

Ohara, K. (1961). A study on the factors contributing to suicide: from the standpoint of psychiatry. *Seishin Shinkeigaku Zasshi* 63, 107–66 (in Japanese).

Ohara, K., M. Shimizu, S. Aizawa, and H. Kojima. (1963). Suicide in children (Part 1). *Seishin Shinkeigaku Zasshi* 65, 468–481 (in Japanese).

Ojima, T., Y. Nakamura, and R. Detels. (2004). Comparative study about methods of suicide between Japan and the United States. *Journal of Epidemiology* 14, 187–92.

Ono, Y. (2006, June). Current status of mood disorders and suicide of children and adolescents in Japan. Paper presented at the 4th Congress of Asian Society for Child and Adolescent Psychiatry and Allied Professionals. Manila, Philippines.

Pfeffer, C. R. (2002). Suicidal behaviors in children and adolescents: Causes and management, in M. Lewis (ed.), *Child and Adolescent Psychiatry: A Comprehensive Textbook*, third edition. Philadelphia: Lippincott Williams & Wilkins, pp. 796–805.

Phillips, M. R., X. Li, and Y. Zhang. (2002). Suicide rates in China, 1995–1999. *Lancet* 359, 835–40.

Rajagopal, S. (2004). Suicide pacts and the Internet. *BMJ* 329, 1298–99.

Roy, A., N. L. Segal, B. S. Centerwall, and C. D. Robinette. (1991). Suicide in twins. *Arch. Gen. Psychiatry* 48, 29–32.

Roy, A., N. L. Segal, and M. Sarchapone. (1995). Attempted suicide among living co-twins of twin suicide victims. *American Journal of Psychiatry* 152, 1075–76.

Russell, S. T. and K. Joyner. (2001). Adolescent sexual orientation and suicide risk: Evidence from a national study. *American Journal of Public Health* 91, 1276–81.

Safer, D. J. (1997). Self-reported suicide attempts by adolescents. *Annals of Clinical Psychiatry* 9, 263–69.

Sato, H., M. Nagasaku, K. Kamimura, M. Ishikawa, M. Honda, Y. Matsuda, K. Arai, S. Ishikawa, and Y. Sakano. (2006). A community-based investigation of depressive symptoms in children. *Japanese Journal of Child Adolescent Psychiatry* 47, 57–68 (in Japanese).

Schmidtke, A. and H. Hafner. (1988). The Werther effect after television films: New evidence for an old hypothesis. *Psychol. Med.* 18, 665–76.

Shaffer, D., M. S. Gould, P. Fisher, P. Trautman, D. Moreau, M. Kleinman, and M. Flory. (1996). Psychiatric diagnosis in child and adolescent suicide. *Arch. Gen. Psychiatry* 53, 339–48.

Shaffer, D. and J. Gutstein. (2002). Suicide and attempted suicide, in M. Rutter and E. Taylor (eds.), *Child and Adolescent Psychiatry*, fourth edition. Malden, MA: Blackwell Science, pp. 529–54.

Silverman, A. B., H. Z. Reinherz, and R. M. Ciaconia. (1996). The long-term sequelae of child and adolescent abuse: A longitudinal community study. *Child Abuse Negl.* 20, 709–23.

Smith, P. K., Y. Morita, J. Junger-Tas, D. Olweus, R. Catalano, P. Slee. (1999). *The Nature of School Bullying: A Cross-sectional Perspective*. New York: Routledge.

Stack, S. (1996). The effect of the media on suicide: evidence from Japan, 1955–1985. *Suicide Life Threat Behavior* 26, 132–42.

Sudak, H. S. (2005). Suicide, in B. J. Sadock and V. A. Sadock (eds.), *Kaplan and Sadock's Comprehensive Textbook of Psychiatry*, eighth edition. Philadelphia: Lippincott Williams & Wilkins, pp. 2432–53.

Sugawara, M., T. Mukai, T. Kitamura, M. Toda, S. Shima, A. Tomoda, T. Koizumi, K. Watanabe, and A. Ando. (1999). Psychiatric disorders among Japanese children. *Journal of American Acad. Child Adolescent Psychiatry* 38, 444–52.

Takei, A., K. Mera, K. Miyazaki, Y. Sato, and Y. Haraoka. (2006). A clinical study of patients with self-mutilation in an adolescent psychiatric clinic. *Seishin-Igaku* 48, 1009–17 (in Japanese).

Thompson, M. P., C. H. Ho, and J. B. Kingree. (2007). Prospective associations between delinquency and suicidal behaviors in a nationally representative sample. *Journal of Adolescent Health* 40, 232–37.

———. (2006). Korea's suicide rate highest in OECD in 2005. September 18, 2006.

U.S. Department of Health and Human Services. (1999). *Mental Health: A Report of Surgeon General*. Rockville, MD: U.S. Department of Health and Human Services. National Institute of Health.

U.S. Public Health Service. (1999). *The Surgeon General's Call to Action to Prevent Suicide*. Washington, DC: Department of Health and Human Services.

Wasserman, D., Q. Cheng, and G. Jiang. (2005). Global suicide rates among young people aged 15–19. *World Psychiatry* 4, 114–20.

World Health Organization. (1992). *ICD-10: The ICD-10 Classification of Mental and Behavioural Disorders: Clinical Description and Diagnostic Guidelines*. Geneva: World Health Organization.

World Health Organization. (2007). Suicide prevention (SUPRE). http://www.who.int/mental_health/prevention/suicide/suicideprevent/en/index.html

Yamamura, T., H. Kinoshita, M. Nishiguchi, and S. Hishida. (2006). A perspective in epidemiology of suicide in Japan. *Vojnosanit Pregl* 63, 575–83.

9

Transgenerational Parent/Child Transmission of Mental Health Problems, Parental Stress, and Posttraumatic Stress Disorder

Per-Anders Rydelius and Atia Daud

INTRODUCTION

The aim of this chapter is to focus upon the situation of children of refugee families arriving in a new country with a history of parental posttraumatic stress disorder. Data support the existence of parent/child transmission of posttraumatic stress in vulnerable children, and this has implications for the assessment and care of these families. Psychiatrists, psychologists, social workers, and teachers need to be aware of such possible transmission of parents' traumatic experiences to their children in order to develop treatment methods for affected children and to make it easier for them and their parents to adjust to the living conditions in the new country. Our experiences also indicate that there is a true advantage for professional teams to have staff members with ethnic, language, and cultural competence when meeting affected families.

BACKGROUND

Over the past thirty-five years refugees from different parts of the world have come to Sweden from their home countries to seek protection from violence and persecution due to civil war and other causes such as political

191

and criminal activities. In this way, groups of refugees with very different cultural backgrounds have arrived from South America, the Middle East, the Balkans, and the new East Asian Republics emerging from territories of the former Soviet Union.

Refugees either come alone or in groups with parents, children, and relatives in order to stay in Sweden until the situation in their home countries stabilizes, when they intend to return. Usually, those coming alone try to have their families and relatives join them in Sweden. Before coming to Sweden, some have witnessed or experienced violence toward their family members and/or themselves. The different types of violence include assault, rape, torture, and/or death threats of different kinds. Many suffer from mental problems in different degrees including posttraumatic stress symptoms.

In 1993, due to the great number of refugees coming to Sweden from the war in Yugoslavia, the Swedish government, the Swedish National Board of Health and Welfare, and the different county councils developed programs to support refugees and their children. The programs had a focus on mental health. The Child and Adolescent Unit at the Department of Women and Child Psychiatric Health at the Karolinska Institutet in Stockholm was involved in this work to (1) establish an overview of the current knowledge in the field of refugee children as a basis for providing mental health services, and (2) to investigate children of parents who had been tortured in order to give the children special help if needed (Näreskog, 1997).

There is an overwhelming bulk of literature on traumatized children including children's emotional reactions to "external" environmental stress such as accidents, disaster, and war, as well as emotional reactions to "internal" familial stress from neglect and abuse.

THE RELATIONSHIP BETWEEN PARENTAL MENTAL HEALTH AND PSYCHOSOCIAL FUNCTIONING, AND CHILDREN'S BEHAVIOR, MENTAL HEALTH, SCHOOL ACHIEVEMENT, AND LATER ADJUSTMENT

In Swedish research in child and adolescent psychiatry there has been a special interest in the relationship between parental mental health and psychosocial functioning and the children's behavior, mental health, school achievement, and risk for deviant behavior and delinquency later in life.

This interest goes back to the pioneering genetic research in the 1940s as exemplified by Otterström's study on "children from bad homes" (Otterström, 1946). Otterström followed up 2,346 of the children who had come into contact with the Child Welfare Board of Malmö, Sweden, between 1903 and 1940, four to thirty-one years after their referral, with special reference to the relationship between parental psychosocial function and the risk for delinquency among the children. For her study, Otterström used a contemporary genetic design. However, she found that genetics alone could not explain the effect on children's outcome. It was necessary to include the effects of a "social inheritance" in order to understand how the psychosocial functioning of the parents affected the children. In 1968, her study was commented upon by John Cowie, Valerie Cowie, and Eliot Slater from the Medical Research Council's Psychiatric Genetics Research Unit at the Maudsley Hospital in the following way: "A prognostic study of great importance was carried out in Sweden by Edith Otterström (1946). She had the advice and help of Gunnar Dahlberg, at that time one of the world authorities on psychiatric genetics and epidemiology, and a statistical expert of the highest order. The poor lady was, accordingly, set to do her statistical work along the soundest lines, with the result that, though she complains of the laboriousness of the arithmetic, her estimates of expectancy of criminality in her sample are in the right form for comparison with corresponding expectancies calculated by Dahlberg for the general population" (Cowie et al., 1968).

In her book, *Deviant Children Grown Up*, Lee N. Robins (1966) wrote: "Although little notice has been given this study in the American literature, it is an extraordinary achievement in length of follow-up, size of sample, variety of the criteria for adult adjustment, and objectivity of methods used both in the original categorizing of the subjects and in their later evaluation. This monograph also provides an exhaustive search of the literature up to the date of publication."

CHILD PSYCHIATRIC STUDIES OF CHILDREN SUFFERING FROM EMOTIONAL STRESS

Discussion of how genetic and "social" inheritance interacts to explain deviant behavior in children of deviant parents resulted in Ingvar Nylander's child psychiatric study of "children of alcoholic fathers" (Nylander, 1960). He tested the hypothesis that "children who live under stress due to serious emotional disturbances in the home" react with special symptoms. He compared children of alcoholic fathers with matched control children of nonalcoholic fathers using a design with "social twins." This means that "for every subject of school age, a control of the same sex was chosen who lived in the same area, went to the same school and was in the same class as the subject, whose father was in a similar employment to that of the subject's father but not registered for any kind of alcohol problems." Further, "it was stipulated that the subject and the control should be born in the same year and the age difference should not exceed 6 months" and "the

Table 9.1.   Children of alcoholic fathers showed the following symptoms and behavioural problems more often than control children

- School problems
- Headache
- Abdominal pain
- "Growing pains," joint pain
- Tiredness
- Nausea, vomiting
- Hysterical symptoms
- Anorectic behavior
- Sleep problems
- Emotional lability
- Anxiety
- Obsessive-compulsive symptoms
- Depression
- Aggressive behaviour
- Motor restlessness
- Difficulty to concentrate
- Peer problems

subjects and controls should have the same or similar school report in all school subjects except physical training, singing and handwork."

Due to the Swedish legislation against alcohol at that time (this changed over the coming years) Nylander found when investigating parental health that the wives of alcoholic men were often depressed and suffered from different mental symptoms but were seldom alcoholics themselves. He found obvious differences when comparing the children of alcoholic fathers with the control children of nonalcoholic fathers as shown in table 9.1.

Nylander also found that the subject girls' mental status was more dependent on the mental status of the mother than of the father, while boys' tended to be more related to their fathers' situations. Of special interest was his finding that treatment of the alcoholic father had a positive impact on the children's symptom and behavior.

In another study, Nylander (1959) investigated 465 consecutive patients (228 boys and 237 girls) treated in pediatric or pediatric surgery wards for somatic symptoms where no somatic explanation could be found. In this study it was found that dissociative symptoms (table 9.2) in children could be linked to long-standing serious emotional stress.

For the coming decades, the findings of these pioneering studies in the 1940s and 1950s had an important impact on Swedish child and adolescent psychiatric research into both parental factors and child adjustment.

Table 9.2.   Symptoms seen in children who have experienced long-standing emotional stress

- Rumination
- Hysteria, paralysis, deafness, loss of vision
- Limping
- Extreme tiredness, apathy, bedridden
- Astasia-abasia
- Simulation

A PSYCHOSOCIAL STRESS THEORY

The results from a series of longitudinal and cross-sectional studies (Rydelius 1981, 1994) indicated clearly a need to investigate further the relationship between parenting, parental psychosocial stress factors, vulnerability in the children, and the children's later adjustment (Rutter et al., 2001; Sandberg et al., 2001). Nylander's findings of specific symptoms (Nylander, 1959) in children suffering from long-standing emotional stress has recently been the subject of renewed interest in Sweden, as a great number of refugee children from the new East Asian Republics and from territories of the former Soviet Union have been treated because of severe apathy on arrival to Sweden.

A LONGITUDINAL STUDY OF GREEK CHILDREN CONFINED WITH THEIR MOTHERS IN PRISON DURING THE GREEK CIVIL WAR, 1946–1949

During the Greek civil war, 1946–1949, Mando Dalianis, a young Greek female doctor, had the opportunity to study mothers and children confined to prison for political reasons. Mando Dalianis later left Greece and became a child and adolescent psychiatrist in Sweden. Based on her early observations and using the design described above, she investigated factors in both parents and children. She followed up three groups of Greek children coming from 143 partisan families, longitudinally over three generations. One group consisted of 119 children from 106 partisan families who were confined to prison with their mothers, before, during, and after the Greek civil war. The mothers were political prisoners. At the time of the mothers' arrests (between 1945 and 1950), 39 children were expected and 80 were being breast-fed. At the age of 2 to 5 years, a majority of children were separated from the imprisoned mother and placed in an institution or with relatives. Only 26 children remained in the mother's care.

In summary, Dalianis investigated short- and long-term developmental effects of repeated exposure to diverse, multiple, sequential, and massive traumatic experiences from prenatal life or infancy through childhood and during adult life, including the long-term health consequences of imprisonment and separation traumas suffered by children during their first years of life.

The results from the 35-year follow-up indicated (Dalianis, 1994) that despite the traumatization, a majority of the children had achieved an adequate psychosocial adult adaptation. Most of the grown-up children were parents in good physical and mental health. On average, they were socially well adapted as regards education, work, and marital adjustment. In order to analyze the relation between background variables, traumatic experiences, protective factors, and outcome, a statistical model was used based upon theoretically traumatizing and protecting factors. The traumatizing factors were:

- Parents' socioeconomic status
- Mother's mental health
- Mother's physical health
- Traumatic factors for mother during detention
- Factors influencing child's psychosocial situation and mental health
- Child's physical health
- Specific traumatic factors relating to the child.

The protective factors were:

- Parents socioeconomic status
- Mother's physical health during pregnancy
- Factors related to parents' mental strength
- Possible factors favoring the child's resilience
- Parent attitude to the child's situation during childhood and to school proficiency

The outcome measures of good health (good health outcome) were taken from Werner and Smith (1992), who defined health as an ability to "work well, play well, love well and expect well." Data were analyzed in the model described in figure 9.1. This analysis indicated that the child's emotional and intellectual capacity and support form caring persons, not necessary a parent, were factors related to a positive outcome. Dalianis herself said that it seems likely that a combination of individual factors, probably to large extent traits inherited from the parents, and various supportive environmental factors, together with their interaction, helped these children develop into rather well-functioning adults.

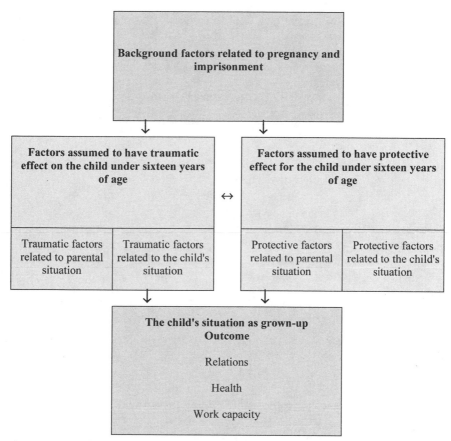

Figure 9.1. Relationship between background variables, traumatic experiences, protective factors and outcome—a statistical model

TRANSGENERATIONAL PARENT/CHILD TRANSMISSION OF POSTTRAUMATIC STRESS DISORDER IN FAMILIES FROM MIDDLE EASTERN EXTRACTION

Through a grant from the Swedish National Board of Health and Welfare program to support refugees and their children, a study was designed (Daud et al., 2005a, 2005b) to investigate tortured refugee parents coming to Sweden with their children. Families were recruited to the study from the Swedish Red Cross' Centre for Tortured Refugees and the Centre for Trauma Treatment and Diagnostics in Stockholm (CTD), if they had been living in Stockholm for at least two years and if one parent had experienced episodes of torture in the home country of at least one month's duration before coming to Sweden.

Fifteen intact families with both fathers and mothers coming from Iraq and Lebanon fulfilled the inclusion criteria. The mean age for the fathers was 43.5 years and for the mothers 38.7 years. They had 45 children between the ages of 6 and 17 years. The mean age of the 29 boys in the group was 12 years and that of the 16 girls 11.3 years.

A comparison group of 15 intact families from the same Arabic ethnicity and with the same language, religious, and cultural background (from Egypt, Syria, and Morocco) were recruited. They had also been living in Sweden for at least two years. The mean age of the fathers was 45.8 years and of the mothers 38.7 years. These parents may have experienced violence in some form, but they had not been subjected to systematic torture. They had a total of 31 children between the ages of 6 and 17 years. The mean age of the 15 boys in this group was 11 years and of the 16 girls 12.6 years.

Both parents and children were investigated. The parents were investigated using interviews, the Karolinska Scales of Personality (KSP) (Schalling, 1986), and the Swedish version of the Harvard/Uppsala Trauma Questionnaire (H/UTQ) (Ahmad, 1999). An interview was carried out to identify the family's socioeconomic status, ethnicity, nationality, and educational background, with special emphasis on psychosocial stress factors related to parents' everyday function at home with their children and with other adults. Somatization symptoms/diagnoses were elicited with the KSP muscular tension subscale and PTSD with the H/UTQ test.

The children were assessed using the DICA-interview and DSM-IV diagnostic criteria (APA, 1994, 2000). Posttraumatic stress disorder (PTSD) or posttraumatic stress symptoms (PTSS) and psychological distress were assessed by means of the children's self-rating on the posttraumatic stress symptoms checklist, assessed by means of the Diagnostic Interview for Children and Adolescents (DICA-R) in both a parents' and a children's version (Reich et al, 1995).

Their intellectual capacities were tested using the WISC-III-scales (Wechsler, 1991) and their emotional state was assessed by means of the Machover Draw-A-Person test (DAP) (Blomberg and Cleve, 1997). The children completed the "I think I Am" (ITIA) questionnaire, which is a Swedish self-report scale developed and standardized on a sample of over 3,465 children between eight and sixteen years of age (Ouvinen-Birgerstam, 1985).

The ITIA questionnaire consists of seventy-two items divided into five factors that measure the child's ideation about him- or herself with respect to: (1) physical components, (2) skills and talents, (3) psychological well-being, (4) relations with family, (5) relation with others, and last, the child's total score. The child has to choose between four alternatives: "exactly like me," "almost like me," "not quite like me," and "not at all like me." The ITIA total composite score ranges between +144 and -144. A high score on the scales reflects adequate mental health.

Teachers and parents rated the children according to the Strengths and Difficulties Questionnaire (SDQ) (Goodman, 2001, Malmberg et al., 2003) and the Yale Children's inventory (YCI) (Shaywitz et al., 1986, 1988).

On the H/UTQ test, traumatized parents scored higher than the comparison group with respect to posttraumatic stress disorder, depression, somatization, anxiety, and psychosocial stress symptoms. On the KSP, they scored higher on nine of the fifteen subscales. The fathers in the tortured group scored higher than their wives only on the subscale for guilt.

According to the DICA-interviews, the children of tortured parents had more symptoms of anxiety, depression, posttraumatic stress, attention deficits, and behavioral disorders compared to the comparison group.

The findings from the DAP test indicated clear differences in the emotional state of the children in the two groups. The children in the traumatized parent group showed increasing signs of insecure attachment and an inadequate (negative) prosociality in comparison with the children in the nontraumatized parent group. The test subjects obtained high scores on the depressiveness variable and low scores on the aggressiveness variable. On the secure/insecure attachment variable, 70 percent of the children of the traumatized parent showed insecure attachment compared with 31 percent of the children in the comparison group.

The results from the "I think I am" (ITIA) questionnaire was used to compare children with and without PTSS/PTSD from parents suffering from PTSD in order to explore possible factors of resilience and protection. Those children who did not develop PTSS possessed adequate relations with the family ($p<0.06$), adequate peer relations (without problems) ($p<0.001$), they displayed adequate emotionality ($p<0.01$), and had a low total ITIA score ($p<0.001$). This gives an indication of the quality of the children's relationship to their significant others (family members and peers), which in turn may indicate that these families had been supportive in promoting a healthy adjustment (Antonovsky, 1979) despite the parents' own lack of well-being. These findings emphasize the importance of a supportive environment (good family and peer relations) for children's well-being, something to be promoted by clinicians and schools supporting them.

FINAL COMMENTS

Several studies, designed to assess possible links between the mental health of parents and their children, support the existence of a parent/child transmission of mental problems. This has been found examining alcoholic fathers and their children as well as parents with PTSD and their children. The data support the conclusion that children who live under stress due to serious emotional disturbances in their homes have an enhanced tendency to react with symptoms and behavioral problems that may impair their school achievement and their relationships with peers. There is evidence that treatment of parental mental health problems can also have a positive effect on their children's symptoms.

However, all children from the same families do not react in the same way. Some children are more vulnerable than their siblings while others are more resilient. The child's emotional and intellectual capacity (probably to a large extent inherited from their parents) and support form caring persons, not necessary a parent, are factors related to resiliency and to a positive outcome.

Refugee families should be offered a psychiatric and psychological assessment when coming to a new country in the same way as their somatic health is evaluated. In families found to have a history of serious traumatic experiences (i.e., rape, murder, and torture) both parents and children should be evaluated for PTSD/PTSS. If such disorders exist, both parents and children should be offered mental health services. Psychiatrists, psychologists, social workers, and teachers should develop treatment programs jointly to treat both parents and children and to support the children's relationships with their family members and with peers. Children with slow learning capacity will need special attention at day care and school.

REFERENCES

Ahmad, A. (1999). Childhood Trauma and Posttraumatic Stress Disorder. A Developmental and Cross-Cultural Approach. A Comprehensive Summaries of Uppsala Dissertations from the Faculty of Medicine 874.

American Psychiatric Association (APA). (1994). *Diagnostic and Statistical Manual of Mental Disorders,* fourth edition (DSM-IV). Washington, DC: American Psychiatric Association.

American Psychiatric Association (APA). (2000). *Diagnostic and Statistical Manual of Mental Disorders,* fourth edition (DSM-IV-TR). Washington, DC: American Psychiatric Association.

Antonovsky, A. (1979). *Health, Stress, and Coping: New Perspectives on Mental and Physical Well-being.* San Francisco: Jossey-Bass.

Blomberg, B., and E. Cleve. (1997). *Machovers test. Handbok med utvecklingsteoretiska perspektiv.* Stockholm: Psykologiförlaget.

Cowie, J., V. Cowie, and E. Slater. (1968). *Delinquency in Girls.* London: Heinemann Educational Books Ltd.

Dalianis-Karambatzakis, A. M. (1994). "Children in Turmoil During the Greek Civil War 1946–1949: Todays's Adults. A Longitudinal Study on Children Confined with Their Mothers in Prison." Thesis. Stockholm: Karolinska Institutet.

Daud, A., E. Skoglund, P.-A. Rydelius. (2005a). The emotional state of children of traumatized and nontraumatized Parents. *Egypt Journal of Psychiatry* 24(2): 171–82.

Daud, A., E. Skoglund, and P.-A. Rydelius. (2005b). Children in families of torture victims: Transgenerational transmission of parents' traumatic experiences to their child. *International Journal of Social Welfare* 14(1): 23–32.

Goodman, R. (2001). Psychometric properties of the Strengths and Difficulties Questionnaire. *Journal of American Academic Child and Adolescent Psychiatry,* 40(11): 1337–45.

Malmberg, M., A.-M. Rydell, and H. Smedje. (2003). Validity of the Swedish version of the Strengths and Difficulties Questionnaire (SDQ-Swe.). *Nordic Journal of Psychiatry* 57(2): 357–63.

Näreskog, M. (1997). *Flyktingbarn—Psykisk Hälsa och mottagande. En kunskapsöversikt ochett planeringsunderlag för hälso-och sjukvård.* Research Report No. 12, ISSN 1400-5891. Stockholm: Karolinska Institutet.

Nylander, I. (1959). Physical symptoms and psychogenic etiology. An investigation of consultation material. *Acta Paediat.* 48, Supplement 117: 69–77.

———. (1960). Children of alcoholic fathers, *Acta Paediatrica Scandnavica* 49, supplement, 121.

Otterström, E. (1946). "Delinquency and Children from Bad Homes." Thesis. The State Institute for Human Genetics. Uppsala University. Uppsala

Ouvinen-Birgerstam, P. (1985). *Jag tycker jag är.* (I Think I Am). Stockholm: Psykologi-Förlaget.

Reich, W., N. Leacock, and K. Shanfeld. (1995). *Diagnostic Interview for Children and Adolescents—Parent Version.* St. Louis, MO: Washington University.

Robins, L. N. (1966). *Deviant Children Grown up.* Baltimore, MD: The Williams & Wilkins Company.

Rutter, M., A. Pickles, R. Murray, and L. Eaves. (2001). Testing hypotheses on specific environmental causal effects on behavior. *Psychological Bulletin* 127: 291–324.

Rydelius, P.-A. (1981). Children of alcoholic fathers, their social adjustment and their health status over 20 years. *Acta Paediatrica Scandinavica,* Supplement 286, 1–89.

———. (1994). Children of alcoholic parents: At risk to experience violence and to develop violent behaviour, in C. Chiland and Y. G. Young, eds., *Children and Violence.* London: Jason Aronson, Inc., pp.72–90.

Sandberg, S., M. Rutter, A. Pickles, D. McGuinness, and A. Angold. (2001). Do high-threat life events really provoke the onset of psychiatric disorder in children? *Journal of Child Psychology and Psychiatry* 42: 523–32.

Schalling, D. (1986). The development of the KSP inventory, in B. af klinteberg, D. Schalling, and D. Magnusson, (eds.), *Self-report Assessment of Personality Traits. Reports from the Project Individual Development and Adjustment* (Vol. 64, pp. 1–8). Stockholm: Department of Psychology, Stockholm University, Sweden.

Shaywitz, S. E., C. Schnell, B. A. Shaywitz, and V. R. Towle. (1986). Yale Children's inventory (YCI): An instrument to assess children with attentional deficits and learning disabilities I. Scale development and psychometric properties. *Journal of Abnormal Child Psychology* 14: 347–64.

———. (1988). Concurrent and predictive validity of the Yale Children's Inventory: An instrument to assess children with attentional deficits and learning disabilities. *Pediatrics* 81: 562–71.

Wechsler, D. (1991). *Manuel for the Wechsler Intelligence Scale for Children*, third edition. San Antonio, TX: Psychological Association.

Werner, E. E. And R. S. Smith. (1992). *Overcoming the Odds: High Risk Children from Birth to Adulthood*. Ithaca, NY: Cornell University Press.

III

TRAINING AND INTERVENTIONS

meet their needs. This in turn has highlighted the importance of training in cultural psychiatry.

This chapter addresses training or the acquisition of knowledge and skills in child psychiatry—that is, psychopathology, symptomatology, and management of child and adolescent mental health disorders—in a transcultural context, across different cultures. This is often taken to mean multicultural training or work with client or patient groups from diverse ethnic and cultural backgrounds. However the term also refers to trainees from one culture being taught by trainers from another. The third and most relevant term—and the one followed in this chapter—refers to a transcultural perspective within the curriculum for training in child psychiatry.

There is no argument about the need for training and capacity building for experts in child mental health across different countries, whether high or low in income (Kim, 2003; Patel et al., 2007). Where countries differ is in how much they recruit to the speciality, the resources made available, but also the content of training itself. There is increasing emphasis on making best use of the strongest empirical evidence base available (March et al., 2005, Hodes, 1998) and there is much to be said for consistency of purpose (Hodes, 1998). However, a recent survey has demonstrated wide variation in content within training programs even in comparatively homogenous areas such as the European community (Karabekiroglu et al., 2006).

This chapter will describe objectives of transcultural training, content, and who should have access to such training, with special reference to an on-going international course in the United Kingdom. Additionally, there will be consideration of questions such as what are effective teaching strategies, different ways of increasing capacity through training, and of the use of expertise across countries and cultures. The chapter draws on experience by the author in teaching and training within the United Kingdom and elsewhere. It does not deal specifically with efforts to sensitize clinicians for work with cultural or ethnic minorities, except through the provision of knowledge about how different cultures may affect child and adolescent mental health.

OBJECTIVES OF TRANSCULTURAL TRAINING

What are the challenges of developing objectives and a curriculum for transcultural training? First there is the issue of how best to present evidence, most of which has arisen from research and clinical work in Europe and North America. It is obviously important to make use of the best material available, while at the same time avoiding a homogenization of thought about child development and behavior that could stifle exploration of culture related issues, including therapeutic approaches. This has been discussed in a review of psychiatric services in South East Asia by Higginbotham and Marsella (1988), highlighting the desirable as well as undesirable consequences of diffusion of Western psychiatric thought to less developed countries.

Multicultural training has been the subject of attention at both medical student and postgraduate level in the Western world, responding to its increasingly multiethnic and multicultural population. This addresses the clinical skills required to work in these populations and includes teaching on diversity, cultural specifics of different ethnic groups, raising awareness among trainers and trainees about the influence of their own ethnic identity, and their cultural attitudes and preconception (Bhui and Bhugra, 1998; Foulks et al., 1998).

In the United States, Foulks et al. (1998) outlined the core psychiatric curriculum for medical students, psychiatric residents, and cultural psychiatrists. For all three groups they defined objectives for knowledge acquisition of culture relevant research, skills, and attitudes, and teaching/learning methods for achieving these objectives. They highlighted the importance of opportunities for trainees to develop cultural sensitivity, acknowledging the existence of cultural biases and ethnocentricities. The curriculum includes specific knowledge on how cultural factors can influence psychiatric epidemiology, psychopathology, assessment, therapeutic approaches, and service development.

Any curriculum needs to relate to training objectives. Training in child psychiatry must always aim to equip clinicians with a comprehensive knowledge of developmental psychopathology, psychopharmacology, and psychological treatments, with adequate clinical skills in the assessment, diagnosis, and management of children and adolescents. Knowledge of legal frameworks and research skills is also a core element of training in the United Kingdom (Royal College of Psychiatrists, 1999).

Objectives for transcultural training will include these. However, in some countries, specialist child mental health clinicians will be a scarce commodity. In addition to the core objectives, training should equip them to work on resource development, the methodology of service planning and evaluation, and in teaching others.

CONTENT OF TRAINING: IS A FOCUS ON CULTURE NECESSARY?

Child psychiatry is seeing significant developments in the establishment of biological causal links for a number of disorders and an increasing emphasis on evidence-based medicine, particularly with regard to therapeutic approaches. It has now been demonstrated that most diagnostic groups, particularly the more biologically based, can be diagnosed reliably across cultures. There is therefore a broadly applicable core content featuring child development, attachments, family dynamics, risk, and resilience. Emerging evidence indicates that most established treatments—both pharmacological and psychological—can also be used effectively in different countries. To a large extent, therefore, the fact that most of the research evidence stems from Europe and North America will not introduce a significant cultural bias, and it should be relatively easy to prepare a core curriculum that can be effectively transferred to different cultural contexts and countries.

Nevertheless, there are also a number of areas where cultural factors do make a difference. This applies to perceived roles and value assigned to children, protective or risk factors arising from varying sociocultural norms of behavior, family structures and dynamics, child-rearing practices, ways of expressing distress, and beliefs about mental health and their effect on service use (Nikapota, 2002; Karnik et al., 2007; Patel et al., 2007).

The primary challenge in developing content for transcultural training is achieving a balance between basic knowledge and skills that is applicable across cultures, and an acknowledgement of the role of sociocultural influences, ensuring that practice, service innovations, and research are culture and context appropriate, that is, feasible in terms of context and resource availability.

One objective of transcultural training is to extend the evidence base in the field. It is essential, therefore, that course reading includes research done in different parts of the world, even if methodologies are comparatively less sophisticated.

Although it is not the aim of this chapter to review the cross-cultural literature, inevitably a curriculum will examine content areas where evidence suggests that social and cultural factors do play a significant role for psychopathology. For example, cross-cultural and cross-national studies on children's behavior styles demonstrate the feasibility of using empirically derived behavioral constructs across cultures, similarities across cultures in terms of rates by age and gender. However, there were also differences by culture in rates that could relate to sociocultural norms. Externalizing behavior is commoner in boys across all groups and it reduces in rate with age, but the gender difference increases or decreases depending on gender-based cultural norms for behavior (Crijnen et al., 1999). A further example of how sociocultural norms influence behavior is provided by work comparing Thai and U.S. youth, which demonstrates differences in coping styles and strategies used by youth to achieve their goals when coping with stress. Thai youth have been found to be more likely to use covert methods of achieving their coping goals, while U.S. youth used overt strategies. This related to sociocultural expectations of behavior and respect shown to responsible adults (McCarty and Weisz, 1999). Recent research among the Puerto Rican population demonstrated the importance of recognizing culture specific forms of distress, in this case "ataques de nervios," as children displaying these are at risk for psychiatric disorder (Guarnaccia et al., 2004).

The core curriculum for cultural psychiatrists outlined before by Foulks et al. (1998) is similar to that developed for the training program with which the author is involved at the Institute of Psychiatry in the United Kingdom, and which seeks to train clinicians in child psychiatry or child and adolescent mental health. The course is transcultural not only in terms of the curriculum, but also because trainees come from many parts of the world, the training is done by trainers many of whom themselves come from different country cultures to that of the trainees', and it is delivered in a multiethnic and multicultural population (see Institute of Psychiatry Web page, www .iop.kcl.ac.uk). The author's experience of developing and running this course will be outlined here.

WHO SHOULD BE TRAINED?

A purpose of developing a course of this nature must be capacity building and resource development. Hence it should best be available to a variety of professional groups and the curriculum should include essential components that in some countries may be considered to be discipline specific, such as psychopharmacology and psychological assessment. The curriculum may thus be appropriate for child mental health professionals working in health services, for those working within education or social welfare, or within established nongovernmental organizations (a recent review of child mental health in low- and middle-income countries or LAMIC gives examples of services provided by nonstatutory organisations [Patel et al. 2007]). This may include psychologists, now well established within multidisciplinary child and adolescent mental health services or CAMHS teams, pediatricians who are increasingly recognized as providing significant CAMHS input in countries such as Japan (Watanabe 1998) and the United States (Goodfriend et al., 2006), and primary care practitioners (Ani and Garralda, 2005). Accordingly, the Institute of Psychiatry's transcultural course has a broad interdisciplinary curriculum that can be accessed by clinicians with a professional training in pediatrics, psychiatry, or psychology.

THE CURRICULUM FOR TRANSCULTURAL TRAINING

A main focus is the development of an appreciation of the influence of social, cultural, or political factors for child mental health. The main components

evidence base for the use of cognitive behavior therapy for depression and for the use of this technique in different settings (Brent et al., 2002). There should also be some content on innovative treatment approaches. For example, traditional healers have been used effectively to treat dissociative reactions in India, using a standard treatment protocol (Kapur, 1995). Content on the use of psychoeducation is crucial, as this may be the only feasible initial option where there is a dearth of resources.

Teaching on risk and resilience will address culture specific *high risk groups*, such as vulnerable children and adolescents exposed to war, either as victim or combatant (Richman, 1993; Somasundaram and Vanderput, 2006), of refugees, child laborers, and "street children" (Campos et al., 1994; Lalor, 1999), and children subject to abuse and substance abuse. The validity of posttraumatic stress disorder (PTSD) in these contexts and the use of established therapeutic approaches will require discussion in the light of practice arising from local cultural norms (Oleke et al., 2005; Wolf and Fesseha, 2005). Political situations may be considered where adolescents voluntarily join a political movement such as Palestine's Intifada (see the chapter by Punamakki in this volume), together with its possible effects on mental health.

Extended discussion on *child protection issues* and procedures and on clinicians' response to this will be required, taking into account the different operating legal structures.

Additionally, social and cultural attitudes may lead to real differences in the way children respond to more common stresses and traumas such as parental separation, divorce, bereavement, bullying, and corporal punishment. There is more clinical evidence than empirical research in this area. Available work should be presented such as on physical discipline (Lansford et al., 2004). Particular high-risk health issues for mental health may be expected in the case of children suffering from HIV (Bassols et al., 2007; Collins et al., 2006).

The marked increase in recent knowledge accrued from research into child and adolescent health psychiatry (Remschmidt, 1996) calls for a good understanding of *research methodology*, both quantitative and qualitative. Training in this field requires the formulation of hypotheses and setting realistic and feasible projects, as well as techniques for writing up papers and to achieve publication. Far less research literature is available from low- and middle-income countries (LAMIC) than from high-income countries (HIC) countries (Patel and Sumathipala, 2001; Saxena et al., 2006; Jenkins, 2007). It is essential, therefore, that careful attention is paid to the issue of how to ensure that transcultural research methodology is rigorous and publishable.

Attention to the *ethics of research* is important. Many countries fail to have clearly formulated ethical processes established and there is a danger that exploitative research is conducted by researchers from other parts of the world. *Legal frameworks* can similarly vary. The principles and purposes underlying child protection, compulsory treatment, and forensic psychiatry will need to be understood using country-specific examples.

The skills of mental health professionals can be much sought after for *teaching other professionals in how to communicate* with children, young people, and families, and have a place in the curriculum.

More than expertise in management alone should be part of transcultural training. What is required is an understanding of the basics of *service planning*, different models of service delivery for child mental health, service inputs that may be required for feasible mental health promotion and for the delivery of care in primary care in addition to that provided at specialist secondary and tertiary levels. It helps to outline historical developments of secondary and tertiary child psychiatric services in countries such as the United States and the United Kingdom, as similar processes may be followed elsewhere (Higginbotham and Marsella, 1988). Guidance issues by the World Health Organisation (WHO 2005b) and policy examples pertinent to the development of child mental health services will be of interest (Malhotra, 1998; Celia, 1998; HAS 1995; WHO 1992, 1997). The objective here is to equip trainees with knowledge and understanding to allow them to join in a debate on what may be most appropriate within their setting. Strategies for advocacy in addition to the methodology required for monitoring and evaluating treatments and services, and an understanding of economic evaluation—a driver for policy makers (Knapp and Henderson, 1999)—are all relevant.

TEACHING CLINICAL SKILLS

Supervised clinical experience is a core component of training. Multicultural training perceives clinical contact with other cultures as a key way of developing cultural competence. Where transcultural training takes place in a country other than the trainee's, several barriers to learning arise, not least difficulty in appreciating nuances of language and culture. Nevertheless these can be incorporated into training as ways of enhancing cultural sensitivity, a generalizable skill when trainees return to their own country. Specific issues are consent and confidentiality, as these will be determined by social expectations about the role of children and adolescents within families.

TEACHING METHOD

This needs to incorporate reflection and experiential role play in addition to the acquisition of knowledge. Where possible, teaching sessions should follow a seminar format that encourages trainee participation, extended discussion, and the exploration of different views arising from contextual differences as well as the identification of gaps in knowledge. The curriculum must provide the time and space for trainees to critically evaluate the evidence presented to them, reflection, and discussion on how this may be relevant to different country contexts, what issues require further exploration. This requires an atmosphere where cultural difference are treated with respect, there is a genuine wish on the part of the teacher and group to know more about different cultures, and teachers and trainees are able to recognize and guard against their own attitudes and biases.

ASSESSMENTS

This is an important and sensitive area for all students. Assessments of competency in child psychiatry should be multimodal (Sargent et al., 2004). Accordingly, the Institute of Psychiatry's transcultural course involves ongoing assessments of participation in seminars, understanding of clinical issues, formative assessments of set work, and final summative written short-answer examination and dissertation. Prior to the final examination, mock exams are held with extensive feedback, to familiarize students with the style of answers expected. The fact that many students do not have English as their first language is taken account in exam marks. However the crucial aspect of assessment is that graduates from the course should be competent and clinically "safe." This is particularly an essential obligation when graduates return to a variety of diverse settings.

ADVANTAGES AND DISADVANTAGES OF
AN INTERNATIONAL COURSE IN CHILD PSYCHIATRY

The Institute of Psychiatry course (Institute of Psychiatry, "MSc in Child and Adolescent Mental Health," http.ww.iop.kcl.ac.uk/courses/?id=12.) has been ongoing since 1987. Bringing a transcultural group of trainees to a center of excellence has advantages, since both clinical and academic teaching may be expected to be of a high standard. Trainees are able to observe specialist clinical work. However, the downside is that fees can be high for students from other countries. Employers in countries of origin rightly expect students to have clinical experience, but some trainees have difficulty with fluency of spoken language and understanding of regional accents. Furthermore, in countries such as the United Kingdom there is a requirement that all professionals working with children within the health service undergo a police check, to make sure that they will not represent a risk for child patients. This causes practical difficulties, particularly when trainees come from countries where policing systems are very different. Ensuring acceptance of trainees and support by host clinical teams, not just by their clinical supervisor, is an essential requisite for a successful placement, as team members act as cultural brokers for the student. In turn, trainees are sometimes able to enrich and interpret cultural aspects of ethnic minority patients, due to their own knowledge and experience.

A major limitation of a course combining clinical and academic training over the course of one year is the time limitation. It is not possible to equate it with professional training in child psychiatry in the United Kingdom, as this extends over a three- or four-year period, and students and sponsors need to understand this. The course, moreover, has to be flexible to incorporate the particular interests and priorities of individual trainees.

The multidisciplinary mix of students has not posed any major problems. In fact having different perspectives has made for richer discussion. This means, however, that some students will require specific guidance where there are gaps in knowledge—for example, on mental illness and schizophrenia for pediatricians.

The introductory period for the course spans several weeks with information about the host country and living in London. George Mikesh's amusing books *How to Be an Alien* and *How to Be Decadent* have been invaluable as a means of introducing humor to these sessions. Students are encouraged to discuss their perceptions and their fears about life in another country. Some have concerns about safety. An Islamic student had worries relating to her acceptance by the group. A Japanese student was very critical about what she felt was the backward nature of UK banking systems. Students who have had positions of authority in their home countries find coping with student status difficult.

Over a twenty-year period, there has been regular feedback from students through individual interviews and focus group discussion. Students report that their own perception of their role as clinicians is enhanced by group discussions and by listening to other people's views on cultural customs, attitudes, beliefs, and practices. They have felt empowered by the appreciation that many clinicians from different parts of the world face similar issues and problems. They are very appreciative of receiving teaching from academic and clinicians of international repute.

However, this also has a negative counterpoint. Exposure to highly developed specialized services and academically stringent research can cause a sense of disempowerment when students return to their own countries of origin, to be faced with poorly resourced services and the economic constraints that affect service delivery and research opportunities. Course organizers therefore set aside time for discussion on how such problems may be tackled.

What has happened to graduates from the course? Thus far, there have been ninety trainees from Brazil, Chile, Columbia, Cyprus, France, Gaza,

Greece, Iran, Iraq, India, Italy, Japan, Jordan, Libya, Malaysia, Mexico, Pakistan, Philippines, Qatar, Saudi Arabia, Singapore, Spain, Sri Lanka, Sudan, Thailand, Taiwan, United Arab Emirates, Uruguay, and Yemen. Each course has had trainees from four or five world regions. The current course has students from Europe (Italy, Spain), the Far East (Japan), South America (Brazil, Chile), and Southeast Asia (Pakistan, Thailand).

All except three trainees have returned to their countries of origin, although two have subsequently returned to the United Kingdom and a further two work in neighboring countries. Three graduates are now heads of psychiatric services in their own countries. One has developed child psychiatry as an academic subspecialty and carried out pioneering epidemiological research in Bangladesh. Graduates from Brazil and Gaza have published important research from these countries. A graduate from India has developed pioneering services in Cambodia with Caritas, an international nongovernmental organization. It is noteworthy that trainees sponsored by their governments or employers become on return more easily and firmly established within a service or academic teaching provision in child mental health or child psychiatry. This has been the case, for example, for trainees from Thailand and Malaysia. Where trainees have been sponsored in other ways or self-financed, future career progression has been more variable. It is also noteworthy that where students have researched and published in peer reviewed journals, this has been facilitated through having retained an academic link with the United Kingdom.

THE WAY FORWARD

An international course is an important means but not the only one for using transcultural expertise. As an example, a group of trainers from the United Kingdom was successfully supported by an international charity and recruited to teach child psychiatry to a group of psychiatrists in Kosovo, as part of service developments in the country (Jones et al., 2003). Transcultural expertise can be used for capacity development as documented by a working party commissioned in the United Kingdom by the Royal College of Psychiatrists' Faculty for Child Psychiatry (2001). This highlighted ways in which such expertise could be deployed for training child mental health professionals. A feature of the work was a guide to transcultural training that emphasizes the need to consult with the groups to be trained, and to be guided by their perception of their needs. This approach is exemplified in an Indian case study (Dogra et al., 2005).

In the current technological era we need to consider how to make best use of advanced knowledge across countries and cultures. Information and communication technologies are increasingly being used in medical education, and the evidence of efficacy has been the subject of review (Vlacke et al., 2006). Internet training has been used to enhance multicultural exposure in Sweden (Ekblad et al., 2004), and computer technology for child psychiatry supervision of clinicians in Pakistan by child mental specialists in the United Kingdom (Rahman et al., 2006). The author is currently involved in developing Internet supervision for trainees in Sri Lanka. An Australian initiative has produced CD-ROMS for multidisciplinary distance learning in mental health (Tarren-Sweeney and Carr, 2004). The transcultural course at the Institute of Psychiatry is developing Internet-based modules that should eventually become part of a distance-learning package.

CONCLUSION

This chapter has outlined a standard curriculum for child psychiatric extended and adapted for transcultural training. Many aspects of this course could in fact form part of standard training; doing so would promote cultural sensitivity not only for multicultural groups, but also with regard to subcultures within a trainees' own culture and help promote further research on transcultural child and adolescent mental health. The chapter has addressed specifically ways in which transcultural training may be offered by focusing on an international course available in the United Kingdom. This can be complemented by transcultural research links that may in turn help extend the knowledge base in the field.

REFERENCES

Ainsworth, M. *Patterns of Attachment: A Psychological Study of the Strange Situation.* New York: Lawrence Erlbaum Associates, 1978.

Ani, C., and E. Garralda. "Developing primary mental healthcare for children and adolescents." *Current Opinion in Psychiatry* 18 (2005): 440–44.

Bassols, A. M., R. A. Santos, L. A. Rohde, F. Pechansky. "Exposure to HIV in Brazilian adolescents: The impact of psychiatric symptomatology." *European Child Adolescent Psychiatry* 16 (2007): 236–42.

Bhui, Kamaldeep, and Dinesh Bhugra. "Training and supervision in effective cross-cultural mental health services." *Hospital Medicine* 59, no. 11 (November 1998): 861–65.

Bird, H. "Epidemiology of childhood disorders in a cross cultural context." *Journal of Child Psychology and Psychiatry* 37 (1996): 35–49.

Brent, D., S. Gaynor, and V. Weersing. "Cognitive-behavioral approaches to the treatment of depression and anxiety," in *Child and Adolescent Psychiatry*, 4th ed. Oxford: Rutter & Taylor, Blackwell, 2002, 921.

Campos, R., M. Raffaelli, W. Ude, M. Greco, A. Ruff, J. Rolf, C. M. Antunes, N. Halsey, and D. Greco. "Social networks and daily activities of street youth in

Belo Horizonte, Brazil." Street Youth Study Group. *Child Development* 65 (1994): 319–30.

Canino, G, P. E. Shrout, M. Rubio-Stipec, H. R. Bird, M. Bravo, R. Ramirez, L. Chavez, M. Alegria, J. J. Bauermeister, A. Hohmann, J. Ribera, P. Garcia, and A. Martinez-Taboas. "The DSM-IV rates of child and adolescent disorders in Puerto Rico: Prevalence, correlates, service use, and the effects of impairment." *Arch. Gen. Psychiatry* 61 (2004): 85–93.

Celia, S., "Planning Mental Health services for Children and Adolescents in Brazil," in G. Young and P. Ferrari, eds., *Designing Mental Health Services and Systems for Children and Adolescents—A Shrewd Investment*. Philadelphia: Brunner/Maazel, 1998, 61–370.

Collins, P. Y., A. R. Holman, M. C. Freeman, and V. Patel. "What is the relevance of mental health to HIV/AIDS care and treatment programs in developing countries? A systematic review." *Aids* 20 (2006): 1571–82.

Crijnen, A. A. M., T. M. Achenbah, and F. C. Verhulst. "Problems reported by parents of children in multiple cultures: The Child Behavior Checklist syndrome constructs." *American Journal of Psychiatry* (1999): 156, 569–74.

Croll, J. K., D. Neumark-Stzainer, M. Story, and M. Ireland. "Prevalence and risk and protective factors related to disordered eating behaviors among adolescents: Relationship to gender and ethnicity." *Journal of Adolescent Health* (2002): 31, 166–75

de Jong, J., and Van Ommeren. "Combining qualitative and quantitative research in transculatural contexts." *Transcultural Psychiatry* 39, no. 4 (December 2002): 422–33.

Dogra, N., C. Frake, K. Bretherton, K. Dwivedi, and I. Sharma. "Training CAMHS professionals in developing countries: An Indian case study." *Child and Adolescent Mental Health* 10 (2005): 74–79.

Ekblad, S. et al. "The use of international video-conferencing as a strategy for teaching medical students about transculatural psychiatry." *Transcultural Psychiatry* 41, no. 1 (March 2004): 120–29.

Evans, D. L., E. B. Foa, R. E. Gur, H. Hendin, C. P. O'Brien, M. E. P. Seligman, and B. T. Walsh. *Treating and Preventing Adolescent Mental Health Disorders: What We Know and What We Don't Know. A Research Agenda for Improving the Mental Health of Our Nation*. New York: Oxford University Press, 2005.

Fleitlich-Bilyk, B., and R. Goodman. "Prevalence of child and adolescent psychiatric disorders in southeast Brazil." *Journal of American Acad Child Adolescent Psychiatry* 43 (2004): 727–34.

Foulks, E., J. Westermeyer, and K. Ta. "Developing curricula for transculatural mental health for trainees and trainers." *Clinical Methods in Transcultural Psychiatry* (1998): 339–62.

Giel, R., M. V. De Arango, C. E. Climent, T. W. Harding, H. H. A. Ibrahim, L. Ladrigo-Ignacio, R. S. Murthy, M. C. Salazar, N. N. Wig, and Y. O. A. Younie. "Childhood mental disorders in primary health care: Results of obsevations in four developing countries." *Pediatrics* 68 (1981): 677–83.

Goodfriend, M. et al. "A model for training pediatricians to expand mental health services in the community practice setting." *Clinical Pediatrics* 45, no. 7 (2006): 649–54.

Goodman, R., D. Neves dos Santos, A. P. Robatto Nunes, D. Pereira de Miranda, B. Fleitlich-Bilyk, N. Almeida Filho. "The Ilha de Mare study: A survey of child mental health problems in a predominantly African-Brazilian rural community." *Soc. Psychiatry Psychiatr. Epidemiol.* 40 (2005a): 11–17.

Goodman, R., H. Slobodskaya, and G. Kayazev. "Russian child mental health: A cross-sectional study of prevalence and risk factors." *European Child and Adolescent Psychiatry.* 1 (2005b): 28–33.

Guarnaccia, P. J., I. Martinez, R. Ramirez, and G. Canino. "Are *ataques de nervios* in Puerto Rican children associated with psychiatric disorder?" *Journal of the American Academy of Child and Adolescent Psychiatry,* 44 (2005): 1184–92.

Hackett, R, L. Hackett, and P. Bhakta. "The prevalence and associations of psychiatric disorder in children in Kerala, South India." *Journal of Child Psychology & Psychiatry* 40 (1999): 801–7.

Health Advisory Service (HAS). *Child and Adolescent Mental Health Services: Together We Stand.* London: HMSO, 1995.

Higginbotham, N., and A. Marsella. "International consultation and the momogenization of psychiatry in Southeast Asia." *Society of Scientific Medicine* 27, no. 5 (1988): 553–61.

Hodes, M. "A core curriculum for child and adolescent psychiatry." *European Child and Adolescent Psychiatry* 7, no.4 (December 1998): 250–54.

Institute of Psychiatry. "Masters in Child and Adolescent Mental Health." http://www.iop.kcl.ac.uk/courses/?id=12. (accessed July 18, 2007).

Jenkins, R. "Health services research and policy," in Kamaldeep Bhui and Dinesh Bhugra, eds., *Culture and Mental Health.* London: Hodder Arnold, 2007, pp. 70–86.

Jones, L., A. Rrustemi, M. Shahini, and A. Uka. "Mental health services for war affected children: Report of a survey in Kosovo." *British Journal of Psychiatry* 183 (2003): 540–46.

Kapur, M. *Internalising Disorders in Mental Health of Indian Children.* New Delhi: Sage Publications, 1995.

Karabekiroglu, K. et al. "Child and adolescent psychiatry training in Europe: Differences and challenges in harmonisation." *European Child and Adolescent Psychiatry* 15, no. 8 (2006): 467–75.

Karnik, N., N. Dhogra, and P. Vostanis. "Child psychiatry across cultures," in Kamaldeep Bhui and Dinesh Bhugra, eds., *Textbook of Cultural Psychiatry.* (In press.)

Kim, W. J. "Child and adolescent psychiatry workforce: A critical shortage and national challenge." *Academic Psychiatry* 27, no. 4 (2003): 277–82.

Kleinman, A. "Anthropology and psychiatry: The role of culture in cross-cultural research on illness." *British Journal of Psychiatry* 151 (1987): 447–54.

Knapp, M., and J. Henderson. "Health economics perspectives and evaluation of child and adolescent mental health services." *Current Opinion in Psychiatry* 12, no. 4 (1999): 393–97.

Lalor, K. J. "Street children: A comparative perspective." *Child Abuse Negl.* 23 (1999): 759–70.

Lansford, J. et al. "Ethnic differences in the link between physical discipline and later adolescent externalising behaviors." *Journal of Child Psychology and Psychiatry* 45 (2004): 801–12.

Malhotra, S. "Challenges in providing mental health services for children and adolescents in India," in J. G. Young and P. Ferrari, eds., *Designing Mental Heath Services and Systems for Children and Adolescents: A Shrewd Investment.* Philadelphia: Brunner/Mazel, 1998, pp. 321–34.

Malhotra, S., and S. K. Chaturvedi. "Patterns of childhood psychiatric disorders in India." *Indian Journal of Pediatrics* 51, no. 409 (1984): 235–40.

Malhotra, S., A. Kohli, and P. Arun. "Prevalence of psychiatric disorders in school children in India." *Indian Journal of Medical Research* 116 (2002): 21–28.

March, J. S. et al. "Using and teaching evidence-based medicine: The Duke University child and adolescent psychiatry model." *Child and Adolescent Psychiatric Clinics of North America* 14, no. 2 (2005): 273–96.

McCarty, C., and J. Weisz. "Culture, coping, and context: Primary and secondary control among Thai and American youth." *Journal of Child Psychology and Psychiatry* 40, no. 5 (1999): 809–18.

Meltzer, H., R. Gatwood, R. Goodman, and T. Ford. *Mental Health of Children and Adolescents in Great Britain.* London: TSO, 2000.

Mullick, M. S., and R. Goodman. "The prevalence of psychiatric disorders among 5-10 year olds in rural, urban and slum areas in Bangladesh: An exploratory study." *Soc. Psychiatry Psychiatr. Epidemiol.* 40 (2005): 663–71.

Nikapota, A. D. "Culture and ethnic issues in service provision," in Rutter and Taylor, eds., *Child and Adolescent Psychiatry,* 4th ed. Oxford: Blackwell, 2002.

Oleke, C., A. Blystad, and O. B. Rekdal. "When the obvious brother is not there: Political and cultural contexts of the orphan challenge in northern Uganda." *Soc. Sci. Med.* 61 (2005): 2628–38.

Palen, L. A., E. A. Smith, L. L. Caldwell, A. J. Fllisher, and E. Mpofu. "Substance use and sexual risk behavior among South African high school students." *Journal of Adolescent Health* 39 (2006): 761–63.

Patel, V., and A. Sumathipala. "International representation in psychiatric journals: A survey of 6 leading journals." *British Journal of Psychiatry* 178 (2001): 406–9.

Patel, V., A. L. Fisher, A. D. Nikapota, and S. Malhotra. "Promoting child mental health in low and middle income countries." *Journal of Child Psychology and Psychiatry.* (Accepted for publication.)

Prince, M. "The epidemiological method and its contribution to international and cross cultural comparative mental health research," in Kamaldeep Bhui and Dinesh Bhugra, eds., *Culture and Mental Health.* New York: Hodder Arnold, 2007, pp. 24–36.

Rahman, A., A. Nizami, A. Minhas, R. Niazi, M. Slatch, and F. E. Minhas. "Mental health in Pakistan: A pilot study of training and supervision in child psychiatry using the internet." *Psychiatric Bulletin* 30, no. 4 (April 2006): 149–52.

Remschmidt, H. "Changing views: New perspectives in child psychiatric research." *European Child and Adolescent Psychiatry* 5, no. 1 (1996): 2–10.

Richman, N. "Annotation: Children in situations of political violence." *Journal of Child Psychology and Psychiatry* 34, no. 8 (1993): 1286–1302.

Robertson, B. A., K. Ensink, C. D. Parry, and D. Chalton. "Performance of the Diagnostic Interview Schedule for Children Version 2.3 (DISC-2.3) in an informal settlement area in South Africa." *Journal of American Acad. Child Adolescent Psychiatry* 38 (1999): 1156–64.

Royal College of Psychiatrists. Child and Adolescent Psychiatry Specialist Advisory Sub-Committee (1999). A Higher Specialist Training Committee paper. London. http://www. rcpsych.ac.uktraindev.

Royal College of Psychiatrists. *Report of the Overseas Working Group Council Report CR93.* London: Royal College of Psychiatrists, 2001.

Rutter, M., and J. Silberg. "Gene-environment interplay in relation to emotional and behavioral disturbance." *Annual Review Psychol.* 53 (2002): 463–90.

Rutter, M., J. Silberg, T. O'Connor, and E. Simonoff. "Genetics and child psychiatry: Advances in quantitative and molecular genetics. *Journal of Child Psychology and Psychiatry* 40 (1999): 3–18.

Rutter, M., J. Tizard, and K. Whitmore, eds. *Education, Health and Behavior.* New York: Robert E. Kreiber Publishing, 1970.

Rutter, M., J. Tizard, W. Yule, P. Graham, and and K. Whitmore. "Research report: Isle of Wight studies 1964–1974. *Psychological Medicine* 6 (1976): 313–32.

Sargent, J. et al. "Assessment of competency in child and adolescent psychiatry training." *Academic Psychiatry* 28, no. 1 (2004): 18–26.

Saxena, S., G. Paraje, P. Sharan, G. Karam, and R. Sadana. "The 10/90 divide in mental health research: Trends over a 10-year period." *British Journal of Psychiatry* 188 (2006): 81–82.

Somasundaram, D. J., and W. A. van de Put. "Management of trauma in special populations after a disaster." *Journal of Clinical Psychiatry* 67, supplement 2 (2006): 64–73.

Srinath, S., S. C. Girimaji, G. Gururaj, S. Seshadri, D. K. Subbakrishna, P. Bhola, and N. Kumar. "Epidemiological study of child & adolescent psychiatric disorders in urban & rural areas of Bangalore, India." *Indian Journal of Med. Res.* 122 (2005): 67–79.

Tarren-Sweeney, M., and V. Carr. "Principles for development of multidisciplinary mental health learning modules for undergraduate, postgraduate and continuing education." *Education for Health* 17, no. 2 (July 2004): 204–12.

Thabet, A. A., Y. Abed, and P. Vostanis. "Emotional problems in Palestinian children living in a war zone." *The Lancet* 359 (2002): 1801–4.

Vlacke, M. and B. de Wever. "Information and communication technologies in higher education: evidence-based practices in medical education" *Medical Teacher* 28 (2006): 40–48.

van Ijzedoorn, M. H., and A. Sagi. "Cross-cultural patterns pf attachment: Universal and contextual dimensions," in J. Cassidy and P. H. Shaver, eds., *Handbook of Attachment: Theory, Research and Clinical Applications.* New York: Guildford Press, 1999, pp. 713–34.

Verhulst, F. and T. Achenbach. "Empirically based assessment and taxonomy of psychopathology: Cross-cultural applications." *European Child and Adolescent Psychiatry* 4 (1995): 61–76.

Watanabe, H. "Child Psychiatry training for paediatricians: Japanese perspectives in infant psychiatry." *Psychiatry & Clinical Neurosciences* 52 (December 1998): 285–87.

Weisz, J. R., C. A. McCarty, K. L. Eastman, W. Chaiyasit, and S. Suwanlert. "Developmental psychopathology and culture: Ten lessons from Thailand," in S. S. Luthar, J. A. Burack, D. Cicchetti, and J. R. Weisz, eds., *Developmental Psychopathology:*

Perspectives on Adjustment, Risk, and Disorder. Cambridge: Cambridge University Press, 1997, pp. 568–92.

Wild, L., A. J. Flisher, A. Bhana, and C. Lombard. "Associations among adolescent risk behaviors and self-esteem in six domains." *Journal of Child Psychology and Psychiatry* 45 (2004): 1454–67.

Wolff, P. H., and G. Fesseha. "The orphans of Eritrea: What are the choices?" *American Journal of Orthopsychiatry* 75 (2005): 475–84.

World Health Organization. *Child Mental Health and Psychosocial Development. Technical report.* Series 613. Geneva: WHO, 1977.

World Health Organization. *Regional Gguidelines for the Development of Health-promoting Schools. A Framework for Action.* Geneva: WHO, 1992.

World Health Organization. *Life Skills Education in Schools.* Geneva: Programme on Mental Health, World Health Organization, 1997.

World Health Organization. *Atlas: Child & Adolescent Mental Health Resources.* Geneva: WHO, 2005a.

World Health Organization. *Mental Health Atlas.* Geneva: WHO, 2005b.

11

Setting Up a Mental Health Care Program with Children in Situations of Wars, Disasters, or Crises

Twenty Years of a Humanitarian Experience

Dalila Rezzoug, Thierry Baubet, Christian Lachal, Oliver Taïeb, Gessine Sturm, T. Ferradji, and Marie Rose Moro

INTRODUCTION

Medical activities in emergency situations such as natural catastrophes, wars, or refugee camps are now common practice. They have been defined and evaluated. Psychological and psychiatric evaluations and treatment activities and experience in this field are more recent. Are medical emergencies of this kind also a psychological emergency? If so, how do we plan, implement, and evaluate the effectiveness of psychological interventions? We do not yet have operational criteria which allow us to define why, when, and how to set up a mental health care mission. We therefore need to better define our perception of humanitarian psychiatry. This is not enough to define operational criteria but there are now a lot of situations that have been experienced and we can say that we have made "good progress." We have to take into account the recent evolution of humanitarian psychiatry over the last twenty years. Here, we suggest some basic ideas as an outline for guidelines on setting up mental health care missions.

A BRIEF HISTORY

Since 1989, we have been actively involved in setting up a number of mental health programs, mainly in Armenia, Palestine, Kosovo, Rwanda, Sierra Leone, Afghanistan, Guatemala, and Peru, but also in Columbia, Sudan, and Indonesia.

Armenia

Our first assignment was in Armenia after the earthquake in early 1989. This terrible earthquake encouraged us to answer such questions and to establish a new framework for intervention adapted to the seriousness of the situation and to the political, geographical, cultural, and social contexts. This pioneering experience was forced on us by the intensity of the psychological distress experienced in the field, especially among children.

On December 7, 1988, one of the most deadly earthquakes of the previous twenty years took place in Armenia. In a population of 3.3 million in Soviet Armenia, an estimated 25,000 to 100,000 people died. Another 15,000 people were wounded and 500,000 to 700,000 left homeless, bringing the total of those affected to close to 60 percent of the population living in the region of the earthquake.

In order to manage with the specificity of the context and our way of working (to help the children and to respect the possibilities of the professionals and the parents and to train the psychologists and psychiatrists), we decided on a plan of action-training (doing things *with* them), rather than the choice of substitution (doing things *instead* of them) or affiliation (affiliating them to a psychoanalytic school, for example). We thought of this action-training plan as true cobuilding between the Armenians and ourselves. It was therefore necessary to train the Armenians in a local clinic. Our goal was to welcome the children who had suffered from the earthquake, to treat them, and to take this opportunity to train local teams who would then be able to accomplish this work on their own. Given the urgency and the lack of clinical training we chose a very pragmatic solution. The work would be done by the Armenians themselves, under the supervision and training of the French—a kind of on-the-job training, day to day, according to the care needed.

Taking into account all of these clinical and technical difficulties, we defined the operating principles of a permanent care center associating clinicians and educators, French and Armenians, care and training. Within this context, these principles had to be as economical and practical as possible; that is, starting with local possibilities, whatever their advantages and limitations.

West Bank and Gaza

Another different mission was an exploratory mission to the occupied Palestinian Territories in the West Bank and Gaza where we were to establish the criteria necessary for starting a mental health mission. Strangely enough, these criteria were all assembled in the situation in Palestine at that time. The needs and the means were there—people traumatized by the seven years of the first Intifada, especially the children, adolescents, and families who had taken an active part in the conflict; the director of a Palestinian NGO (nongovernmental organization) who had come to Paris requesting Medecins sans Frontieres's (MSF) help; a network of local professionals to work with and train in the field who had a concept of psychology and psychopathology that was reasonably similar to our own; MSF's desire to be involved just as the Washington peace accords were attracting hundreds of NGOs into Palestine.

It was an ambitious project—setting up a consultation center for children and their families who were suffering from secondary problems having lived through the first Intifada; the staff were mixed, each expatriate team member having his or her professional Palestinian counterpart. We set up the project with a Palestinian NGO, who was to take it over after the initial phase. The place: Jenin, a town which had been very militant during the first Intifada, and therefore had many victims, far beyond the reach of all the humanitarian organizations then flocking to Gaza. The time: shortly afterward. The Washington accords had just been signed, security wasn't a serious problem, and it was time to care of the "hidden wounds" of this sad period.

And yet, while all the elements necessary for a successful program seemed to be in place, the project suffered a series of setbacks and was closed down at the end of eighteen months, having failed to reach all its objectives. The main reason for this closure was that after the acute period the professionals, but even more so the parents, were able and wanted to take care of their children alone; they did not need us any more. When setting up a mental health program, the evolution of the social, cultural, and political contexts is critical—whether in giving the project its positive and dynamic impetus, or, on the contrary, in impeding its development and effectiveness.

Other highly successful programs have been set up in haste and amid all sorts of difficulties and uncertainty. This was the case, for example, with a program aimed at helping released detainees from Israeli prisons after the Oslo accords. We had to work with a Palestinian team who, for the most part, were ex-prisoners themselves, and who themselves had problems—however, it was forbidden to mention them. This demonstrates the difference between the collective and the individual aspects of trauma: one can talk about the collective experience of the suffering endured in prison, of

semiparalysed or confining its activity to Gaza City where certain populations were deemed important for political reasons, namely, families of the
martyred or wounded, and so we needed to provide substitute care. This did
not exclude collaborating closely with the people already in place; on the
contrary, we invested heavily and immediately in the team—the translators,
the drivers, and all the staff without whom this kind of work (which involved immediate access to the Gaza community and its families) would
have been impossible.

The fourth point was for us to move about, to go out to the people who
were unable to come to us: the project was designed to be mobile. In fact,
the people themselves knew very well what help they needed, whether this
be medical or psychological care, or both. The fifth point was to quickly assemble a mixed team of doctor and psychologist. Strangely enough, the
objections to the project had less to do with problems of security—a crucial
issue, nevertheless—or the criteria we had identified, than with a clinical
discussion about posttraumatic stress disorder (PTSD): we knew how to
treat PTSD, we knew about the problems that would surface some time *after* the trauma, but we had no idea about treatment *during* conflict or war,
at the very moment these traumas occur.

There are many other examples to illustrate the following point: that at
the present time it is difficult to be absolutely definitive about the criteria
for setting up a mental health mission. We believe that such criteria need to
be drawn up separately for each individual project after an initial evaluation, which takes into account not only our previous experience, but also
the discussions, which, as we have seen, can sometimes raise unexpected issues. These are all issues that psychologists and psychiatrists simply must
address. The arguments *against* setting up a project are just as important as
those *for*; they allow for careful elaboration, even though psychologists and
psychiatrists see them as presumptions. We shall now discuss some of these,
and then attempt to extract some generally agreed principles for setting up
mental health care missions in a humanitarian situation.

SOME PRESUMPTIONS IN HUMANITARIAN PSYCHIATRY

Humanitarian Psychiatry is a Superfluous Luxury
When There Are so Many Unmet Medical Needs

We shall quote Dominique Martin, an MSF head of mission (1995: 18)
who made the point that "Humanitarian aid is not only concerned with
physiological needs; it must take into account the complexity of Man, his
very being. Restoring his capacity to choose freely and to influence the
world is as essential as providing him with food, shelter and medical care."

We can add to this a certain number of additional arguments, especially for the children. The first is quantitative: the high incidence of psychological problems in the context of war is now a well-established fact for babies, children, and adolescents (Moro and Lebovici, 1995, 1998; Rousseau, 2003; Rezzoug and Co., 2005). This means that we are not talking about exceptional cases or people who are especially fragile or sensitive, but about a health issue of considerable importance. The most vulnerable (infants, children, adolescents, or women), those who are present with an illness or a deficiency are particularly affected.

There is consensus about the almost obvious conclusion to be drawn from this: that psychological intervention should be introduced *after* certain urgent and primary measures have been implemented. It is a question of intervention strategy (Moro and Lebovici, 1995), but the rule *psychological after somatic aid* is not an absolute one. We have seen (as in Gaza) that the medical and the somatic can function concurrently. We can also mention the mother-infant program in Hebron, which targets the dyads and the families where a child's life is in danger due to malnutrition—often severe—associated with the mother's psychological problems. Baubet, Gaboulaud, and Grouiller (2003) carried out a study of this program, and demonstrated the importance of *psychological care* first in certain cases: Of the 382 children studied over the four-and-a-half-year program, 57 percent presented with malnutrition as the result of an isolated psychological cause. With an average treatment time of five months, 65 percent of the children had improved (i.e., had not died from malnutrition) and had started to put on weight; 5 percent had died.

Treating People with Psychological Problems Resulting from War Makes no Sense, Since Such People are Not "Sick" in the True Sense of the Word

We know that this problem exists and how to tackle it (as in Gaza) by identifying families, groups, or geographical zones which are particularly at risk. We can also ask ourselves, as in a refugee camp in Sierra Leone: Do we treat everyone? How are we going to decide who does/doesn't need our help? Among all these children who have been through the same traumatic experiences, how do we identify "the traumatized"? To clarify these issues, it is useful to distinguish several *levels of psychological suffering*. It is true that many children experience traumatic events that do not trigger any significant problems; others, on the contrary, develop problems that can be very incapacitating. It is difficult to define each individual's resilience, his vulnerability, or his breaking point. Once this stage has been reached, the person will appear with genuine psychological problems, even though he was previously "normal," that is, before experiencing the traumatic events/the war. Our first priority is therefore to distinguish very carefully between the traumatic experience (the horror of the events), the reactions that should be considered as normal adaptations to such events, and those that should be described as pathological.

When you work with small groups of people who have been through the same experiences together, you note that they can *clearly identify* those among them who are suffering beyond the limits that the group recognizes as "normal." It is therefore extremely important to take note of what *they* take to be an indication of suffering or failure to adjust. An example of this comes from the Kenema Refugee Camp in Sierra Leone: If an adolescent refuses to go and fetch wood, or to take part in other communal duties, there is obviously something very wrong—it is a cry for help which has real meaning for the entire community. Another example in another context: a little boy of five or six, in Tabbah, southern Gaza. We were in a house that had been half-destroyed by Israeli gunfire. The families living there were all together in a room on the ground floor. Shots flew past the house as we talked, and the acrid smell of tear gas was everywhere. This is to say that everybody in that room—including ourselves—was frightened; we were all experiencing the same *traumatic event*. And yet, the mothers identified this one particular child as suffering psychologically, as being traumatized.

When we carry out this process of identification and differentiation, it is important not to label people as "sick"; at the same time we must not forget the—sometimes very serious—impact such events can have. In collective terms, we have learned that the *most vulnerable* individuals within a population (infants, adolescents, women), and in a wider context, *vulnerable populations*, help us identify needs and determine our intervention methods more accurately.

Treating People When War or Conflict is Ongoing Makes Even Less Sense, Since They Will be Repeatedly Retraumatized

There are two clinical points to distinguish and consider: the issues of *recurrent and accumulated traumas* and *when to intervene*. It is a fact that we always work with people who have accumulated traumatic events and very rarely with those who have just had a single experience. Bereavement, loss of all kinds, inhuman acts, fear, lack of schooling, violence (both inflicted, as well as received), deprivation: the number of blows to a person's integrity is often far greater than the traumatic event itself. It is not necessarily the same people who are traumatized each time, but it is often the case that an individual person experiences a series of traumas—a series of losses, several attacks, a number of constraints, and the like. We are always faced with complex individual or family backgrounds. Traumatic events are an integral part of these backgrounds—they are not something external, a "foreign body" that can be extracted like a bullet from a wound. They are interwoven with memories, with the collective account of events, and with the way in which a particular community construes and portrays what is (and what is not) traumatic.

The second issue (direct intervention during ongoing conflict versus delayed "dressing of psychological wounds") has made us revise our working practices in line with military psychiatry for some of our projects. If one follows military principles of care—for instance, those of Salmon (1917)—it is better to intervene immediately, in situ, and provide basic care, which focuses on symptoms. The moment of intervention (the "when") determines the problems needing treatment and the way in which such care will be managed (the "how").

One of the distinctive aspects of working in the middle of a war is to see at close hand what people are going through, to be plunged into "the eye of the storm" with them: the storm destroys everything around you, but at the center of it, there is a strange sense of stability—what might be called the "neoculture" of war and survival. Being there at that moment obviously reduces the distance that always exists between caregivers and receivers to a minimum, but it is impossible to say whether this emergency care has a preventative value in terms of reducing the impact of future trauma. In Goradje, Hebron, in places where the conflict is ongoing, we are more concerned with psychological *intensive care* (helping the most damaged to get over a critical phase) than with curative or preventative issues. Deciding on the right time to start a mental health mission does not just depend on clinical judgement. The political philosophy of the NGO, its standpoint in a particular country, security—these are all factors to be taken into consideration. A conflict is always perceived and interpreted in different ways, and psychological input has to fit into the sometimes contradictory ebb and flow of such perceptions.

The Cultural Differences between Caregivers and Receivers Are Such that Mental Health Care is Impossible

One might think from the above that this is a problem specific to mental health and therefore not relevant to surgeons or nutritionists; this is absolutely not the case. An international literature review on problems of nutrition in humanitarian settings clearly demonstrated the importance of *cultural factors* in malnutrition and its management (Baubet et al., 2003a). In terms of mental health, we often work in contexts where the local traditional methods can be very different—even contradictory—to our own. This is true of humanitarian medicine in general. In certain famine situations, the elderly (as the guarantors of social cohesion) claim priority for food, whereas our moral hierarchy would feed the most vulnerable and the

These examples may illustrate how much the work with an interpreter increases the degree of complexity of the interrelations in therapy. Coping with this complexity demands a clear definition of the therapeutical setting and of the role the interpreter is supposed to take. It may also be extremely helpful to discuss the emotional dynamics of the triangular relation between patient, interpreter, and therapist with the interpreter in order to help him to deal with the challenges relied to his intermediate position. In supervision settings, the discussion of the emotional dynamics of the therapeutic relationship should include an analysis of the patient's transference on the interpreter and the interpreter's countertransference on the patient.

Talking about Cultural Representations and Emic Conceptions of Distress

Symbolization and the construction of narrations play a central role in psychotherapy with children and their parents. This is why we should think about the way we work with cultural representations patients use as frames in their narrations: theories about the origins of their pain and the possibilities of healing, conceptions of family and social bounds, religious or metaphysical conceptions of the world, and ideologies or positions in a field of political conflicts. Anthropology of the last decades has shown that these frames are constantly changing, transformed by globalization, mass media, and the dialogue between different symbolic systems (Hannerz, 1991). This means that we have to deal with the dynamic character of collective representations and the interrelation of different symbolic universes. Translation and the shifting between different social and symbolic universes becomes a central aspect of therapy. If we insist on the importance of collective representations, this does not mean that patients reproduce them without any transformation. On the contrary, collective representations may be used in a very personal way. They may be commented, questioned, or reinterpreted; they may be reorganized in a *bricolage* using different symbolic universes. In any case, they play a central role for the process of symbolization in therapy (Moro, 1998b).

Cultural representations provide a frame for the construction of narrations and help to establish connections between the present and the past or to think about the sense of painful or frightening experiences. Sometimes they may help bridging gaps between disconnected aspects of the patient's life experience. In other cases they permit acceptance of the experience of rupture and the impossibility to attribute a sense to certain experiences. Cultural representations may also help patients communicate their suffering to their social environment, molding subjective experience into a narration formulated in socially acceptable terms.

If we learn how to discuss cultural representations, we not only help children and parents use their symbolic resources. We also have the possibility of creating a dialogue about different symbolic universes, different social environments, and different periods in the patient's life. While engaging in such a discussion about cultural frames and contexts, we introduce a double dialogue into therapy. We create a dialogue about the patient's history, his feelings and his inner-psychic conflicts, and complete this dialogue with a discussion about the different social and symbolic universes he refers to. French clinical approaches have insisted on the necessity of such a double dialogue in transcultural therapies (Nathan, 1986; Moro 1998a). In accordance with the propositions made by George Devereux (1985), the two levels of the therapeutic dialogue should not be confounded. This means that we should avoid "psychological interpretations" with regard to collective representations. Rather, we should consider them as a frame or a container the patient uses in order to think and communicate his subjective experience. Transcultural therapies are characterized by a constant shifting between a discussion about the social and symbolic contexts patients introduce and the inner psychic dynamics they express in their narrations.

Mental Health Care is Time-Consuming, Costly in Terms of Human Resources, and Directed at so Few People that It Is Not Worth the Trouble

There is no doubt that psychological temporality is different from factual temporality. This is why, at first, it was thought that mental health care projects could not coincide with emergency situations involving care for millions of people at the same time; mental health care on that scale does not, in fact, exist anywhere. This has prompted some NGOs to use a psychosocial or community approach that aims to mobilize and train mental health workers in basic skills so that they can treat or help a greater number of people. As already mentioned, this is also what drives us to look for more rapid treatment methods: we target the trauma, we use very quick techniques (debriefing), and those workers who seem best able to implement such methods are targeted for accelerated training schemes. Unfortunately, the effectiveness of these techniques is far from established; they may even, at times, prove to be more harmful than therapeutic (Summerfield, 1995). In addition, to isolate the trauma and to focus solely on the PTSD is to ignore a large number of contextual problems and reactions which—although linked to war or displacement—cannot strictly be considered as part of the posttraumatic state (e.g., depressive, anxious or psychotic states, bereavement, psychosomatic problems, etc., or, in children, difficulties with sleeping, learning, feeding, enuresis, etc.).

MSF, along with other French NGOs, has opted for a dual strategy: to *measure the complexity of situations* and at the same time, to *set limits*. Sierra Leone, for example, has no mental health care system to speak of—virtually no psychologists and only one psychiatrist to cover the whole country. There is no way we can pretend we are going to resolve problems on a nationwide scale. And so, our decision has been to select a refugee camp for *returnees*[3] where we have set up training mental health auxiliaries who will benefit from complementary training provided by other NGOs. In Gaza, we go out to the families who live in precise zones of the Gaza Strip. Such decisions and ways of working do not mean that we are unaware of the country as a whole; they are objectives, which, although sometimes challenging, are attainable within our limitations. The therapies we offer are not particularly time-consuming (indeed in some cases, they can be of very short duration) but they must be adapted—on a number of levels—to the complexity of a situation: the social group, the family, the mother and child, the individual. The worst possible thing is to do nothing because we can't provide care for everyone; on the other hand, we must not delude ourselves by thinking we can deal with the traumas of an entire population.

We could analyse many other common presumptions. For example, psychologists and psychiatrists differ so widely in their conception of psychological problems and their treatment methods that it is impossible to draw up guidelines or standardized techniques. Programs revolve around the notion of PTSD and those people who have reactional, rather than chronic, pathologies—independent of war or disaster. Since the programs do not focus on the mentally ill, they exclude the very people most in need of help. On this last point, I would simply say that although the mentally ill do not fall into the target population for most mental health programs, they tend to be included anyway, since they figure among the most vulnerable and fragile. In the mother-baby project in Hebron, for example, our initial objectives did not include the care of children with developmental pathologies (genetic, perinatal, etc.). A significant number of these children were nonetheless included in the program because they were malnourished; their mothers were unable to feed them because of complex problems and the vicious circle of a personal pathology influenced by a number of other factors: psychological, familial, economic, and the like.

WHY? WHEN? HOW?

Having made the above points, we think it is clear that at the present time, we do not have the operational criteria that allow us to respond to these issues in any definitive way. It is worth remembering that mental health care programs in MSF have been in place for some twenty years since the Ar-

WHY? Ethics in humanitarian psychiatry
- Fight "inhumanity" with humanitarianism.
- Populations in danger.
- Needs to be identified by us and by the people themselves.
- Specific damage to social structure.
- Humanitarian space/an enclave of humanity.

WHEN? A question of strategy
- When we can associate the moral and political representation of the facts with a psychological and cultural one.
- When the situation is urgent.
- When a population requests help.
- When it is logistically feasible (criteria).
- When there are no time constraints (duration).

HOW? Constructing "resilient" programs
- Take into account local resources.
- Take into account NGO resources.
- Work with cultural mediators: the "scouts."
- The five aims of a mental health program: To console, to provide care, to provide training, to witness, to evaluate input.
- Make clinical work the core of the program.

Figure 11.1.   Why, when, and how to set up a mental health program?

menian project after the earthquake in Gumry in 1988 and since this date in MSF France we have organized more than fifty programs and the others MSF sections are doing the same in Belgium, Holland, Spain, Switzerland, and, more recently, New York (Etherington et al., 2007). We will nonetheless attempt to make some basic suggestions as a prelude to establishing recommendations for the implementation and follow-up of mental health missions. In the interest of clarity, we have detailed five parameters for each of the three questions in the title: Why, When, How (see figure 11.1).

Why? A Question of Ethics

Our primary motivation in setting up a program is a *moral* one: people have experienced suffering, loss, and the constraints imposed upon them by war or disaster. Their own resources are insufficient to cope with this, and they need help. This is a simple premise, but one which needs to take into account both the type of suffering and its causes.

Fight Inhumanity with Humanitarianism

Numerous psychological strategies are used during conflict. War does not only use weapons to kill and injure, it perfects methods—whether instinctively

discussed, but other factors tend to get in the way—the NGO's political philosophy, the current situation in a given country, the gathering of witness reports, and the like. We are ready to implement a program when:

We Move from Empathy to Trauma and from Witnessing to Care

We decide to associate the moral and political representation of the facts with a psychological and cultural one. This is the transition from *empathy* to *trauma*: aid workers obviously feel empathy for the distressed populations with whom they work. Their first reaction is to say "This is awful—we must bring in some psychologists to help these poor people." We have to get past this initial emotional reaction, which is of short duration, and move on to a *clinical* approach, which may or may not focus on concepts of traumatism and the posttraumatic state. In the same way, the legal aspect—more and more a part of humanitarian work—will reveal situations where people are suffering as a direct result of attacks on their integrity (communal, familial, physical, and psychological). Here, we move from humanitarian rights to considering the harm done when individuals and their culture are the objects of violence: how this modifies such things as child care, growing up, adolescence, starting a family, and the like. Everyday human behavior can be greatly impaired when basic rights are denied or ridiculed. Here again, we have to make the transition from *rights* to *intervention*, from *witnessing* to *care*.

The Situation is Urgent

This may be due to a medical emergency (the infants in Hebron, for example, could have died from malnutrition without psychological intervention), or an emergency in terms of the current situation (as in Gaza, where the living conditions imposed by war necessitated both medical and psychological input).

A Population Requests Help

Requests for help may be either direct or indirect, for instance, when the local medical teams recognize a need for psychological input. Medical and logistical work implies close contact with a population; the teams are therefore ideally placed to identify psychological impairments resulting from war or disaster, and can then request additional psychological/psychiatric help (as in the medical program in the refugee camps in Kenema, Sierra Leone).

It is Logistically Feasible

A minimum level of security is essential—both for expatriates and the local population.[5] It is obviously important that the NGO is in place in the field beforehand—for example, it would have been unthinkable to implement a medicopsychological program in Gaza at the end of 2000 had MSF not been involved in Palestine since 1993.

There are No Time Constraints

Reservations about the length of a project are often raised when discussing mental health programs. In fact, it is possible to provide treatment over relatively short periods of time, that is, ones that last no longer than programs of a purely medical nature. We must, however, bear in mind the following two points: (1) that posttraumatic disorders do not just stop when the war stops—here again, note the vital distinction between events, traumatic experiences, and problems which are secondary to trauma. The postwar phase is one that is busy with the reconstruction process and full of hope—but it is also one that is marked by all sorts of psychological and psychosocial problems. One has to take treatment times into consideration, but above all, we must not forget that certain kinds of posttraumatic problems can be of long duration. (2) It is always necessary to consider the perspective of the mental health program in the context of the war and the postwar phase, and to consider individual experiences alongside the collective experience.

Mental health care does not take place in the abstract; it is strongly influenced by contextual evolution. The personal development of refugees in the Sierra Leone camps, for example, will be greatly affected by being able (or unable) to return to their own villages. On the other hand, this in no way implies that all their psychological problems will be resolved once they return to their homes. We must not confuse the communal *collective background* with each individual's *personal background*, but rather be aware of the way in which the two interact with each other.

How? The Issue of "Resilient" Programs

One of our most crucial problems in designing mental health programs is to make them resilient, that is, solid or strong enough to absorb the shocks caused by the events and difficult contexts that surround them. When we say programs, we are in fact referring more to the people who implement them, because such projects depend above all upon the personalities of the people in the field, whether expatriate or local. So, how can we make our mental health programs sufficiently resilient?

We have to draw up plans that take local resources into account on a number of levels. These resources allow a population to maintain a certain level of organization in the midst of all the upheaval and disarray that war creates—for example, by producing a collective account which lends meaning to traumatic events, even though this account may be a blend of reality and imagination which represents real and imagined fears. Traditional local resources (including familial and group solidarity) which help people cope with psychological, somatic, and physical suffering exist in all societies; we also need to explore the pre-existing care networks and those which will be able to endure and continue afterwards.

Human resources must be evaluated with particular care: professionals, people who can participate in the process, those who have ideas, and can sometimes take on the responsibility for the program. They may be doctors (highly competent, but caught up in the maelstrom of war) or carers with varying levels of training, but they can also be social workers, teachers, volunteers, and the like. The associative network has an important role to play: we depend on this to help run programs, but also with a view to taking them over or continuing them should the NGO decide to withdraw. The issue of taking over projects is always an important part of the logistics of humanitarian aid, that is, ensuring that the people we help do not become dependent on us, and can eventually utilize our input to help themselves.

On the other hand, we must not worry if they take over and run programs in a way that is different to ours. There have been a number of programs that have developed along very different lines from those we had at first imagined, namely, in the West Bank. The project in Jenin consisted of a consultation center providing psychological support for children and families, which was due to be taken over by a trained local team and the NGO which had requested our help. In fact, by the end of the first year, the team had broken up and its members dispersed throughout the new Palestinian administration to become school psychologists, project managers, and the like. As they were still able to utilize their skills in their new surroundings, the project was closed down.

NGO resources also need to be considered. We would just emphasize two points. The methods employed by psychologists and psychiatrists involve a great deal of personal investment: to counteract this, they have to be able to stand back from their work and put it into perspective, which is why we try to ensure we set up supervision systems. Advice and support from consultants is also valuable. Planning is an essential phase in mental health programs and needs to be worked on in more detail.

Collaboration with cultural mediators is of the utmost importance, namely, the translators (who have a fundamental role since they take part in consultations and translate not only the language, but also the culture), the drivers, the logistics experts, the different individuals and members of the community who help NGOs in one way or another. This makes us think of the programs in Palestine, where Israeli psychologists supervised both our expatriate and our Palestinian psychologists, thereby allowing the two sides to communicate with each other in the context of conflict. These mediators open doors for us, they guide us and protect us, and clarify things we might otherwise not understand: they act as our "scouts."

An intervention must integrate the five classical objectives of a mental health program, which are as follows: (1) *to console*—working with a group or a community, and implying presence, dialogue, empathy, and sometimes prevention; (2) *to provide care*—using techniques appropriate to the context; (3) *to provide training*—using tutoring and other more "academic" methods; (4) *to witness*—mindful of the fact that psychologists and psychiatrists have a particular role here, and must clearly differentiate between this and their clinical work; and last, (5) *to evaluate*.

The clinical work must, of course, form the core of the program. There are a number of specificities in clinical psychology and psychiatry: although mental health professionals are part of the medical team, they have their own distinct techniques and pace of work, and it requires efforts on both sides to produce a real medicopsychological collaboration. In my opinion, treatment and concurrent staff training programs in the field cannot be mixed up with social support. An example: street children need both medical and social aid, but we also need to offer them a specific psychological or psychiatric approach. This is not an educational support or just a friendly helping hand, but rather a specific approach that targets the secondary psychological problems caused by their individual backgrounds (Lachal and Co., 2003).

There is a great deal of reflection and rethinking going on in the field of humanitarian psychiatry today. It is a big deal for all the children all over the world.

NOTES

1. Cognitive behavioral-based therapy centered on difficulties encountered by patients.

2. *Cleansing ceremonies* are traditional purification rituals for people who have broken taboos. For such ceremonies in Mozambique and Angola, see Green et al., 1999.

3. Displaced people either within Sierra Leone or in Guinea and Liberia, and unable to return to their region because of continued fighting.

4. The first, in 1992, was edited by François Jean.

5. We must mention here the possibility of putting certain people at risk as a result of psychological input—namely, when treating combatants—when treatment involves hearing eye-witness accounts, or when setting up healthcare with different factions; even with a comprehensive understanding of the local situation, mistakes are always possible.

REFERENCES

Abdelhak, M. A., and M. R. Moro. "L'interprète en psychothérapie transculturelle," in M. R. Moro, Q. de La Noë, and Y. Mouchenik, eds., *Manuel de Psychiatrie Transculturelle. Travail clinique, travail social.* Grenoble: La Pensée sauvage, 2004, 239–48.

Amselle, J. L. *Logiques métisses. Anthropologie de l'identité en Afrique et ailleurs.* Paris: Payot, 1990.

Arendt, A., *La nature du totalitarisme.* Paris: Payot, 1990.

Baubet, T., C. Desjardins, R. Oosrow, B. Vasset, and E. Drouhin, eds., "Quels soins pour la souffrance psychique des travailleurs humanitaires locaux?" *L'autre* 7, no. 1 (2006): 129–46.

Baubet, T., V. Gaboulaud, K. Grouiller, F. Belanger, P. P. Vandini, P. Salignon, D. Bitar, and M. R. Moro. "Facteurs psychiques dans les malnutritions infantiles en situation de post-conflit. Evaluation d'un programme de soins de dyades mères-bébés malnutris à Hébron (Territoires palestiniens)." *Annales Médico-Psychologiques* 161, no. 8 (2003a): 609–13.

Baubet, T., K. Leroch, D. Bitar, and M. R. Moro, eds., *Soigner malgré tout. vol. 1: Bébés, enfants et adolescents dans la violence.* Grenoble: La Pensée sauvage editor, 2003.

———. *Soigner malgré tout. vol. 1: Traumas, culture et soins.* Grenoble: La Pensée sauvage editor, 2003b.

Baubet, T., and M. R. Moro. "Cultures et soins du trauma psychique en situation humanitaire," in T. Baubet et al., eds., *Soigner malgré tout* (vol. 1). Grenoble: La Pensée Sauvage Editor, 2003c, 71–96.

Beradt, C. *Rêver sous le IIIe Reich.* Paris: Payot/Rivages, 2002.

Devereux, G. *Ethnopsychanalyse complémentariste.* Paris: Flammarion, 1985.

Doray, B. *L'Inhumanitaire ou le cannibalisme guerrier à l'ère néolibérale.* Paris: La Dispute/Snédit, 2000.

Etherington, C., K. Gnauck, N. Levy-Carrick, C. Moore, R. Osrow, and M. Spitzer. *Mental Health in MSF, A White Paper for Internal MSF Review.* June 2007.

Garland, C. *Understanding Trauma. A Psychoanalytical Approach.* London, New York: Karnac Publications, 1999.

Green, E., and A. Honwana. *Indigenous Healing of War-affected Children in Africa.* Washington, DC: IK-Notes, 1999.

Hannerz, U. *Cultural Complexity. Studies in the Social Organisation of Meaning.* New York: Columbia University Press, 1991.

"Hospitality." *L'autre* 6, no. 3. Grenoble: La Pensée sauvage Editor.

Human Rights Watch. *Mauritania's Campaign of Terror: State-Sponsored Repression of Black Africans.* New York: Human Rights Watch, 1994.

Labaume, C. "Paroles d'ex-détenus palestiniens." *L'autre* 1, no. 3 (2000): 531–33.

Lachal, C., and M. R. Moro. "Treatment for sorrow, trapped by war." *Medical News* (2002): 11–16.

Lachal, C., L. Ouss-Ryngaert, and M. R. Moro, eds., *Comprendre et soigner le trauma en situation humanitaire.* Paris: Dunod, 2003.

Lebigot, F. *Soigner les troubles psychotraumatiques.* Paris : Dunod, 2005.

Martin, D. "Psychiatrie et catastrophes: le point de vue d'un humanitaire," in C. Chiland and J. Gerald Young, eds., *Psychiatrie humanitaire en ex-Yougoslavie et en Arménie. Face au traumatisme.* Paris: PUF, 1995: 17–20.

Moro, M. R. "Psychiatric interventions in crisis situations: Working in the former Yugoslavia" *The Signal* 2, no. 1 (1994a): 1–4.

———. "Earthquake in Armenia. Establishment of a psychological care center," in C. Chiland and J. Gerald Young, eds., *Children and Violence. Vol. 11: The Child in the Family.* Northvale, NJ: Aronson, 1994b, 125–44.

———. *Parents en Exil.* Paris: PUF, 1994c.

———. "The Armenian earthquake: The reanimator and the psychiatrist." *Medical News* 7, no. 2 (1998a): 27–43.

———. *Psychothérapie transculturelle des enfants de migrants.* Paris: Dunod, 1998b.

———. "Parents and infants in changing cultural context: immigration, trauma and risk." *Infant Mental Health Journal* 24, no. 3 (2003): 240–64.

———. *Enfants d'ici venus d'ailleurs.* Paris: Hachette, 2004d.

———. *Aimer ses enfants ici et ailleurs. Histoires transculturelles.* Paris: Odile Jacob, 2007.

Moro, M. R., and S. Lebovici, eds. *Psychiatrie humanitaire en ex-Yougoslavie et en Arménie, Face au traumatisme.* Paris: PUF, 1995.

Nathan, T. *La folie des autres. Traité d'ethnopsychiatrie clinique.* Paris: Dunod, 1986.

Obeyesekere, G. *Medusa's Hair.* Chicago: University of Chicago Press, 1981.

———. *The Work of Culture. Symbolic Transformation in Psychoanalysis and Anthropology.* Chicago: University of Chicago Press, 1990.

Rezzoug, D., G. Sturm, and T. Baubet. "Le traumatisme psychique en situation transculturelle." *Psycho-Média* no. 4 (2005): 59–62.

Rousseau, C. "Violence organisée et traumatismes," in T. Baubet and M. R. Moro, eds., *Psychiatrie et Migrations.* Paris: Masson, 2003, 148–54.

Salmon, T. W. "War neuroses (shell-shock). Lectures, illustrated with motion picture films, prepared by direction of the surgeon general for use in the medical officers training camps, N.Y. National Comm. Mental Hygiene. *Mil. Surg.* 41 (1917): 674–93.

Sturm, G. "Les thérapies transculturelles en groupe 'multiculturel.' Une ethnographie de l'espace thérapeutique." Dissertation, University of Paris 13 (France) and Bremen (Germany), 2005.

Summerfield, D. A. "Debriefing after psychological trauma. Inappropriate exporting of western culture may cause additional harm." *BMJ* 311, no. 7003 (1995): 509.

Turner, V. *The Ritual Process. Structure and Anti-structure.* Chicago: Aldine, 1969.

Van Gennep, A. *The Rites of Passage.* London: Routledge, 2004.

12

Child Mental Health Services in War and Peace

Perspectives from Lebanon

John Fayyad, Mariana M. Salamoun, Elie G. Karam, Aimee N. Karam, Zeina Mneimneh, and Caroline C. Tabet

Child mental health awareness and services in most countries are not well developed nor are governmental policies to support them in existence (Belfer, 2007). Depending on the healthcare structure within a given country, promotion and development of child mental health services is dependent on the efforts of individuals and organizations in the private sector as well as nongovernmental organizations. Given the lack of awareness about child mental health needs in the community as well as among policy and decision makers, it is often challenging to create sustainable and long-term programming that necessitates steady availability of funds. This is usually challenging in peacetime, let alone in times of wars and disasters. This chapter will highlight these issues using the country of Lebanon as an example. We begin by addressing the importance of conducting research on a local level, followed by shedding light on the development of child mental health services around specific issues such as child abuse, pervasive developmental disorders, attention deficit hyperactivity disorder (ADHD) and learning disorders, the dissemination of evidence-based practices into the community, as well as the impact of war on child mental health service development.

IS LOCAL RESEARCH IN MENTAL HEALTH IMPORTANT?

While some authors imply that conducting research in mental health on a local level may not be necessary to develop and implement services in developing countries (Rahman, 2000), it is always advisable to align science and practice wherever and whenever possible (Hoagwood, 2003). The development of mental health epidemiologic research in Lebanon illustrates this point.

It was the research efforts of members of the Institute of Development, Research, Advocacy and Applied Care (IDRAAC) and the Department of Psychiatry and Clinical Psychology at the St. George Hospital University Medical Center and Balamand University Faculty of Medicine in Beirut, Lebanon, that shed light on the relation between war and depressive disorders among adults and, along with several cross-national collaborators, noted the higher risk of depression with successive younger birth cohorts (Karam, 1998; Weissman, 1996). These findings caught the eye of governmental officials from the Lebanese Ministry of Health, which paved the way in the aftermath of the 1996 Grapes of Wrath military operation to another epidemiologic study of children and adolescents exposed to war and the implementation of a classroom-based intervention to 2,500 students in six of the most affected villages (Fayyad, 2002; Fayyad, 2003; Karam, 1996, 1997, 2002). Additionally, a group of orphans who lost one or more parents and other family members after the bombing of a UN shelter in Qana were followed prospectively in a comprehensive child-care program that met their psychological, medical, social, and educational needs for many years (Cordahi-Tabet, 2002).

In the area of substance use and abuse, it was commonly held by both local and international observers that rates of substance abuse in Lebanon were high after the years of wars that plagued that country from 1975 until 1990. Epidemiologic research in Lebanon dispelled these beliefs when it was demonstrated that rates of substance abuse and dependence in a large sample of university students were lower than comparable international samples (Karam, 2000). This sample of students was followed a decade later in order to monitor trends over time. Moreover, the team at IDRAAC was commissioned by the United Nations Office of Drug Control and Crime Prevention to conduct a Rapid Situation Assessment of Substance Use and Misuse in Lebanon. Using both qualitative and quantitative methods, this assessment became a national benchmark as the results stemming from it were endorsed by a national Parliamentary committee in charge of creating a national action plan for substance use. Additionally, it was data from this study which revealed that nicotine smoking and substance using adolescents in Lebanon have an onset of use in their early adolescent years leading to the development of various prevention programs targeting this age group and younger ones in schools and in the community (United Nations Office of Drug Control and Crime Prevention).

Given the need to understand the extent and burden of mental disorders on a national scale, Lebanon was the first Arab country to join the World Mental Health Survey Initiative (WMH) led by Harvard University and the World Health Organization (WHO), Geneva. Thus, the first epidemiologic study of a nationally representative sample of Lebanese adults was conducted, highlighting the need for early interventions among children and youth given the early onset of disorders in nearly half of all individuals with disorders (Demyttenaere, 2004; Karam, 2006). In addition, this study shed light on the very low rates of treatment seeking in Lebanon, most of it taking place in the primary health care sector, bringing to the fore the need to raise awareness about mental health as well as improve the readiness of primary care personnel in managing mental disorders. Childhood mental disorders like ADHD were also examined in the WMH Surveys and the cross-national prevalence of adult ADHD was examined in developing and developed countries alike (Lebanon included) bringing to the fore the burden and lifelong impact of ADHD on education, employment, and comorbidity with other conditions (Fayyad, 2007).

Data from this national study has for the first time provided policy makers and officials a portrait of the mental health of the entire Lebanese population along with data on treatment-seeking patterns, burden of mental disorders, as well as their comorbidity with other medical conditions. This has created an opportunity heretofore unprecedented in Lebanon to create a national mental health plan that is based on national data, with reliable and valid information on local needs of the population while at the same time providing comparable data from many other cultures in the world.

The above series of studies illustrate how national research in a developing country can be fundamental in shedding light on local needs with subsequent setting up of local and national programming built on a solid foundation of science.

DEVELOPMENT OF SERVICES FOR AUTISM AND PERVASIVE DEVELOPMENTAL DISORDERS

While awareness efforts can be geared toward global child mental health issues, the public eye is often caught by focusing on one particular set of problems during childhood. One successful example of developing awareness and services around one particular set of disorders is that of pervasive developmental disorders.

A series of pioneering actions have been undertaken by a group of dedicated parents of children with autism who founded the Lebanese Autism

Society (LAS). The LAS advocates for the rights of individuals with autism and provides them and their families with support and services. Since its initiation, it has been involved over the years with activities that address the needs of children and adolescents with autism in Lebanon through emphasizing early diagnosis and intervention with the development of highly structured, specialized educational programs tailored to the individual needs of the children with autism disorders, the promotion and support of the social and economic integration of autistic children and adolescents, supporting and expanding the professional capabilities of personnel and institutions providing services to autistic children in Lebanon, and upgrading public awareness in what relates to autism spectrum disorders.

One of the pioneering projects of the LAS in Lebanon was the development of classes for children with autism by setting up a school integration program that aims at providing special education for children with autism in an integrated academic setting. This was followed by the launching of a technical school for adolescents with autism. Current programming also includes the decentralization of services for families with children affected by autism through training parents and personnel of nongovernmental organizations serving remote regions in Lebanon.

Despite these pioneering efforts, much remains to be done on a national scale as the early identification of autism and related disorders continues to lag among primary care health professionals, and given the paucity of early and special education programs in school settings.

DEVELOPMENT OF SERVICES FOR ADHD AND LEARNING DISORDERS

At the time of drafting a chapter on systems development of child mental health services in developing countries a few years ago, one of the authors (J.F.) detailed the efforts undertaken in Lebanon to raise awareness on ADHD and to make stimulants available for treatment (Fayyad, 2001). The foundation of the Lebanese ADHD Association by the networking of a group of parents and mental health professionals added to the spectrum of services the availability of support groups for parents of children and adolescents with ADHD.

Although there was no organized campaign to raise awareness about ADHD in Lebanon, this awareness increased on a national scale due to two main factors: school lectures and media appearances by child mental health professionals. In the first instance, a concerted effort was made by child mental health professionals to give lectures and conduct workshops on ADHD at schools in various regions in Lebanon targeting school personnel (teachers, councilors, administrators) as well as parents. In the second instance, most local television and radio stations developed an interest in topics related to child development, education, and mental health, and began hosting mental health professionals on talk shows that air during daytime, targeting mostly mothers and homemakers.

Given that academic attainment is highly valued in Lebanese culture, any disorder or condition that impacted learning of children and their academic progress was easily accepted by families as one that needed addressing. Therefore, as awareness about these conditions increased, there was far less stigma about seeking consultation for ADHD and learning disorders for children and adolescents than otherwise anticipated. The impact of school lectures and workshops also served to increase dialogue between parents and school administrators about starting programming at schools to implement special interventions within regular classrooms in order to accommodate students with special needs. While there is no law in Lebanon mandating schools to implement special education procedures within the education setting, many schools have taken it upon themselves to implement individual educational plans and initiatives to develop such programming. Additionally, a law was passed two years ago whereby students with ADHD or learning disorders were exempted from sitting for the official national exams and were allowed to advance to the next academic year based on their school performance alone, thereby optimizing their chances for successful completion of a high school education and transition to university.

Media appearances by professionals also led to media appearances by parents of children with ADHD, learning disorders, and other conditions such as autism and anxiety disorders. This has had a tremendous impact on destigmatizing mental disorders in childhood in the general population as families in their homes heard firsthand accounts of other families' experiences with these disorders on their television and radio sets.

DISSEMINATION OF EVIDENCE-BASED PRACTICES

As awareness about ADHD and behavioral problems in childhood increased, the need for more services in the community increased commensurately. In developing countries, the great lack of qualified child mental health professionals makes specialized services virtually unavailable to many in the general population, let alone issues related to the expense of seeking health care and commuting to centralized tertiary health care facilities. There is therefore a need to disseminate services and practices in a way that makes them accessible to the general population on a wide scale.

In 2002, the World Psychiatric Association (WPA) Presidential Programme on Child Mental Health developed a comprehensive set of tools to address different countries' needs for systematic, evidence-guided treatment of child and adolescent mental health problems. This program consisted of three components: community awareness, prevention, and integrated services. Each of these components was developed by a task force of international experts, under the guidance of a steering committee, and implemented in multiple sites in different countries. The integrated services taskforce included mental health professionals from Lebanon and other developing countries who together participated in implementing manual-based interventions for externalizing and internalizing disorders in childhood in various cultural settings. This project demonstrated the feasibility of taking evidence-based psychological approaches and applying them successfully across diverse cultural settings in preparation for their wider dissemination (Bauermeister, 2006; Jensen, 2006; Murray, 2006; So, 2006).

Following the successful initial testing of this program in the clinical setting, the authors and their colleagues undertook a project of training social and health workers from service centers and dispensaries of the Lebanese Ministry of Social Affairs and Lebanese Ministry of Health respectively in coordination with the Lebanese Higher Council for Children (HCC). In this project, social and health workers from impoverished regions in Lebanon were trained in recognizing common behavioral problems in young children and in administering a manual-based intervention to mothers of children with these problems in their own communities. Each trained worker undertook the screening of mothers who sought services at their local centers followed by training sessions of these mothers to give them appropriate specialized skills in handling their children's behavioral difficulties. The results of this project demonstrated that maternal corporal punishment of the children greatly diminished as did many other negative parental responses with resulting improvement in children's behavioral ratings as well as parent-child relations (IDRAAC, 2006). In addition, another main advantage of this project was making tools that were not available except at specialized clinics widely available within the reach of families who needed them the most and who otherwise would not seek mental health consultation. This project served as a model pilot project that could be replicated and disseminated further into all communities.

PUBLIC AND PRIVATE SECTORS JOIN TOGETHER TO COMBAT CHILD ABUSE

While in some developing countries efforts to combat child abuse or other important social issues may begin with a top-down approach by the decision of a ruling royal family member or a highly influential governmental official to develop these services, in other countries these efforts begin at a grassroots level with individual local nongovernmental organizations each working alone in the absence of central governmental policy on child abuse and neglect. The latter was indeed the situation in Lebanon until a governmental organization, the Higher Council for Children (HCC), grouped under its umbrella a multidisciplinary taskforce of academic experts, researchers, legal experts, pediatricians, mental health professionals, and representatives of various nongovernmental organizations active in the field of child abuse and neglect. The purpose of this taskforce was to bring together stakeholders from both private and public sectors to discuss the needs in this area and to make recommendations to address these needs. This taskforce will ultimately develop a national action plan for child abuse and neglect and the related services.

In the same vein, HCC has gathered together various taskforces with similar missions to the one on child abuse and neglect to address issues such as homeless and street children, child labor, institutionalized children, and integrating handicapped children into the regular educational system.

THE IMPACT OF WAR ON
CHILD MENTAL HEALTH SERVICES

Lebanon has gone through several wars since the 1940s, the last being the July 2006 war where there was massive destruction to infrastructure, more than one thousand citizens were killed, and hundreds of thousands internally displaced. Many national and international organizations, governmental and nongovernmental alike, became involved in the relief effort. A major focus of interventions for these organizations fell into the psychosocial domain. In the absence of a national emergency plan following disasters and wars, there was no central governmental committee to regulate and organize this psychosocial relief effort. Additionally, there was also very little agreement on what constituted priorities for interventions, even among mental health professionals themselves. Given that various international organizations had drafted and circulated a documented titled the "Inter-Agency Standing Committee Guidelines on Mental Health and Psychosocial Support in Emergency Settings" (Inter-Agency Standing Committee, 2007), many professionals and others in decision-making capacities thought that there was a dichotomy between "psychosocial" and "mental health" issues and actually interpreted this to mean that "mental health" issues were related only to psychopathology and psychiatrically ill children with subsequent resistance to address these particular needs. Following the end of the war it thus became imperative to get an accurate idea of what the psychosocial/mental health needs of children and adolescents in the affected regions were and what services were there to meet those needs.

The Higher Council for Children (HCC) commissioned the Institute for Development, Research, Advocacy and Applied Care (IDRAAC) in association with the Department of Psychiatry and Clinical Psychology at Balamand University and St. George Hospital University Medical Center to conduct a psychosocial needs assessment of children and adolescents in Lebanon in the areas mostly affected by the recent July 6 war events (South Lebanon and Beirut's southern suburbs), to map available community psychosocial resources and make recommendations for short- and long-term interventions to help guide policy and planning by HCC. In order to undertake this needs assessment and mapping, funding was secured from the European Commission Humanitarian Aid Department ECHO Program and Handicap International.

In order to map all available resources in the target regions, a good source of information that covered all villages in the target regions was required. There were two available sources of information: either the municipalities in all the villages of the target regions (n=255) or the Social Development Centers of the Ministry of Social Affairs (n=29). Since it was not clear which was a better informant, IDRAAC conducted a pilot study whereby a sample of both was contacted the kinds of information available to both these sources were compared. The outcome favored the municipalities, and thus it was decided to contact the municipality in each of the villages in order to locate the existing active and nonactive facilities and organizations concerned with psychosocial services as well as to identify the stakeholders who offered any psychosocial activities during and after the war to children and adolescents. A list of potential stakeholders who might have offered or were still offering psychosocial services was compiled.

The next phase was to contact each of the stakeholders and administer a questionnaire developed by the IDRAAC team via a telephone interview (10–15 minutes), or via e-mail or fax. Additional stakeholders were added to the list because they were known to the HCC as potential psychosocial service providers. The questions asked of each center pertained to the geographic location, catchment area and identity (type) of the stakeholders; the types of professionals available; the specific types of services provided (medical, psychological, recreational, support groups, play groups, educational groups, etc.); the types of professional training provided (workshops, training programs, etc.); the various population groups targeted; the accessibility or obstacles preventing community members from reaching them, as well as utilization of these services.

The data gathered from the municipalities and the stakeholders offered a wide range of results. A detailed cadastral map of the target region was marked to display the number of stakeholders offering psychosocial services by village. This allowed a visual display of areas where there was a lack of services. Additionally municipalities were able to identify who were the active stakeholders during and after war. This was validated and modified by interviewing the stakeholders themselves. Contacting the stakeholders complemented the work whereby results from the questionnaires were tabulated to describe the following categories for each organization: characteristics of the service providers, the availability of services to various age groups, areas in the target regions that are potentially served as reported by the service providers, the time frame of activities for each service provider (before the July war, during war, after war [September–December 2006], and since January 2007), personnel of service provider (specialty of paid professionals and volunteers), type of services offered: psychological treatment (individual therapy, family therapy, group therapy), referral to specialized centers for clinical health care, sports activities, psychosocial activities (drama/theater, recreational/play, support group, parental training), availability of safe space programs, workshops/training, and any other services. In addition, stakeholders were asked to identify who the national and international partners who worked together were, and how much of the organization's capacity was used during and after war.

Limitations of this mapping method included the possibility that not all psychosocial service providers were identified, due to either missing information from the municipalities or being unable to contact every local service providers in remote villages using the study means (phone, e-mail, and fax). In addition, there might have been smaller villages with no municipalities that received psychosocial services and were not included in our study. However, this mapping was able to show that there is a need for building on the already existing facilities and available organizations as well as allocating much more resources for psychosocial and mental health services to children and adolescents.

It is worth noting here that this mapping survey probably would not have taken place (at least not in the time frame it did) had it not been for war ravaging these affected areas. While issues related to child mental health like child abuse and neglect had been given importance on a governmental level during peace time, mental health in childhood per se had not received much attention on such a wide scale until this latest war.

The fact that the psychosocial and mental health needs assessment included a large representative sample of children and adolescents from all affected regions, combined with the comprehensive mapping of all regions, allowed the team at IDRAAC to come up with specific recommendations related to psychosocial and mental health needs emanating from these surveys (IDRAAC, 2007). These recommendations were also classified according to the relevant ministerial bodies concerned with their execution. Hopefully the HCC and all concerned ministries and organizations will use the momentum of the war and the resulting psychosocial and mental health needs to start developing the needed programming. It will be crucial for all concerned governmental and nongovernmental agencies to work in harmony and to cooperate together in setting up building blocks and mechanisms for what could be the blueprints of a national child mental health service. This is particularly so since the psychosocial and mental health needs of children and adolescents are not only related to times of war but rather, as the results of the survey indicated, to times of peace as well.

CONCLUSION: MEETING THE CHALLENGES

Service development related to child mental health in Lebanon has depended so far on initiatives of individuals and organizations in the private sector rather than on governmental efforts. Research activities have guided progress in various domains, but major challenges remain to be met. Foremost among them is the creation of a national plan related to child mental health and implementing it nationwide. This will not be achieved alone by one agency or ministry but rather with the collaboration of various concerned ministries in one concerted effort. Another challenge is the paucity of qualified child mental health professionals: there are simply not enough trained professionals to deliver services in all regions. More training programs are needed, and the project highlighted earlier in this chapter serves as an example and model of what could be achieved in dissemination of expertise and services. In this vein, the World Health Organization (WHO) office in Beirut embarked after the war on a series of mental health training seminars to primary care physicians and primary health care personnel all over Lebanon and not just in war-affected regions. This has served to sensitize professionals in primary care to mental health needs in the general population and has given them the basic tools for interventions that they themselves could implement prior to networking with more specialized mental health care professionals. Needless to say, much more remains to be done.

Additional challenges revolve around the cost of mental health care. Currently in Lebanon, insurance companies do not cover mental conditions. Governmental funds are available for psychiatric hospitalizations and outpatient physician consultations, but they cover only a minor portion of the cost. Most families seeking mental health services from psychiatrists, psychologists, or other allied professionals have to pay out of pocket in order to have access to such care.

Finally, funding is direly needed not only to support services and patient treatment, but also to support research and sustainable programming. Unfortunately, even in the aftermath of war when funds for mental health were urgently needed and international funding became available, donations from the involved international organizations earmarked for mental health constituted only a very small portion of the overall support provided, and when such financial support was given, most of it came with strings attached to execute what international organizations themselves designated were the psychosocial needs and priorities rather than what the true community needs were. Mental health professionals have a major role to play in developing and developed countries alike in order to inform and guide governmental policies related to mental health based on solid local research and local experience rather than on imported standards.

REFERENCES

Bauermeister, J. J., C. Y. So, P. S. Jensen, O. Krispin, A. S. El Din, and the Integrated Services Program Task Force. "Development of adaptable and flexible treatment manuals for externalizing and internalizing disorders in children and adolescents," *Revista Brasileira de Psiquiatria* 28 (2006): 67–71.

Belfer, M. L. "Critical review of world policies for mental healthcare for children and adolescents," *Current Opinion in Psychiatry* 20 (2007): 349–52.

Cordahi-Tabet, C., E. G. Karam, G. Nehmé, J. Fayyad, N. Melhem, and N. Rashidi. "Les Orphelins De La Guerre: Expérience Libanaise et Méthodologie d'un Suivi Prospectif," *Stress et Trauma* 2 (2002): 1–9.

Demyttenaere, K., R. Bruffaerts, J. Posada-Villa, I. Gasquet, V. Kovess, J. P. Lepine, M. C. Angermeyer, S. Bernert, G. de Girolamo, P. Morosini, G. Polidori, T. Kikkawa, N. Kawakami, Y. Ono, T. Takeshima, H. Uda, E. G. Karam, J. A. Fayyad, A. N. Karam, Z. N. Mneimneh, M. E. Medina-Mora, G. Borges, C. Lara, R. de Graaf, J. Ormel, O. Gureje, Y. Shen, Y. Huang, M. Zhang, J. Alonso, J. M. Haro, G. Vilagut, E. J. Bromet, S. Gluzman, C. Webb, R. C. Kessler, K. R. Merikangas, J. C. Anthony, M. R. Von Korff, P. S. Wang, T. S. Brugha, S. Aguilar-Gaxiola, S. Lee, S. Heeringa, B. E. Pennell, A. M. Zaslavsky, T. B. Ustun, S. Chatterji, WHO World Mental Health Survey Consortium. "Prevalence, severity, and unmet need for treatment of mental disorders in the World Health Organization World Mental Health Surveys," *Journal of the American Medical Association* 291 (2004): 2581–90.

Fayyad, J., R. De Graaf, R. Kessler, J. Alonso, M. Angermeyer, K. Demyttenaere, G. De Girolamo, J. M. Haro, E. G. Karam, C. Lara, J. P. Lepine, J. Ormel, J. Posada-Villa, A. M. Zaslavsky, and R. Jin. "Cross-national prevalence and correlates of adult atten tion-deficit hyperactivity disorder," *British Journal of Psychiatry* 190 (2007): 402–9.

Fayyad, J., E. G. Karam, A. Karam, C. Cordahi-Tabet, Z. Mneimneh, and M. Bou Ghosn. "PTSD in children and adolescents following war," in Raul R. Silva, ed., *Posttraumatic Stress Disorders in Children and Adolescents.* New York: W. W. Norton & Company, 2003, 306–52.

Fayyad, J. A., C. S. Jahshan, E. G. Karam. "Systems development of child mental health services in developing countries." *Child and Adolescent Psychiatric Clinics of North America* 10 (2001): 745–62.

Fayyad, J. A., E. G. Karam, A. Karam, C. Cordahi-Tabet, N. Melhem, Z. Mneimneh, V. Zebouni, G. Kayali, P. Yabroudi, N. Rashidi, and H. Dimasi. "Community group therapy in children and adolescents exposed to war," in abstracts of the

49th Annual Meeting of the American Academy of Child and Adolescent Psychiatry, San Francisco, CA, 2002.

Hoagwood K, "The policy context for child and adolescent mental health services: implications for systems reform and basic science development." *Annals of the New York Academy of Science* 1008 (2003): 140–48.

IDRAAC. *Assessment Study of the Psychosocial Status of Children and Adolescents in the South of Lebanon and the Southern Suburbs of Beirut After the July 06 War*, Final Report, 2007.

IDRAAC/Oxfam-Quebec/CIDA. *Parenting Skills Treatment Program for Mothers of Children with Behavioral Problems*, 2006.

Inter-Agency Standing Committee (IASC). *Guidelines on Mental Health and Psychosocial Support in Emergency Settings*, February 25, 2007 version, www.humanitarian-info.org/iasc/content

Jensen, P. S. "Disseminating child and adolescent mental health treatment methods: An international feasibility study." *Revista Brasileira de Psiquiatria* 28 (2006): 1–2.

Karam, A., E. G. Karam, V. Zbouni, P. Yabroudi, C. Cordahi-Tabet, and J. Fayyad. "Traumatismes De Guerre: Prévention Psychologique à Large Echelle en Milieu Scolaire." *Stress et Trauma* 2 (2002): 169–77.

Karam, E. G., D. B. Howard, A. N. Karam, A. Ashkar, M. Shaaya, N. Melhem, N. El-Khoury. "Major depression and external stressors: The Lebanon wars." *European Archives of Psychiatry and Clinical Neuroscience* 248 (1998): 225–30.

Karam, E. G., A. Karam, C. Mansour, N. Melhem, S. Saliba, P. Yabroudi, and V. Zbouni. "The Lebanon Wars Studies: The Grapes of Wrath Chapter. Phase I. The Final Report." Beirut, Lebanon: UNICEF, 1996.

Karam, E. G., N. Melhem, A. Karam, P. Yabroudi, V. Zbouni, C. Mansour, and S. Saliba, "Acute Responses to War Trauma in Children and Adolescents: The Lebanon Wars." *Traumatic Stress Points. News for The International Society for Traumatic Stress Studies (ISTSS)* 11 (1997): 1–7.

Karam, E. G., N. Melhem, C. Mansour et al., "Use and abuse of licit and illicit substances: Prevalence and risk factors among students in Lebanon." *European Addiction Research* 6 (2000): 189–97.

Karam, E. G., Z. N. Mneimneh, A. N. Karam, J. A. Fayyad, S. C. Nasser, S. Chatterji, and R. C. Kessler. "Prevalence and treatment of mental disorders in Lebanon: a national epidemiological survey." *The Lancet* 367 (2006): 1000–6.

Murray, L. K., J. Fayyad, P. S. Jensen, K. Hoagwood, M. Azer, and the Integrated Services Program Task Force. "An examination of cross-cultural systems implementing evidence-based assessment and intervention approaches." *Revista Brasileira de Psiquiatria* 28 (2006): 76–79.

Rahman, A., R. Harrington, M. Mubbashar et al. "Developing child mental health services in developing countries." *Journal of Child Psychology and Psychiatry* 41 (2000): 539–46.

So, C. Y., J. S. Hung, J. J. Bauermeister, P. S. Jensen, D. Habib, P. Knapp, O. Krispin, and the Integrated Services Program Task Force. "Training of evidence-based assessment and intervention approaches in cross-cultural contexts: Challenges and solutions." *Revista Brasileira de Psiquiatria* 28 (2006): 72–75.

United Nations Office of Drug Control and Crime Prevention. *The Rapid Situation Assessment of Substance Use and Misuse in Lebanon*. Report. May 2003.

Weissman, M. M., R. C. Bland, G. J. Canino, C. Faravelli, S. Greenwald, H. G. Hwu, P. R. Joyce, E. G. Karam, C. K. Lee, J. Lellouch, J. P. Lepine, S. C. Newman, M. Rubio-Stipec, J. E. Wells, P. J. Wickramaratne, H. Wittchen, and E. K. Yeh. "Cross-national epidemiology of major depression and bipolar disorder." *Journal of the American Medical Association* 276 (1996): 293–99.

Index

Index

About the Editors and Contributors

Dr. **Cornelius Ani**. Specialist registrar and honorary lecturer in child and adolescent psychiatry, Imperial College London, United Kingdom.

Dr. **Asma Bouden**, MD. Department of Child and Adolescent Psychiatry, RAZI Hospital, La Manouba, Tunisia.

Professor **Maurice Eisenbruch**, MD, MPhil, FRCPsych. School of Psychology Psychiatry & Psychological Medicine, Monash University, Australia.

Dr. **John Fayyad**, MD. Department of Psychiatry and Clinical Psychology, St. George Hospital University Medical Center, Beirut, Lebanon.

Professor **Elena Garralda**, MD MPhil, FRCPsych. Academic unit of child and adolescent psychiatry, Imperial College London, and Honorary Consultant in Child and Adolescent Psychiatry, CNWL NHS Foundation Trust, United Kingdom.

Dr. **Matthew Hodes**, PhD FRCPsych. Senior lecturer in child and adolescent psychiatry, Academic Unit of Child and Adolescent Psychiatry, Imperial College London, United Kingdom.

Professor **Marie Rose Moro**, PhD MD. Professor of child and adolescent psychiatry, University Paris 13, Avicenne Hospital, Bobigny, France.

Dr. **Anula Nikapota**, FRCPsych. Senior tutor, Institute of Psychiatry, Kings College London, and emeritus consultant in child and adolescent psychiatry, South London and Maudsley, United Kingdom.

Dr. **Yoshiro Ono**, MD, PhD. Wakayama Prefecture Children and Disabled Person's Guidance Center, Kemi, Wakayama, Japan.

Dr. **Berna Pehlivanturk**, MD. Associate professor of child and adolescent psychiatry, Hacettepe University, Ankara, Turkey.

Professor **Raija-Leena Punamäki**, PhD. Department of Psychology, University of Tampere, Finland.

Professor **Jean-Philippe Raynaud**, MD, PhD. Professor of child and adolescent psychiatry, Hopsital La Grave-Casselardit, Toulouse Cedex 9, France.

Professor **Per-Anders Rydelius**, MD, PhD. Karolinska Institute, Astrid Lundgren Children's Hospital, Stockholm, Sweden.

Professor **Frank C. Verhulst**, MD. Department of Child and Adolescent Psychiatry, Erasmus University Medical Center–Sophia Children's Hospital, Rotterdam, The Netherlands.